The Ultimate
Hunting Dog
Reference Book

A Comprehensive Guide to More Than
60 Sporting Breeds

Vickie Lamb

Skyhorse Publishing

Visit our website at www.skyhorsepublishing.com.

10 9 8 7 6 5 4 3 2 1

Library of Congress Cataloging-in-Publication Data is available on file.

Cover design by Richard Rossiter
Cover photographs credit: Thinkstock

Print ISBN: 978-1-63450-444-7
Ebook ISBN: 978-1-63450-462-1

Printed in the United States of America

Contents

Foreword

Whenever you read something in a book or magazine, the author sounds just like you—ever noticed that? My favorite authors over the years have all sounded like me in my head when I read them. Sometimes I'll get tapes or CDs of a book I've read and listen to the authors read in their own words and I think, "Wow, I liked me better!"

It's too bad things are this way, because I wish you could hear Vickie Lamb read her own words in her soft south Georgia accent, so full of patience and calm, moving at that steady, inexorable speed that accomplishes things, things like contract negotiations, explaining curfews to your teenager, and getting somebody to spill the beans in court. And training dogs.

There's a short section in chapter 15, "Training Philosophy," titled "Art of Speaking Canine." Vickie speaks canine. There are trainers who specialize in hounds, others in retrievers, and still others in pointing dogs. But ever since wolves moved to our side of the campfire, dogs have been dogs, regardless of the shapes they've been twisted into and the talents they've had instilled in them through selective—and sometimes just plain lucky—breeding. So a Walker is a Labrador is a shorthair is a Jack Russell. If you know how to speak canine, and Vickie does, you can train just about any dog to do just about anything a dog is capable of. And through all of this so far, I hope you have taken the time to admire my restraint in not using the term "dog whisperer."

A few years back, I was putting together what the publisher hoped would be a comprehensive volume called *Encyclopedia of North American Sporting Dogs*. It covers all the hunting breeds, as the name implies, and I was restricted to using only about a half-dozen authors, and since encyclopedias have a way of being in print for a lot of years, I was very careful in the experts I selected. Vickie was one of them.

I have seen Vickie's dogs work, I have seen the high regard in which she's held by her peers—trainers, trialers, and trial judges—and have been editing her copy at *The Retriever Journal* for going on a decade, and her depth of knowledge always pleases us at the magazine's editorial office when it's time to put an issue together—her stuff just "fits."

I'll tell you a dirty little secret of magazine publishing, if you're interested. When you have columnists and you also run full-length feature stories, you have to make sure that what you publish does not have redundancy in it—three columns and a feature on teaching "Sit" to a puppy is a little like overkill. So, a year ahead, we ask the columnists to send in their ideas for the upcoming year, and then we decide on the mix of those and then which features would complement the columns. It's a jigsaw puzzle, but a fun one to put together if you have good people, and we do.

But here's the secret: In a lot of magazines, a lot of columnists ran out of ideas years ago, and the ideas they end up writing about are fed to them by the editors. We've never had to do that with Vickie; the well is deep, the rope is strong, and the bucket is large.

If you read and follow her advice in this book, you'll end up with a trained dog, one that wants to please you, one that will hunt to your gun, one that will make you a fine companion at home, and one that will make you proud for years.

But unless you're a pretty little lady from south Georgia, you sure won't sound as good in your own head.

Steve Smith, Editor
The Retriever Journal
The Pointing Dog Journal
Traverse City, Michigan

Acknowledgments

Without a doubt, the success of a book of this nature requires the contributions of many folks. The exceptional photos are a testament to that fact, and my profuse thanks go out to all that contributed images.

I wish to thank Kim Kuhlman, Rossella Di Palma, Chip Laughton, Dennis Ingram, Claudio Cerutti, Brian Schmidt, Shannon Nardi, Sharon Potter, Pamela Kadlec, Eli Reichman, Lisa and Judd Street, and Vince Robinson for their help, which was "over the top." Many thanks to Marilyn Fender, PhD., Ed Aycock, DVM, Rick Jackson, DVM, and Steve Smith. Also, I appreciated the help from various breed enthusiasts, as well hunters, from around the globe, including Oddur Magnusson, Pippa Mattinson, Eric Begbie, and Deb Wall.

Many thanks to my editors and everyone else who lent their expertise throughout the publishing process.

Thanks also to my parents, who have always supported my dreams; to my daughter, for loving the dogs as I do; and to the dog trainers, from whom I have learned throughout my life. Finally, I wish to thank the dogs; they have taught me most of all.

Introduction

Something about the unique relationship between dogs and hunting has intrigued me for nearly as far back as I can remember. Of course, as a child I was precocious and curious, and as you find with many children, I was inexplicably drawn to animals. It seemed that anything with fur or feathers had a unique attraction for me, and I fancied that I might be able to talk to all creatures great and small, tame or wild. And I tried to do just that and was quite sure I succeeded any number of times, after all.

I tamed numerous wild creatures—sort of—and patched up many injured ones over the years. I constantly wandered in the woods, often on my own, and got into more than my share of scrapes because of it, but I always managed to emerge none the worse for wear and, hopefully, a bit wiser. I was a student of animals in general and how they lived and communicated, but in particular I was drawn to horses and dogs and how they coexisted with each other and with humans.

And I read books. All those you might imagine for someone of my background, ones such as *Old Yeller* and *Big Red* and *Where the Red Fern Grows*, and others that might surprise you, such as Edgar M. Queeny's *Prairie Wings* and authors including Burton Spiller, Havilah Babock, Nash Buckingham, Col. Harold P. Sheldon, Archibald Rutledge, and Gordon MacQuarrie.

At the same time I was learning about hunting, mostly by tagging along every chance I could with my dad—much to the chagrin of my mother—and also by listening to endless stories from my elders. I never tired of hearing the tales of wary ducks and wayward geese, of sneaking pheasant and exploding partridge, and of zigzagging rabbits, wily foxes, elusive bobcat, and raccoon and bear.

But the recurring theme as I grew up was that no matter if the game was feathered or furred, there was always a special dog attached to the equation, a canine hunting companion that gave more meaning to each experience. You see, my grandpa and my dad were always accompanied by dogs on these hunting excursions, and I grew up around those dogs and that kind of hunting.

Indeed, it was always the dogs that captured my attention; I wanted a dog with me at every bend in the road. In college and afterward,

I volunteered at different pro trainers' facilities in an effort to learn more about training dogs. It wasn't enough to know the basics; I had a thirst for knowledge and wanted to soak it all in. So for a period of several years I traversed the country and worked and apprenticed with dog trainers from South Carolina to Minnesota to California.

And I learned a lot. There are many different means to the same end, some more successful than others, and no two dogs are alike. I gradually came to realize the most valuable lesson of all: *there is always something else to learn*. It might be how to do something or how *not* to do something, but every day around dogs offers the potential for something new.

And that brings me here, to these pages. For you see, while I've been fortunate to have some really good dogs over the years in several different breeds, and while I've had competitive success in some varied sporting dog arenas and been blessed to hunt in many wild and beautiful places, I still remember. My dogs have been all over this great country of ours, and some have graced the pages of magazines or been on television. But I still remember—just like it was yesterday.

I remember the first time I saw a retriever watch three birds down and then recover them for his handler. I was awestruck. I remember the first time I saw a pointer whirl and lock on a bird and the first time I heard a hound's music in the hardwood bottoms. I remember how I wanted to train my dog and couldn't find anyone to help me, much less find anywhere that I could buy the most rudimentary of supplies.

I remember the first training rope I ever made, and the metal coach's whistle I used. I remember throwing oversized plastic boat bumpers from the local marina for my dogs and hand-making canvas dummies out of fire-hose material. I remember making a drag from worn-out hide, and tying a bird's wing to a cane fishing pole. Back then it didn't matter if you needed dog training supplies or hunting gear, the pickins were slim. And I remember taking my dogs to the fields, the woods, and the marshes in pursuit of wild adventures. I remember duck hunting and bird hunting and coon hunting "when hunting wasn't cool."

In some ways, times have changed. Today, entire television networks are devoted to hunting and fishing programming. Multimillion dollar companies specialize in retailing all types of hunting paraphernalia: These superstores and smaller ones all cater to the needs of hunters and anglers, and most of them have extensive selections of dog training supplies. What you can't get in these stores, you can find in catalogs or on the Internet. If you want it you can probably find it.

However, in other ways time has stood still. It is still tough to get started. Where do you turn? How do you find help? Once you are under way, what things will help you become more advanced? How do you transform dog training and hunting experiences into priceless memories?

You will find the answers to all these questions, and more, in the pages ahead. I want to help you avoid the painful, time-consuming mistakes I've learned from doing it the hard way over the years. I also share some valuable things I've learned about people, dogs, and the wild outdoors in the hopes that this knowledge will help you on your journey with your dogs.

Yes, I remember. And it is my fervent wish—whether you are a newcomer to dog training and hunting or a veteran—that you will enjoy what you find here, as we all ultimately share in these experiences of living with dogs, loving them, and taking them afield.

PART ONE

Hunting Dogs . . . So Many Choices

CHAPTER
ONE

Hunting and Training Dogs

Hunting and dogs. Such a pairing seems perfectly natural, doesn't it? Indeed, those words describe the oldest working relationship humans have shared with dogs. Take into consideration all the shooting sports that involve dogs, and participating *without* them can become a pretty empty proposition. How many dove fields have you visited with a few good dogs that were a pleasure to watch and gun beside? What about the duck blinds, pheasant country, and grouse woods with dogs that knew their job well? How about rabbit or raccoon hunting or following the scent of bear or mountain lion or bobcat?

Hunting with dogs encompasses varied pursuits, including riding with a pack of hounds and exciting bird hunts with canines that become staunch pointing wonders at the whiff of scent, whether it's southern bobwhite quail or Huns, chukars, or another upland species. Then, we may be on the sweeping tundra of Iceland, or the moors of Ireland, plains of Africa, the rolling hills of Italy, or South America.

Of course, many of us can recall plenty of occasions where we have gunned in dove fields with totally unruly dogs—you know the ones, those wild, out-of-control dogs that attempt to retrieve everyone else's birds. Or in duck blinds where dogs were constantly breaking to shot. Or in the uplands where dogs were chasing pheasants, busting grouse, or blowing through entire coveys of quail totally out of your gun's reach. Then there were the coonhounds that refused to come in even when not running a track, and there you sat.

How about the places, such as in some South American countries, where people are used for retrieving instead of dogs? The shooting is fantastic, but an element is missing for those of us who appreciate good dog work. Even in some U.S. dove fields many people simply pick up their own birds. But for me it just doesn't seem like the total experience to go without a dog. And I suspect you feel the same way.

Indeed, what makes any of these hunting adventures complete is a *trained* dog, a dog that knows his business and loves to do his job with style, is a pleasure to hunt with, and a joy to own. This book is going to give you more than one way to achieve this goal.

You will have to make at least one major decision as you approach this business of hunting with your dog: choosing the breed that will best suit your interests. If you are essentially a waterfowl hunter, you will likely be interested in one of the retriever breeds. If you hunt ducks as well as upland game, you may want a retriever, spaniel, or versatile hunting dog. If you primarily hunt upland birds, you may choose one of the pointing breeds.

Perhaps you like to squirrel hunt, in which case you may want to choose from various breeds of cur dogs or a Jack Russell terrier. Several hound breeds satisfy most coon and big game (bear and mountain lion) hunters. Airedales are effective for many types of hunting. If you like to coyote or fox hunt, several different breeds might suit you, while beagles are solid choices for rabbit and hare hunting and dachsunds do earth work and even some retrieving.

Decisions, decisions! All these choices bring up an interesting question: how did all these different dog breeds develop? Most experts agree that dogs originally evolved from wolves, and the human/dog relationship extends well beyond the ancient Egyptian and Babylonian civilizations. Art from the third and fourth centuries depicts dogs hunting game to be captured by trained hawks and falcons. Unfortunately, we have too much ground to cover on the nuts and bolts of hunting dogs to delve into the particulars on the history of the dog. (Several good books on the subject are included in the Resources section at the end of this book.) But suffice it to say that as humans domesticated the dog they cultivated the canine for many different uses, such as for protection, transportation (e.g., sled dogs), companionship, work, and, of course, hunting. Dogs were used to hunt any number of species, and hundreds of years ago certain breeds were even trained to hunt humans.

In today's world we are raised with the saying that dog is man's best friend. What does this mean exactly? If you ask a roomful of people, you may get as many answers as there are people.

Airedale (DogAds Photo)

Without a doubt, the dog is an amazing animal. Pets in general can provide therapeutic benefits to the sick. A dog can often detect physiological changes in a person, such as when someone is about to have a seizure. A dog can sense impending storms and earthquakes. And a dog certainly seems to know when his master needs a friend. In short, dogs seem to have additional senses beyond the five we have come to recognize as our own.

Given the proper guidance, opportunities, and circumstances, our dogs will work their hearts out for us. The amount of time we invest in training, love, and companionship will be given back to us in devotion a hundredfold. These moments and memories build over time, to be cherished as the years go by.

Speaking of training, this book is chock-full of various training meth-ods and suggestions for applying them. But your choice of methods must be tailored to you and your hunting dog. For instance, this book won't tell you that starting with a puppy is the only way to go. It's the optimal situation *if*—and this is a mighty big *if* for some folks—you have the time to devote to raising and training a puppy. But if a puppy doesn't fit into your particular circumstances, there *are* other options, including started and trained dogs, and I'll provide plenty of helpful hints and information for this approach. Indeed, whenever puppies are discussed, apply those things to your older dog, if that is what you have.

Also, this book is loaded with lots of additional information you'll need as you go down the sometimes bumpy but inevitably treasured road of life with your new dog.

But beyond all the training advice lies an intangible jewel—the *unmistakable bond* that develops between human and dog. It is a con-nection that transcends description, one that you'll only experience by raising and training some of the best friends you'll ever have the pleasure to know.

CHAPTER
TWO

What's Your Fancy?

Sometimes you just know. It springs from deep inside and there may be no rhyme or reason, but you are absolutely certain that the dog for you is a vizsla. Or a flat-coated retriever, or an Irish setter . . . you just know. Your choice may stem from special childhood memories or other attachments you developed to a particular type of hunting or breed of dog over the years. Then again, you might not have any clue at all about what kind of dog will suit you, except that you know you want to bird hunt or duck hunt or bear hunt.

This dog-buying business signifies a huge commitment from you for the next ten to fifteen years, so you owe it to yourself and your prospective canine companion to give some thought to the breed that will best complement your interests and lifestyle. Even if you think you already *know*. For instance, some breeds take much longer to train than others because they mature and develop more slowly. Can you live with the fact that your dog is still in junior high while your buddy Joe's dog is doing college-level work?

Some breeds have a reputation for being notoriously hardheaded, while others are quite sensitive. Certain breeds are plagued with more health problems than others. These are just a few things that should factor into your decision.

Let's take a gander at all the options available. For further information on any of these breeds, contact the breed clubs and associated kennel clubs listed in the Resources section.

Pointing Breeds

The different pointing breeds offer many choices that may fit your hunting purpose and personality. Do you want a dog that runs big or one that hunts close? Do you want a dog that will point no matter where he is and hold until you arrive on the scene? Some dogs are more adept at pointing and remaining staunch to wing and shot, which typically assists their retrieving ability as they're able to watch the birds down, while others break to shot.

Individual pointing breeds were developed from dogs with a tendency to hold their position in the face of game scent, and before the age of shotguns these dogs signaled to their human counterparts where the birds were hiding. Nets were thrown over the area to trap the birds. As shotguns became available, hunting methods changed and various breeds continued to evolve.

Within this classification are the pointers and the setters. Generally speaking, pointers have a more classic pointing stance, while the setters often assume the "setting" (or crouching) stance, from whence they get their name. Some describe setters as pointers with long hair, although many fanciers claim that setters are a bit softer and more family-oriented than most pointers. Others say that's bunk, and that it depends on how the dogs are raised. Another generalization is that pointers will naturally point sooner than setters, but that setters are easier to break to wing and shot.

French Brittany—a pointing breed (Claudio Cerutti)

The long coats of setters can be an issue in thick or thorny cover, and some believe that setters may be lacking a bit in stamina compared to some of the other pointers. However, enthusiasts of both sides will tell you that many setters are apt to run as big as some of the pointers. In the final analysis, it is primarily how you train them. Indeed, many dogs can switch-hit (run big or hunt close) to adapt to whether you are on horseback or foot.

Your choices among the pointing breeds include the American Brittany, English setter, French Brittany, Gordon setter, pointer, red (Irish) setter, and red and white setter. Other breeds that point are listed in the versatile hunting dog classification because of their ability to perform many tasks well.

American Brittany

Previously known by the name "Brittany spaniel," this breed was originally developed in France and eventually became the American and French Brittany (its recognized predecessor) breeds. The North American Versatile Hunting Dog Association (NAVHDA) recognizes the

American Brittany (Kevin Case)

Brittany as one of the oldest breeds, one that also helped found other versatile continental breeds.

The Brittany is a pointer through and through, but with perhaps closer range than some other breeds. Recognized for its pleasing personality and its ability to learn and develop quickly in the field, the Brittany makes an excellent choice for the neophyte dog trainer and hunter as well as for the veteran. This is a medium-sized, attractive breed that may or may not have a docked tail. The short, fine, slightly wavy coat is colored white and orange or white and liver, with roan or ticking allowed. Males average thirty to forty-five pounds, with females usually slightly smaller.

English Setter

Some sources trace the origin of this elegant breed to the 1300s, although records seem to indicate that the English setter was more clearly defined in the past four hundred years. It was originally called the setting spaniel. The breed developed with tendencies to find birds and assume a "setting" stance, which some of today's setters still do along with the more pronounced pointing stance. English setters embody grace and style in their work.

English setter (Oddur Magnusson)

Serious breeding of two lines of English setters occurred from the early 1800s. At this time, Edward Laverack of England began perfecting his stock, while some years later R. L. Purcell Llewellin of South Wales crossed some Laverack stock with other setters from northern England to produce a slightly smaller setter. Today's Llewellin setters are working descendants of those dogs, along with other strains known as Ryman or Old Hemlock setters.

The modern English setter can range from medium-sized to upwards of eighty pounds for some males, and it typically sports a long, lean body and the characteristic feathered tail. Colors include variations of belton (white background with color flecking in roan or ticking over the body), orange, blue (black on white), tricolor (blue with tan on legs, over eyes, and on muzzle), lemon, and liver. Patches of color are allowed on the head and ears.

French Brittany

Otherwise termed the Epagneul Breton, the French Brittany is credited as the founding breed for the American Brittany. This medium-sized

French Brittany (Nathan Albertson)

breed is known for a tremendous work ethic, delightful personality, and close-working tendencies, which makes it a good choice for hunters. These dogs have a strong natural desire to hunt, point, and retrieve.

The French Brittany comes in five color phases: black/white, orange/white, liver/white, black/orange/white tricolor, and liver/orange/white tricolor. The smallest of the pointing breeds, it is a very hardy, adaptable dog with a number of desirable traits, including keen intelligence and early development.

Gordon Setter

The only hunting breed native to Scotland, the Gordon setter has a storied past dating from several hundred years. Records refer to black and tan "setting" dogs, also a characteristic of English setters, dating from the sixteenth century. The Duke of Gordon perfected the breed in the late 1700s and early 1800s, hence the name for this beautiful hunting dog.

The Gordon setter's coat is similar to that of the English setter, except that its color is black and tan or it has chestnut markings. Typically best on upland birds, the Gordon setter is slower to develop than some

Gordon setter (Jonathan Brandt)

of the pointing breeds, despite its superior scenting ability. Gordons are smart and biddable, and although sometimes accused of being less stylish than the English setter when pointing, they are very reliable. Gordon setters range from medium-large to weights of more than eighty pounds.

Pointer

This classic, flashy breed of noble carriage is often called the English pointer, although there actually is no such recognized breed. Without a doubt the pointer is the favorite choice in field trial circles because of its wide-ranging, tenacious drive and ability to seek and find birds. It is far and away the most winning breed in bird dog competition. References to the pointer date from the 1600s and indicate that the breed evolved from crosses that included the Spanish pointer, Italian pointer, and possibly the foxhound, greyhound, bloodhound, Newfoundland, setter, and even the bulldog.

Pointer (Stacey Wiper)

Many pointing breed enthusiasts agree that the pointer has the greatest amount of stamina during a long day afield. Most pointers also sport the classic twelve o'clock tail position—eye pleasing and stylish as it is—when they point birds.

The pointer's short, close coat may come in white with liver, lemon, black, or orange markings or may be any of these colors in solid form, although pointers with darker solid colors should have a similarly dark-pigmented nose. Adults typically approach sixty to seventy pounds in size but can be smaller. Pointers are extremely active and function well in competition or for hunting purposes. They are often referred to as the Cadillac of bird dogs.

Red (Irish) Setter

Developed in Ireland, this breed probably shares similar ancestors with the English setter, pointer, and Gordon setter, but its present form predominantly descended from the red and white setter. The Irish red setter ranges

Irish setter (Kim Kuhlman)

in color from an almost deep mahogany or chestnut to red, with traces of white allowed. Although this breed nearly disappeared from good working stock for a time, it enjoys a place in history because of the classic book *Big Red* by James A. Kjelgaard (New York: Holiday House, 1945) and the efforts of a number of dedicated people who sought to reclaim its hunting attributes. The history of this breed is well worth exploring.

Today's red setter functions well as a field trial competitor or a class gundog and has a strong network of support in North America. Across the pond representatives of the breed may be more parti-colored. Size ranges from upwards of seventy pounds with a long flowing coat down to a medium size and weight coupled with a dense coat in some of the field lines. The red setter enjoys popularity as a companion and gundog and deserves a closer look if you are partial to the setter breeds.

Red and White Setter

Developed in Ireland in the 1700s, this breed is the closest predecessor of the red (Irish) setter. As the two breeds evolved, two distinct tastes developed among hunters with some preferring the solid red and

Red and white setter (Fiorella Mathis)

others feeling that the red and white variety showed up better against heavily brushed backgrounds. Over time the red setter began edging out the red and white dogs, and at the time of World War I the latter breed nearly disappeared. It took considerable work to restore the red and white setter, which eventually regained a footing and spread from Ireland to England. Currently this breed isn't recognized by the American Kennel Club (AKC) in the United States but is registered with the United Kennel Club (UKC).

Today's red and white setter continues to gain in popularity but can still be difficult to find. The dog is quite pleasing in appearance, with an athletic build and a dense, feathered coat. It is fairly large with white mostly found on the chest and legs and red markings on the head, back, and rump areas. Red and white setters are noted for their friendly but determined personality and bird-finding tenacity.

Versatile Pointing Breeds

As different hunting needs developed, so did the desire to produce dogs that were all-purpose, or versatile, in their abilities to perform a number of tasks with efficiency. All of these breeds, which are typically grouped with pointing dogs, were developed in continental Europe; thus, they are referred to as the continental breeds, or the HPRs (hunt, point, and retrieve). Furthermore, according to NAVHDA, all but four of these breeds developed in the late nineteenth century. The other five—Weimaraner, vizsla, Brittany, small Munsterlander, and Spinone—provided some foundation for these newer breeds.

For hundreds of years hunting with dogs in Europe was primarily a pursuit for the wealthy, those who had the means to keep large kennels of specialized dogs. But after a change in the German hunting law in the mid-nineteenth century, hunting became more accessible to the general populace. Hunters who couldn't afford to keep a variety of dogs needed breeds that were more versatile in their abilities.

Eventually, a number of breeds were developed that were capable of hunting and pointing game, retrieving all types of furred and feathered game on land and water, and tracking wounded game. These versatile gundogs also offered pleasing personalities and temperament as well as trainability.

Wrapping so many good qualities into one package is obviously an attractive proposition. And for many of today's hunters, these breeds present the perfect choice for varied types of hunting and conditions.

Versatile breeds weren't effectively introduced in North America until the twentieth century, and NAVHDA wasn't established until 1969. (See p. 349 for more on NAVHDA.) According to NAVHDA reports, the tracking hound, pointer, and waterpudel provided foundation stock for short- and wirehaired breeds, while the small Munsterlander and flat-coated retriever were the basis for the longhaired breeds.

These breeds include the German longhaired pointer, German shorthaired pointer, German wirehaired pointer (Drahthaar in German), Hungarian vizsla, large Munsterlander, Pudelpointer, small Munsterlander, Spinone Italiano, Weimaraner, and wirehaired pointing griffon, among others.

German Longhaired Pointer, German Shorthaired Pointer, German Wirehaired Pointer (Drahthaar)

In the mid-1900s German pointers began to develop in three different ways dictated by coat and ability, but record keeping of any breeds at that time was sorely lacking. The first German dog shows were conducted in Frankfort in 1878 and 1879, so standards for many breeds recognized by that time, including the longhaired and shorthaired pointers, were written to improve records and develop desirable hunting characteristics. Three years later a breed standard was written for the German wirehaired pointer.

The longhaired pointer was developed over time to become a good-sized dog still capable of speed and also possessed beauty and character along with health and intelligence. Founding breeders shied away from crossing with the large Munsterlander of those days. Today this breed is well regarded for its pointing, retrieving, and hunting ability, as well as its pleasing disposition. These dogs weigh upwards of seventy pounds and possess good, flat, dense coats with some feathering of the legs. Colors include solid brown with white allowed on feet and chest,

German longhaired pointer (Eileen Winser)

dark brown roan with solid patches, white ticking with patches of color, trout roan, and variations of brown and white. No black is permissible.

The shorthaired pointer developed into a dynamic medium-sized dog, neither too large nor too small, with a short, dense coat of solid liver or a mixture of liver and white. This breed evolved by crossing English foxhounds and old German hunting hounds with English and continental pointers. The shorthair is known as a high-performance versatile dog on land and water, with a superior nose and unparalleled stamina for work.

Finally, the wirehaired pointer was developed to accent its versatile traits with a dense, wiry coat that could withstand rugged territory and almost impenetrable cover. This breed descended from the Pudelpointer, which was a product of the German Pudel and the (English) pointer. The Pudelpointer was crossed with griffons, Stichelhaars, Polish water dogs, and some early shorthairs to create the modern German wirehair.

This strong, medium-sized dog has a water-resistant wiry coat on its body with distinctive facial "hair" including medium-length eyebrows and a beard around the jaw area. Wirehairs are either solid liver or variations of liver and white such as ticked and roan, but they usually have a liver head. This breed has become well known for its rugged durability in

German shorthaired pointer
(Sharon Potter)

German wirehaired pointer
(Claudio Cerutti)

harsh climates and its hunting ability. The wirehair is the same breed as the German Drahthaar and is the epitome of the versatile hunting dog.

Hungarian Vizsla

This breed has evolved from the original smooth-haired vizsla to include a second wirehaired vizsla.

The original vizsla (Hungarian for pointer) developed from extensive crosses between a breed known as the Pannonian hound and a yellow Turkish dog; it accompanied Magyar tribes that infiltrated central Europe over a thousand years ago and settled in what became Hungary and Transylvania. The original vizsla has a short, close, shiny coat with no undercoat and has a high degree of intelligence and trainability coupled with hunting instinct and drive. The vizsla's tail is docked one-third in all countries where docking is permitted.

Vizsla (Karen Maurice)

In contrast, the wirehaired vizsla evolved from the desire of many hunters to re-create their beloved vizsla with a coat more able to withstand tough hunting coverts and icy water. The first step was taken by mating an off-haired vizsla bitch and a German wirehaired pointer around 1930. Some vizslas had been produced with this "off" or slightly denser coat, and it was quickly noted that the different coat texture provided more protection in cold water and thick cover. When a female with one of these unusual coats was bred with a German wirehair, the resulting coat was harsh with a dense undercoat and brush on the back of the forelegs.

Wirehaired vizsla (Ton Niessing)

Subsequent breedings were with offspring from those crosses as well as from crosses with a Hertha pointer, an Irish setter, a Pudelpointer, and a Braque. The modern breed has gained respect in the past twenty years in the United Kingdom and in the United States. It possesses classic vizsla characteristics but has a coat more able to withstand challenging hunting conditions, stronger bones, and a more even temperament.

Large Munsterlander

Although this breed was being developed in the same time frame as the German pointers, it didn't become well known until it started claiming the black and white progeny of the German longhaired pointer crosses, as that color was a disqualification in the longhaired pointer breed. This breed has evolved into a hardy, versatile dog, well suited for rough shooting and with a keen nose and hunting ability.

Large Munsters are known for their quick ability to catch on and for their willingness and trainability. Males reach twenty-five inches in height. The coat should be dense and long but not curly or wavy, with

Large Munsterlander (Diane Davies)

feathers on the front and hind legs and the tail; the color should include a black head with a white or blue roan body accented with black patches or ticking.

Pudelpointer

Just as the name implies, this breed evolved from a cross between a German hunting Pudel and a pointer. That first cross occurred in 1881 in Germany. The Pudel offered trainability, retrieving instinct, good water attitude, intelligence, and a good protective coat, while the pointer contributed drive, desire, stamina, and pointing ability. According to the breed history, the Pudel proved more dominant in the cross, and as a result, only eleven Pudels were used to develop the Pudelpointer, as opposed to eighty pointers, with occasional reintroductions of pointer blood over the years.

This breed is solid colored, usually dark brown and sometimes black, with a dense, wiry coat that protects against harsh cover and cold climes. Efforts are ongoing to maintain high standards in this breed,

Pudelpointer (Ben Hong)

which was first imported to North America by Sigbot "Bodo" Winterhelt in 1956.

The Pudelpointer is highly regarded for its versatile hunting ability. Notable traits include a strong desire and drive for work afield and adapting well to training and being a team player.

Small Munsterlander

Longhaired, small pointing dogs existed in the Munsterland region of Germany for a long time, and numerous recordings of other breeds refer to this one as an older variation of the continental dog. But official efforts to keep records and establish the breed didn't occur until the late 1800s and early 1900s. These dogs had notable scenting abilities, were stylish pointers, and could retrieve well.

The small Munsterlander has an alert, pleasing personality, responds well to people, and is quick to learn. It also possesses a keen prey drive and strong gaming instincts. Its elegant carriage and impressive personality round out the qualities that make this medium-sized dog an action-driven hunter that adapts to and works with his owner.

Small Munsterlander (Mike Helms)

Spinone Italiano

This is one of the oldest sporting dog breeds; canines resembling this breed date from the second century AD. Obscure bristle-haired Italian pointing dogs date even further, from 500 BC. What is truly amazing is that this breed, according to its staunch supporters, has remained unchanged over all these centuries and continues to breed true to form. Commonly called the Spinone, this breed is also referred to as the Italian Spinone or Italian Griffon.

Known for working close, these wonderful hunting companions will slow down and stalk scented birds before assuming their point; in other words, they don't traditionally slam into a point like most pointing breeds.

Males approach twenty-seven inches at the shoulder and weigh up to eighty-five pounds. The spinone coat provides superior protection against the elements, which makes the breed a strong swimmer and competent retriever in water. Accepted colors include white, white with orange markings or orange roan, and white with brown markings or brown roan. The persistent and agreeable working attitude of this breed, along with its delightful personality, makes it an interesting choice.

Spinone (Rossella Di Palma)

Weimaraner

Continental pointing breeds and mastiffs are believed to be among this breed's ancestors. Weimaraners were supposedly developed to serve as personal gundogs for the nobility. References to this breed date from the 1600s, with records surfacing in the 1800s. Cultivated for traits necessary in tracking large game as well as hunting small furred and feathered game, the breed developed a strong following in short order. The name is derived from the Grand Duke of Weimar.

Although this breed can be hyperactive around the house and kennel, it tends to hunt slowly in the field—in contrast to its aristocratic build and look of speed and endurance. However, the dog compensates for this slowness with a superior nose and excellent team attentiveness.

Weimaraners can reach shoulder measurements of twenty-seven inches and have a silver or silver-gray coloring. The latter is responsible for its nickname, the gray ghost. Blue Weimaraners aren't recognized by the breed standard.

Weimaraner (Marilyn McLeod)

Wirehaired Pointing Griffon

While references to the griffon date from the 1500s, accurate records begin in 1873 in the Netherlands when Eduard Karel Korthals set out to create the ultimate walking hunter's versatile dog, one that could tackle the low-lying marshes of his country. The breed was called Korthals' Griffon, a name still referred to in certain parts of the world today.

There is much speculation about what breeds were crossed to develop the griffon, and many types of dogs had already been referred to as griffons prior to Korthals's effort. The breed was nearly lost during the world wars, but emerged again because of solid breed support. Two clubs formed after World War II, with one following Korthals's dreams and the other introducing a cross of the Cesky Fousek, a breed from Czechoslovakia that resembled the griffon but possessed traits more akin to the German wirehaired pointer. Those efforts faltered.

Males reach a height of twenty-four inches at the shoulder, and larger specimens are discouraged because the dog should be able to cover difficult terrain with ease and speed while working for his handler. The coat is harsh with a thick undercoat, and colors include steel gray with brown markings, chestnut brown or roan, white and brown, or white and orange.

Wirehaired pointing griffon (Greg Earle)

The griffon was quickly respected for its ability to adapt to varying terrain and climates and to different types of birds and game. It has a refreshing ability to absorb lessons quickly and remains a viable choice for the all-around versatile dog.

Flushing Breeds

Within the flushing breeds are a number of spaniels well-suited to their game. Spaniels were originally bred from the need for close-working dogs that would seek and flush small game and birds from areas with thick cover. Once they did so, sight hounds took over the chase for small game, and falcons and hawks were trained to nab the flushed birds.

As hunting methods changed with technology, smaller flushing dogs excelled in hunting woodcock and were thus nicknamed "cockers" or "cocking" dogs, and eventually cocker spaniels. The larger breeds that "sprang" on their game became springer spaniels. Since modern hunting methods require close-working dogs that can quarter and work in heavy, dense cover within gun range, the flushing breeds have become best suited to hunting game birds such as ruffed grouse or partridge, as well as woodcock, and in many cases, pheasant.

Most spaniels have dense, tough coats that enable them to handle both difficult cover and water with aplomb. However, within some of these breeds, bench enthusiasts have bred to achieve long, luxurious, attractive show ring coats that make those particular dogs nearly useless for hunting, much to the chagrin of fanciers of performance flushing dogs.

Flushing spaniels include the American cocker spaniel, Clumber spaniel, English cocker spaniel, English springer spaniel, field spaniel, Sussex spaniel, and the oldest of them all, the Welsh springer spaniel.

American Cocker Spaniel

In the United States, the American cocker spaniel is simply referred to as the cocker spaniel, as opposed to its kissing cousin, the English cocker

American cocker spaniel (Brian Schmidt)

spaniel. However, throughout the rest of the world it is the other way around, with the English cocker spaniel simply called "cocker."

Once an active field dog, the American cocker spaniel all but vanished from the working ranks because of its beauty and winning ways in the show ring. Yet some breeders are now investing quality time to resurrect the field abilities of this breed and are making good progress. I remember as a child reading a book called *Champion Dog Prince Tom* by Jean Fritz and Tom Clute (New York: Coward-McCann, 1958) that focused on a charming, dynamic American cocker that took the field world by storm.

American cockers are the smallest of the flushing breeds, reaching heights of fourteen to fifteen inches at the shoulder, and they have a very distinctive look, with a rounded head, round intelligent eyes, and a pronounced stop. Most folks think American cockers are all buff colored, but they also come in black and other solid colors and may be parti-colored.

Clumber Spaniel

The history of dog breeds is largely filled with unknowns, and the Clumber spaniel is no exception. One theory holds that the breed originated in France, but when the Duc de Noailles feared for his life—as well as his beloved dogs—during the French Revolution, he gave them all to the Second Duke of Newcastle in England who kenneled them at Clumber Park.

According to another theory the breed was developed by crossing large spaniels with St. Hubert's hounds, and possibly bassets, or with the alpine spaniel and the Saint Bernard, but in either case the Duke of Newcastle, and more specifically his gamekeeper, William Mansell, receive credit for solidifying the breed. First recognized in England, the Clumber was also included in the first group of dogs to be registered by the AKC, although it has only become popular over the past forty years or so.

Everything about the Clumber spaniel signifies power, from its heavy bone structure to its signature massive head. Longer than it is tall, this breed moves with a characteristic "Clumber roll." However, the Clumber is not clumsy, as its build, name, and even movement might suggest. The breed is quite athletic, although slow, and can hunt at a trot all day long. This big, handsome dog is mostly white in color with orange or lemon

Clumber spaniel (Kim Kuhlman)

markings about the face and ears, and colored "freckles" are permissible on the legs and at the base of the tail.

Clumbers can be good water dogs but were bred to be visible while working heavy cover in Europe, and the white coat can be a drawback in some waterfowl and upland hunting conditions. These dogs reach weights upwards of eighty-five pounds.

English Cocker Spaniel

The delightful English cocker coasted along with the American cocker until 1936, when it was recognized as a separate breed. Ten years later it was accepted into registry by AKC. More widely known for its field abilities than the American cocker, the English cocker is a superb water dog that excels on wood ducks and teal yet can also handle bigger ducks. And it's a terrific little upland dog on grouse and woodcock. English cockers also do well in the dove field.

Slightly taller than its American counterpart, the English cocker is very sturdy and built more like a miniature setter, with a longer muzzle, low-set ears, and less prominent eyes. English cockers come in black,

English cocker spaniel (Brian Schmidt)

liver, red, and golden (not to be confused with the buff color character-istic of American cockers). Any of these solid colors can have tan accent points over the eyes, on the throat, muzzle, and feet. The parti-color coat pattern combines the main color with roan, ticked, or open markings. The largest representatives of this breed are around thirty pounds.

English Springer Spaniel

Artworks from the sixteenth and seventeenth centuries depict dogs strongly resembling the English springer spaniel, and lore from that time describes springer spaniels that flushed furred and feathered game for hawks, coursing hounds, and nets. But it wasn't until 1902 that the Sporting Spaniel Society of Britain made the name "springer" official. In 1913 the first dog was imported to Canada from England, and the breed quickly spread to the United States. By 1924 the English Springer Spaniel Field Trial Association was formed. Early on the breed enjoyed combination field and bench popularity, but that ended in the 1940s when the last dual champion was recorded.

English springer spaniel (Brad Eden)

Today's field-bred English springer spaniel is light years away from the dogs bred to a physical standard for the show ring. The field-bred dog was developed for an excellent nose, tractability, soft mouth, marking ability, desire, water prowess, and other qualities necessary for good field work. These dogs are often a bit smaller and also longer than they are tall, with shorter coats and smaller, high-set ears. A few dedicated breeders are still striving to create more dual-purpose dogs despite the seventy-plus-year split between the two.

English springers are dynamic, friendly, game-finding machines that can be surprisingly explosive around the water. They are usually black and white or liver and white, although roans in these colors (blue and liver) are acceptable, as are tricolored dogs with tan markings accentuating the black and white or liver and white color scheme. Most field dogs will range between forty and sixty pounds.

Field Spaniel

The field spaniel is linked by history to the English cocker spaniel. Back when flushing breeds were being developed and were classified as land or water spaniels, the land spaniels were often called "field" spaniels. Over time the spaniels were further divided by size. Those above twenty-five pounds were termed "field spaniels" and those below were called "English cockers."

While the first field spaniel was registered in the United States by the AKC in 1894, the breed experienced a severe decline until 1967 when more stock was imported from England to America. Progress is now being made with field work, as the first Working Dog (WD) certificate was earned in 1992 by a male field spaniel and the first Working Dog Excellent (WDX) certificate was issued in 1995. (For more on certificates, see chapter 4.)

Field spaniel. (Pamela Kadlec)

The field spaniel is slightly larger than the English cocker and exhibits a noble carriage and personality. Built for work in both cover and water, the field spaniel has a solid build resembling the setter, but it stands just seventeen or eighteen inches at the shoulder. Colors include black, liver, golden liver, and roan.

Sussex Spaniel

The Sussex spaniel, too, has suffered hard times as a breed after a modest beginning under the watchful hand of a Mr. Fuller from Rosehill, Sussex, England. By 1945 just five Sussex spaniels remained in England. Then, a British woman named Joy Freer stepped in and devoted nearly sixty years to rejuvenating the breed with an accent on field work. There were a few Sussex breeders in America during this period, and their work also helped to maintain the breed. But it wasn't until the 1970s that serious efforts began in the United States with the Sussex.

This breed is often likened to a miniature Clumber spaniel of rich golden liver, with male dogs weighing over forty-five pounds. The powerful build of this attractive little dog is one of its strongest attributes,

Sussex spaniel (Pamela Kadlec)

although it tends to slow the dog down, just as the Clumber's does. Interestingly, as this dog discovers scent and closes in on the bird, his tail movement often increases in speed; also the breed has a tendency to give voice while working scent.

Today Sussex spaniels are being campaigned in the field in England and the United States. The breed is enjoying a slow comeback in popularity for working purposes. Of note, there is no split between field and show lines in this breed.

Welsh Springer Spaniel

This breed enjoys a rather ancient history dating from at least the 1500s. Its purpose was, of course, similar to other spaniels in that it flushed game, originally for falconry and then for the gun. Founded in South Wales and in much fewer numbers than the English springer, the Welsh springer has remained true to its working characteristics and is just becoming appreciated beyond Wales.

Of compact size and athletic working ability, this breed reaches eighteen to nineteen inches at the shoulder. The Welsh springer sports a unique head and gaze not duplicated by other spaniels. It is red and white in color with a dense, short coat. Although slower than the English

Welsh springer spaniel (Brian Schmidt)

springer and the cocker breeds, the Welsh springer is deliberate and intelligent in its work. It also tends to be slower to mature but possesses a keen nose and excellent tracking ability, as well as a courageous spirit.

Retrieving Breeds

All but one of the recognized retriever breeds were developed in the 1700s and 1800s. Bet you can't guess the identity of the oldest breed—that would be the standard poodle, often scoffed at as a working dog. This breed was established back in the 1500s as a hardy working dog. Today it's enjoying a resurgence of popularity in the field.

Retrievers were developed to retrieve downed game like waterfowl and upland birds to hand. But it soon became apparent that the retriever could easily adapt to quartering and flushing work, and in recent years certain dogs within at least one retriever breed, the Labrador, have been developed for their propensity to point birds.

Retriever work requires close coordination between dog and handler. First and foremost, unless the dog is quartering for upland game, he must wait for his master to shoot game to bring back. However, the team factor really kicks in when the time comes to recover downed or crippled game that the dog hasn't seen fall.

The dog must trust his handler's hand and whistle signals and must also line and hunt dead in an area—or exhibit a combination of those skills—in order to retrieve all game. Because of this teamwork, retriever believers often feel that they develop the closest bonds with their dogs.

Breeds recognized as retrievers include the American water spaniel, Boykin spaniel, Chesapeake Bay retriever, curly-coated retriever, flat-coated retriever, golden retriever, Irish water spaniel, Labrador retriever, Nova Scotia duck tolling retriever, and standard poodle.

American Water Spaniel

This wonderful dog is one of the few breeds developed in the United States, more specifically in the Wolf and Fox River valleys of Wiscon-

American water spaniel (Susan Liemohn)

sin. Its primary uses were to retrieve waterfowl (often from a boat), flush upland game and furred small game, and to be a tractable companion.

The American water spaniel ranges from fifteen to eighteen inches at the shoulder and weighs from twenty-five to forty-five pounds. A dense undercoat supports a wavy or curly topcoat that serves to protect the dog in rough and cold conditions. Colorations are shades of brown, including liver, dark brown, or chocolate.

Its attractive size and intelligence, retrieving and game-finding ability, and abundant personality have made this breed increasingly popular. Without a doubt, this breed warrants a second look in view of its varied abilities in the field, in the duck boat, and at home.

Boykin Spaniel

Another breed "made in the USA," the Boykin spaniel originated in the area surrounding Boykin, South Carolina, near the hunting-rich Wateree River. The breed was developed to assist hunters with retrieving waterfowl from the river as well as hunting wild turkeys in the bottoms.

According to breed lore, a little stray spaniel named Dumpy was rescued by a banker in Spartanburg, South Carolina, who then gave him to close friend L. W. "Whit" Boykin. This dog became the foundation of the lively little Boykin spaniel we know today.

The Boykin ranges from fourteen to eighteen inches at the shoulder and weighs twenty to forty pounds. Its color is a rich liver to chocolate, and its coat is dense and wavy. This little dog can handle demanding swimming conditions and performs well on upland game.

Boykin spaniel (Pamela Kadlec)

Chesapeake Bay Retriever

The Chessie was developed near its namesake, the Chesapeake Bay, which has a rich waterfowling history. At one time the area had a large population of market hunters who needed a tough, courageous dog that could handle the demanding job of retrieving many birds in the icy waters of the bay.

It is thought that the Chessie owes its roots to the Newfoundland, and some claim that a combination of blood from curly-coated retrievers and water spaniels is mixed in. This hasn't been substantiated, and in fact the American Chesapeake Club has an interesting record of data tracing to two unrelated Newfoundland pups named Sailor and Canton that were obtained from a sinking vessel in 1845. Sailor was a dingy red color, and descriptions of his build and coat remarkably resemble today's Chessie. Early on, these dogs were called Chesapeake Bay ducking dogs.

Chessies are relatively large, hardy dogs ranging in color from light deadgrass or sedge to dark brown, with thick oily double coats that can

Chesapeake Bay retriever (Pattie Maye)

withstand ice and cold. They can stand as tall as twenty-six inches at the shoulder and weigh upwards of eighty pounds. This breed is well known for its loyalty as well as its bravado and durability under the most adverse conditions.

Curly-Coated Retriever

One of the oldest retriever breeds, the curly originated in England and was bred to retrieve ducks from the seaboard marshes in the 1700s. Its roots include poodles, Newfoundlands, pointers, setters, and spaniels. This breed is aptly named for its signature black or liver coat, which is composed of tight, dense curls all over the body, including the tail and legs. The dense coat repels water and protects the curly from rough working conditions.

Curly-coated retrievers range from twenty-three inches (females) in height to twenty-seven inches (males), but the standard specifies that oversized dogs with otherwise recognized qualities should not be penalized. This breed can be slower to mature than some other retriever breeds but is hardy, athletic, and smart. The curly was imported to the United States and has enjoyed increasing popularity.

Curly-coated retriever (Ross Round)

Flat-Coated Retriever

The flat-coated retriever dates from nineteenth-century England, reportedly descending from the St. John's dog mixed with a combination of blood from the rather unlikely trio of field setters, sheepdogs, and spaniels. This breed quickly established itself as a class shooting dog for the sporting gentleman, excelling in both upland game and water-fowling. It has remained true to form over the years, without any big rift between field and show lines, as has so often happened with other hunting breeds.

The flat-coat experienced a decline in the United States around World War II, partly because of the increasing numbers of golden retrievers, but since the 1960s it has enjoyed steady growth. This elegant, strikingly graceful retriever is a joy to own for fanciers who can allow for its slower mental working development. Indeed, flat-coats have demonstrated that they can perform shoulder to shoulder with more popular retriever breeds in hunt tests and field trials, and sometimes win.

Tall, lean, and athletic, flat-coats come in black or liver and have a flat, dense coat to protect the dog from the elements; a slight wave in the coat is permissible. These dogs range in weight from sixty to seventy pounds.

Flat-coated retriever (Lorenzo Roncoroni)

Golden Retriever

One of the most popular dog breeds of all, the golden retriever was first developed in the highlands of Scotland by Lord Tweedmouth. In 1865 he purchased a male yellow puppy from an otherwise all-black litter of wavy-coated retrievers and bred him with a Tweed water spaniel (now

Golden retriever (Rossella Di Palma)

extinct) in 1868 and 1871. Puppies from these litters were crossed with wavy and flat-coated retrievers, another Tweed water spaniel, and a red setter. Meticulous records were kept as this breed developed into a working gamekeeper's dog and gentleman's shooting companion. By the early 1900s these dogs had found their way to North America.

The golden retriever has become a sporting dog of many attributes. Generally they are quick learners and have biddable personalities and keen intelligence. The sheer beauty of this breed has been a detriment to field stock because its popularity as a pet and in the show ring has diluted its working blood. However, the golden retriever enjoys strong working lines. If you want one, be sure to choose one from field performance blood.

The golden may reach twenty-four inches at the shoulder and weigh seventy-five or more pounds. Pleasing in symmetry and movement, the golden's physical appeal has few equals. The lustrous coat, ranging from light to a dark golden hue, provides adequate density to protect the dog in all weather conditions and field environments. This breed excels at upland work and as a water retriever and is a terrific companion.

Irish Water Spaniel

This breed developed in nineteenth-century Ireland from poodle blood crossed with other now-extinct ancient water breeds. In fact, its strongest

Irish water spaniel (Jeremy Kezer)

lineage is said to be from the extinct Southern Irish water spaniel that thrived in Ireland for a thousand years

Since its recognition, the Irish water spaniel's appearance hasn't changed: a liver color; dense, kinky curls over the body; a rat tail distinguished by two or three inches of curls at the base that taper to smooth hair at the tip; and a cascade of curls that descends over the forehead to an otherwise smooth face. These dogs should weigh no more than sixty-five pounds and be sturdy, athletic, and structurally sound.

The breed is prized for its hunting ability and companionship, as well as its healthy track record and pleasing personality.

Labrador Retriever

There is some question about where the extremely popular Labrador originated, and from which blood, but the generally accepted story traces to St. John's water dogs, with recorded writings dating from 1662. These St. John's, or smaller Newfoundland or Labrador dogs as they were called in those days, were eventually imported to the United Kingdom where mostly pure breeding continued. The dog was always described in similar fashion—black and about the size of a pointing dog—with exceptional retrieving skills and a short, dense coat that repelled water.

The Kennel Club, based in England, first recognized the Labrador as a breed in 1903, and the AKC followed suit in 1917. Since those days the Labrador has experienced phenomenal growth and popularity as a breed and remains the top registered breed by AKC for several years running.

The Labrador has evolved into three distinct coat colors—black, yellow and chocolate—but no other colors, including the much publicized silver hue, which isn't recognized by the breed standard or AKC. Strains of pointing Labs have been developed, although the Labrador Retriever Club maintains that Labradors should be bred to retrieve downed game.

This breed possesses a number of admirable qualities that make it such a popular one. It is very handsome, sturdy, well built, athletic, and friendly yet protective. The Labrador has great intelligence and early, rapid mental development. The breed standard states that heights for males should not exceed twenty-four and one-half inches at the shoulder or eighty pounds in weight. The breed is the epitome of a multipurpose retriever.

Chocolate Labrador retriever (Charles Tyson)

Black Labrador retriever (Days Afield photo)

Yellow Labrador retriever (Bill Beckett)

Nova Scotia Duck Tolling Retriever

This delightful breed is gaining in popularity and winning hearts with its many endearing qualities, unique working ability, and retrieving prowess. Developed in Nova Scotia, the breed evolved from a technique, known as tolling, for luring ducks into traps or within gun range. The dog was able to "toll" (lure) waterfowl by running and playing along the shoreline.

The active toller is no more than twenty-one inches at the shoulder for males, with a preference listed at nineteen inches, making it a medium, muscled package. Coat color is red, with white permitted on the feet, tip of the tail, and chest, with a blaze on the face; these variations give the toller a foxlike appearance. The coat should be dense, with an undercoat, and be of medium length to withstand icy waters.

While the toller was developed for a specific purpose, it has become popular throughout North America and has successfully adapted to all types of retrieving and upland work, and it's a wonderful companion and pet. The breed's clean health history, genetic lines, and keen intelligence make it worth a closer look.

Nova Scotia duck tolling retrievers (Joe Miano)

Standard Poodle

Too many folks sell the standard poodle short. This is not without basis, of course, as groomed and coifed show dogs have been prancing around for years, effectively wiping out any thoughts of this dog's performance in the field or water.

Although canines resembling poodles have been documented from ancient times, the poodle's history isn't as well understood as one would expect. The modern breed can be traced to western Europe, probably France, four hundred years ago. Its ancestry is more defined; it descended from a nearly extinct French water spaniel called the Barbet and the Hungarian water hound. Although breed historians agree to some extent in giving France the bulk of the credit for the breed, it is thought that "poodle" is derived from the German word *Pudel*, which means "one who plays in the water."

The poodle has what is described as a profuse and curly, wiry coat that requires extensive grooming. The accepted cuts for the show ring are what make many hunters turn up their noses at this breed, but its more recent reentry into working retriever circles as a bona fide performer should do much to dispel naysayers.

Standard poodle (Pamela Kadlec)

Hound Breeds

With records dating from thousands of years in Egypt and Europe, hounds have enjoyed a solid place in the history of hunting. They fall into two categories: sight hounds, which have sharp eyesight, a keen build, and exceptional speed to spot and run down prey; and scent hounds, which possess superior scenting abilities and a stalwart build with stamina and strength.

Hounds once played a significant part in the livelihoods of many families by putting game on the table and by providing furs to exchange for goods or money. In some parts of the world this is still true today. One of the most widespread uses of hounds remains big-game hunting, primarily for wild boar in North America, South America, Europe, Asia, and Australia, as well as other big game species such as bear, mountain lion, and other big cats.

Fox hunting was a European sport that was brought to America centuries ago. George Washington was a noted enthusiast. This sport has enjoyed healthy roots in the States and continues to expand in popularity.

In North America, coon hunting has become not only a serious pastime for sport and night hunters, but has also grown into a recognized competitive sport with many hunts dedicated to charitable causes. Rabbit hunting also continues to grow in popularity within the sport and competitive ranks.

In various parts of the world, hounds are used for everything from hunting deer and stags (as they were thousands of years ago) to hunting coyotes by sight, as well as hunting wild boar, bear, mountain lion, bobcat, foxes, raccoon, squirrels, rabbits, and even opossum. Along with the rough, rigorous conditions that often accompany hunts shared with hounds comes an abiding respect for the quarry and for Mother Nature.

American Black and Tan Coonhound

Most of the six registered North American coonhound breeds weren't recognized until recently by AKC (and some of them are only included with AKC as Foundation Stock Service—FSS—instead of full breed recognition), although they've been registered with UKC for some time. However, AKC welcomed the black and tan in 1945. This breed can be traced to bloodhounds and foxhounds on both sides of the Atlantic.

American black and tan coonhound (Vicki Rand)

Black and tans are fairly tall, gracefully built dogs with rich black color and tan points on the face and legs. They possess a glossy, sleek coat capable of repelling the elements, and the characteristic long, droopy hound ears. This breed is known for a resonant, deep bawling mouth on track, and a ringing, clear chop on the tree. It possesses great speed and is always a threat in competition and a favorite among pleasure hunters.

American Blue Gascon

Linked to the fabled stag and boar hounds in European history, this breed ultimately descended from the Grand Bleu de Gascogne hounds of France. These large dogs resemble North America's bluetick coonhounds but reach nearly twenty-eight inches at the shoulder and weigh up to or over one hundred pounds. Indeed, the breed was originally registered as the bluetick coonhound in North America, with the same black and blue mottling over a white background, but standardization of size and weight excluded the commonly occurring large specimens of the Gascons. As a result, a separate American Blue Gascon Association was formed in the early 1970s.

American blue Gascon (Larry Morgan)

Gascons are very popular for big game because of their ability to take cold scent and work the trail. They are also used for coon hunting and enjoy a unique popularity.

American Foxhound

These hounds are a combination of primarily English and French bloodlines and are commonly referred to as being from Walker, Trigg, or Goodman lines, although these names are commonly thrown about in very general terms describing foxhounds. They have a colorful history in America, starting with a black and tan named Tennessee Lead, famous in the 1800s for his ability of putting a red fox to ground, a talent that eluded many hounds of the times that were more suited to the less challenging gray fox. Foxhounds of all types were bred to Lead in an effort to cross on this ability, and the American foxhound soon emerged as a distinct breed.

Most popular for hunting fox, this medium-sized pack hound breed can be any hound color, including tricolor, red and white, and lemon and white. Foxhounds can be found in traditional horseback pack hunts in America, as well as in the rapidly growing "fox pen" competitions.

American Foxhounds on the trail in Virginia. (Becky Mills)

Basset Hound

Instantly recognizable by its low-slung stature; sad, droopy eyes; and exceptionally long hound ears, the basset has quite a following as a companion dog and hunting hound. With ties to the St. Hubert hounds that crop up in most historical references to hounds in general,

and possibly to the bloodhound, this breed traces to sixth-century France. The basset was bred to be an enjoyable foot-hunting hound and became known for its tenacity after badger, rabbits, and hare. Today the basset is used primarily for rabbit and small game, although it can be used on some game birds too.

Bassets still run in packs in some parts of the world and in competition. They also run in braces in AKC events, and the Basset Hound Club of America

Basset hound (Francesca Capodagli)

recently incorporated a hunt test as well. Although bassets appear small, they average between fifty and seventy pounds. Bassets can be of any recognized hound color, including tricolor, red and white, or lemon and white.

Beagle

References to small hounds can be found in writings throughout much of Europe as far back as two thousand years. In the 1700s these tiny packages emerged as successful rabbit dogs in England; active records were kept by the breed's recognized forefathers, Reverend Phillip Honeywood and Thomas Johnson, both of England, in the 1800s.

AKC first recognized the breed in 1884, and in 1888 the National Beagle Club was established and a first field trial began. Today several different registries host competitive events incorporating a number of methods for running and judging the skill of these delightful dogs for running rabbits.

As with many other hounds, beagles can be any recognized hound color, including the popular tricolor (black, tan, and white) or red and white. They come in two sizes: thirteen inches and fifteen inches.

Beagle (Don McVay)

Bloodhound

The ubiquitous St. Hubert hound is commonly held as the ancestor of today's bloodhound; indeed, the names are often used interchangeably. Early records hint that Talbot hounds were also crossed to produce and perfect the bloodhound breed. The bloodhound has influenced a number of hound breeds, as well as several other hunting breeds, because of its superior scenting ability and its tenacity on trail.

First seen in France and Belgium, the breed migrated to England and North America and was used to cold trail deer, other big game, and even small game. Today the breed is not as common as a hunting dog, although bloodhounds and bloodhound crosses are still used in parts of the world on big game, and active horseback hunts exist in Europe where the dogs hunt actual human scent "to the boot" in packs.

Bloodhounds are widely used in search and rescue and in law enforcement; in fact, evidence turned up by bloodhounds is admissible in a court of law.

Reaching heights of twenty-seven or more inches and weights of over one hundred pounds, this massive breed comes in the classic red color, as well as black and tan, and liver and tan. The dog has a deep, melodious tone to its voice, coupled with droopy eyes, ears, and flews.

Bloodhound (Alberto Velis)

Bluetick Coonhound

The bluetick is an instantly recognizable breed often seen in TV commercials. It shares a history with its larger cousin, the American blue Gascon, and was even paired with the English coonhound for a number of years, in part because of similar coloring.

Shoulder heights range from twenty-two to twenty-seven inches, and males weigh up to eighty pounds and females sixty-five pounds.

Bluetick coonhound (Author photo)

Color should be mottled dark blue and blue-black on a white background, although tan points over the eyes and on the lower legs are permissible, as are black patches on the body.

This dog has deep roots in American history and a strong following for big-game and coon hunting because of its scenting and trailing ability, although it is often teased for "blue-ticking" (bogging down) on some trails. This trait has appeared less often as superior breeding practices continue to improve the best aspects of the bluetick coonhound, one of the six recognized coonhound breeds.

Dachshund

According to breed lore, this low-slung "hot dog" breed has ties to the bloodhound, as well as to other European hounds and terriers. Developed in Germany, the dachshund (literally "badger dog") evolved to scent, chase, catch, and perhaps kill badgers and other ground game, as well as fox and even wild boar. Today the breed is used extensively on rabbits, and the dogs can be amazing little retrievers as well.

Known in America as "wiener dogs," they are often referred to as "Dackels" or "Teckels" in Germany. Dachshunds grow up to nine inches tall at the shoulder, and the standard size can weigh about thirty pounds while

Dachshund, smooth haired (Lorenzo Roncoroni)

Dachshund, longhaired (Lorenzo Roncoroni)

the miniatures weigh just eleven pounds. A wide range of colors and coat variations are possible: black and tan, gray and tan, fawn and tan, or chocolate and tan; solid colors of red, sable, or cream (solid black or chocolate are disqualifying faults); single or double dapple, brindle, wild boar, red boar, blue and tan, black and cream, and piebald. Coat variations include smooth, longhaired, and wirehaired, with slightly shorter body length in the latter. This breed can suffer from spinal and vertebrae problems.

Dachshund, wirehaired (Lorenzo Roncoroni)

English Coonhound

English coonhound (Vicki Rand)

This breed crossed paths with the bluetick coonhound and descended from the original foxhounds, having first been registered as the English fox and coonhound. It also strongly influenced the bluetick and the treeing Walker breeds.

English coonhounds come in three primary color phases, including the most popular redtick (red hairs on a white background), bluetick (as in the bluetick breed but with more red or tan), and tricolor, a striking combination of bluetick, redtick, and tan.

These dogs excel on big game and raccoon and have a fairly high success rate in competition circles, even higher when you consider this breed's impact on the most popular coonhound, the treeing Walker. Known for big bawl mouths on track and for being hard tree dogs, the English coonhound is definitely all hound.

English Foxhound

Originally evolving from several different breeds, reportedly including the greyhound, staghound, and bloodhound, this breed emerged in England and was first brought to North America in the 1600s. Although the English foxhound ranks lowest in number of the three foxhounds—the others being the American foxhound and crossbred foxhounds—recognized by the Masters of Foxhounds Association of North America (MFHA), it is a breed that radiates tradition and quality of bloodline.

Dogs can reach shoulder heights of twenty-seven inches and weights of seventy-five pounds. The most popular color remains tricolor, with combinations of black, tan, and white; but "pies" of the color of

English foxhound (Emily Latimer)

hare or badger, or yellow or tan are allowed. The English foxhound has a certain classic look known as symmetry, which defines the breed.

Greyhound

The greyhound dates from the time of the pharaohs in Egypt and to Alexander the Great, although the origin of the breed's name is unknown. Always a sign of nobility, these dogs were associated with speed (up to forty-five miles per hour) and grace in pursuing game by sight. U.S. Army General George A. Custer traveled with several greyhounds during his campaigns in the West in the 1800s.

In modern hunting, greyhounds are used primarily for sight hunting coyotes and rabbits and hare in certain parts of the States and the world. Greyhound racing is a popular betting sport, although many used-up race dogs end up as rescued dogs.

This breed can reach thirty inches at the shoulder and can weigh seventy-five to eighty pounds. Colors include solid as well as brindle and spotted variations of red, fawn, black, gray and white, with a hard, glossy coat.

Greyhound (Maureen Lucas)

Harrier

Used on hares and foxes for thousands of years, this breed is regarded by many as a smaller version of the English foxhound. It also causes some confusion with the beagle, as it falls between those two breeds in size, roughly twenty-one inches at the shoulder and up to sixty pounds. This breed has a very sturdy build and is meant to hunt game, primarily hare, in packs.

While some beagles are born with rear dewclaws, which are often removed at three to five days but leave a slight scar, and sometimes have blue eyes, harriers reportedly never have either characteristic. Many people use this as a means to differentiate between the two.

Harriers have fallen drastically in numbers in the United States, but are seeing a resurgence of popularity in other parts of the world.

Majestic Tree Hound

This breed resembles the bloodhound, and rightly so, for it specifically descends from the bloodhound and the St. Hubert hound from eighth-century southern France. These hounds were used to hunt deer, big game, and fox and crossed with greyhounds and other hound breeds to develop the majestic tree hound we know in America.

Majestic tree hounds (Lance Morrow)

Today these hounds are used on big game such as bear and mountain lion and have been successful on jaguars in parts of the world, as well. They are well proportioned in size, height, and facial features and can come in any color combination.

Plott Hound

North Carolina's state dog, the Plott hound traces its ancestry to wild boar hounds of Europe. In 1750 Jonathan Plott brought some of these hounds along when he immigrated to western North Carolina from his native Germany. He used them for hunting bear and continued to breed within his family of hounds. Despite a few reported outcrosses with big-game hounds, the breed has largely remained pure to its original foundation.

Today the Plott hound enjoys a reputation for tenacity and toughness on bear and other big game while also displaying talent for running coon with skill.

These dogs are about twenty-five inches at the shoulder. Colors include the popular brindle in dark or light variations of yellow, red, tan, brown, gray, and black brindle, as well as solid black, and brindle with a

Plott hound (Vicki Rand)

black "saddle" permissible. A small amount of white is allowed on the chest and feet.

Redbone
The foxhound and bloodhound are thought to be the foundation of this breed, which may have originated in Ireland and Scotland. Brought to

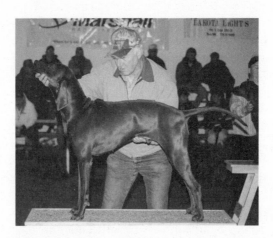

Redbone (Vicki Rand)

the States in the 1700s, the redbone continued to evolve, and color variations once included a black saddle; however, the deep red signature breed color eventually emerged. A small amount of white is allowed.

The redbone should depict grace and symmetry with deep brown intelligent eyes and a pleasing face reflecting wisdom. The popular coming-of-age book (and movie) by Wilson Rawls *Where the Red Fern Grows* (Garden City, NY: Doubleday, 1961) featured two redbone coonhounds.

Rhodesian Ridgeback

This interesting breed originated in South Africa, reportedly near the Cape of Good Hope. In the sixteenth century a breed of hunting dog was found with the hair along the backbone ridge turned forward. The dog evolved as a breed that could handle big game as well as birds and also function as a guard dog while withstanding the rigors of the climate.

Ridgebacks are used successfully on deer, bear, mountain lion, bobcat, raccoon, and wild boar yet also can be trained to hunt and retrieve birds. They are sturdy and fast, with a solid, sleek, muscular build. They stand up to twenty-seven inches and weigh up to eighty pounds. The color of the breed is called wheaten, from light to red. Slight white on the chest or toes is permissible, and the trademark ridge of reverse hair is required.

Rhodesian ridgeback (Sharon C. Johnson)

Scottish Deerhound

The origin of the Scottish deerhound traces to the sixteenth and seventeenth centuries, with vague references to various Irish wolfhounds and deerhounds well before then.

Scottish deerhound (Lyn Robb)

Deerhounds were held in high esteem and only certain nobles could own them, which was similar to greyhounds of that time. They were revered for their great speed and ability to run and subsequently kill Scottish deer, which averaged 250 pounds. And they did so singly or in pairs.

While it is commonly thought that it is illegal to hunt antlered game with dogs in the United States, a number of southern states permit it either statewide or in certain sections, including Georgia, Florida, South Carolina, and Mississippi. Deerhounds are used on wild boars, coyotes, rabbits, and even foxes in some areas.

Keen for human companionship, this breed is tall and stately, with males reaching up to thirty-two inches or more at the shoulder and weighing over one hundred pounds. Symmetry is essential to the overall function of the deerhound, which should resemble a larger version of the greyhound with more bone and substance. The wiry coat—softer on the face, breast, and belly—is colored the popular dark blue-gray, dark or light gray, or brindle or yellow, sandy-red, or red-fawn, with black ears and muzzles.

Treeing Walker

The treeing Walker sprang from American and English foxhounds in the United States. It is one of the six recognized coonhound breeds. The black and tan hound Tennessee Lead influenced the foxhounds and, in turn, the treeing Walker in the 1800s as a dog that could drive a red fox to den. Many breed fanciers feel that this dog put the exceptional track drive of the modern treeing Walker in the breed. The Walker family of Kentucky and George Washington Maupin played significant roles in the evolution of this breed. It was included as an English fox and coonhound in 1905 and later recognized as a separate breed in 1945.

These dogs can reach twenty-seven inches at the shoulder and weigh eighty pounds. Most dogs are tricolor—black, white, and tan—with various combinations, and sport a short, dense coat. They have a wide range of mouth tone but generally give plenty of mouth on track with a hard, ringing chop on the tree.

Treeing Walker (Frank Giddings)

While treeing Walkers have a propensity toward fast game—they're often used as deer dogs where legal—they have a keen prowess for treeing raccoon in sharp fashion and are competitively the most winning of the coonhound breeds.

Terriers and Curs

These are some pretty amazing dogs that have the ability to do all sorts of hunting tasks. The group includes several cur breeds and terriers that have evolved into versatile dogs capable of producing different types of game. Airedales and curs possess many of the attributes of hounds, and to a lesser degree this applies to the rest of the terriers as well.

Airedale Terrier

This breed can be traced to the Aire River area of Yorkshire, England, and

it emerged in the 1800s as a well-rounded hunting dog with many skills. Descended from the otterhound and broken-coated terriers, this dynamic dog was first called the Waterside terrier, then Bingley terrier, and finally the Airedale. This terrier can hunt and retrieve and tree game, and it might be the perfect choice as an all-around dog that isn't a specialist. The Airedale can work on fur and feather.

The sides and upper body of this dog should be black or dark grizzle in color, sometimes with red included, and the legs, underbody, and most of the head should be tan. The coat is dense, wiry, and short, with some crinkle allowed. The Airedale reaches about twenty-three inches at the shoulder and can weigh over fifty pounds.

Airedale terrier (Chris Halvorson-Dog Ads Photo)

Curs—Blackmouth, Camus, Catahoula Leopard, Stephens Cur

The blackmouth cur is actually yellow, or variations thereof, although there is an occasional blue. It has black points about the head and ears and does possess a black mouth. This is a sturdy breed, and males can weigh over sixty pounds. These dogs are mostly silent on track but are hard tree dogs that will stay put. Blackmouths are used on raccoon, squirrels, opossums, hogs, mountain lion, bobcat, and bear. They will retrieve when taught and can help pen cattle.

The Camus cur is accepted as a cross between the Catahoula leopard dog and a Canadian cur, and there are a number of similar cur breeds such as the Kemmer stock mountain cur, treeing Tennessee brindle, mountain view cur, leopard cur, and treeing cur.

Blackmouth curs: Ladner stock, left; Bruno stock, right. (Casimir Bonczewski)

The original mountain cur—colored blue, yellow, or brindle—claims its ancestry from the dogs Spanish explorer Hernando de Soto brought to America in the 1500s. It was further developed in the Shenandoah and Appalachian Mountains and then moved west as the breed expanded and gained popularity. Stephens curs were direct descendants of the mountain cur, but the breed was modified by a hunter named Hugh Stephens and is usually black with white points on the feet, chest, and sometimes a white collar around the neck.

The Catahoula leopard dog has distinctive mottled spotting on the body and usually comes in blue leopard, red leopard, black, light, and dark shades of red or yellow, and brindle, often with white toes and chest. This is

Original mountain cur (Alan Cassell)

the largest of the recognized cur breeds, and some specimens can weigh up to one hundred pounds. This gritty breed can handle wild cattle and hogs and is excellent on big game and very good for raccoon and squirrel.

Catahoula leopard dog (High Plains Journal-Kylene Orbaugh Photo http://www.goldstarcatahoulas.com)

German Jagdterrier

The feisty little Jagdterrier resembles the dachshund in many ways but is thirteen to sixteen inches at the shoulder and weighs up to about twenty pounds. Used for badger, fox, and weasel, this dog was developed in Germany at the turn of the twentieth century. In German, *jagd* means "to hunt" and *terrier* derives from the French word for "earth," or "ground." However,

German Jagdterrier (Sharon Jones)

this dog can also tree game such as squirrels and raccoon, giving voice on track and whining at the tree.

Although a relatively small dog, the Jagdterrier won't back down from big game such as bear, mountain lion, and wild boar. This dog will also blood trail when taught and can track wounded game.

Not recognized by AKC, it was registered with UKC in 1993, which is fairly recent by any standard. With a smooth or harsh coat, the Jagdterrier's most popular color is black with tan, although black or dark brown with tan or red variations on the face, chest, and legs is acceptable.

Jack Russell Terrier

The Jack Russell seems to have an exceptional fan club, and with good reason. These dogs can do just about anything—just ask their owners! The breed traces to the Reverend John Russell from southern England in the 1800s. This man rode with foxhounds and kept his terriers in saddlebags, ready to bolt fox from dens. Consequently, he developed fearless little dogs that would go to ground and root out live game. This breed reaches fourteen inches and can weigh close to twenty pounds.

Jack Russell terrier (Renee Glover, Animals in Action)

It might have a smooth, flat, hard coat or a broken coat that is harsh and straight; both have an undercoat to withstand the elements. The body of this dog is usually white with black, tan, or brown markings, usually about the head.

All of the breeds that go to ground have the tenacity to stay there for a long time, but this is particularly true of the Jack Russell. If you venture into the woodlands with one, *be sure you have the means to dig your dog out of trouble!*

CHAPTER
THREE

Looking for a Dog— Options

From the Cradle—Starting with a Puppy

O nce you reach a decision to add a dog to the household, other things will vault into action. You start involuntarily dreaming of puppies and more puppies. While this occurs out of the blue, it seems like a logical place to start—with a puppy—so your new hunting protégé can grow and become one with you and your ways.

There'll be plenty of work ahead, as the acquisition of a puppy is not unlike the addition of a new infant to the family, but this effort seems minute *before* the fact. Little thought is given to twice or thrice daily feedings, play sessions, and housebreaking lessons, let alone the early training that a new puppy demands. Instead, voluminous visions of a cute little butterball—one that magically transforms into the best hunting dog of all time—dances through your head, consuming every thought.

Perhaps this is as it should be; there *is* something special about a new puppy. Once you bring the little rascal home, he or she will inexplicably invade your world. Soon you're rearranging plans and commitments to accommodate the new character. Your life has probably changed for the next ten to fifteen years, either subtly or drastically, and likely you won't be sorry.

Where to Find Them

So you want a new puppy. Human tendency is to check the Sunday classifieds under "pets" for available puppies nearby. While this is one possible source, it's not necessarily the best for locating good hunting stock. That's not to say it's impossible to strike pay dirt—my first registered dog was a $50 newspaper puppy that became a crackerjack dog—but your odds are lower for finding good prospects than if you'd checked breed and gundog publications. Any number of backyard breedings occurring for all the wrong reasons may produce puppies with all the wrong instincts, or none at all. If you *do* find some litters of interest, phone ahead with specific questions (covered in the next few chapters) before you make a trip.

With research you'll find other sources to consider, such as the many periodicals that are dedicated to all working dogs within each rank. Internet sites can be helpful, too. Ethical breeders offering sound litters from well-bred hunting stock use these opportunities to advertise their puppies. (Sample sources are found in Resources section at the end of this book.)

Check in your area and surrounding states for avid hunters, field trialers, and hunt testers who campaign your chosen breed. Start making phone calls. Ask for suggestions on puppy availability. With a little nudging, you may receive priceless information about characteristics within certain lines of any breed that may help you narrow your search for the right dog.

How to Pick Them

Advice abounds on how to pick the perfect puppy. A popular old sayings is close your eyes, reach in, and pick one when you've chosen a litter with the traits and parentage you desire. There is often merit to that advice. Some experts suggest you observe the puppies and eliminate the shiest and the boldest puppies and pick one that is outgoing yet cautious. Still others use results from the Puppy Aptitude Test (PAT) developed over the years by various professionals and refined by Joachim and Wendy Volhard. The PAT provides screening criteria for each puppy to reveal intelligence, obedience potential, and compatibility, giving an opportunity to evaluate temperaments and relationships to humans. And don't overlook this one: perhaps you should pick the puppy that picks you.

An obvious drawback to puppy observation and testing is that certain variables may affect performance during these sessions. Some puppies may have just drank or eaten or may have played hard.

The Volhard Puppy Aptitude Test

Reprinted by permission of the authors.

PAT uses a scoring system from 1-6 and consists of ten tests. The tests are done consecutively and in the order listed. Each test is scored separately, and interpreted on its own merits. The scores are not averaged, and there are no winners or losers. The entire purpose is to select the right puppy for the right home. Ideally, the test is administered when the puppy is about 49 days of age.

The tests are as follows:

1. Social Attraction - degree of social attraction to people, confidence or dependence.
2. Following - willingness to follow a person.
3. Restraint - degree of dominant or submissive tendency, and ease of handling in difficult situations.
4. Social Dominance - degree of acceptance of social dominance by a person.
5. Elevation - degree of accepting dominance while in a position of no control, such as at the veterinarian or groomer.
6. Retrieving - degree of willingness to do something for you. Together with Social Attraction and Following a key indicator for ease or difficulty in training.
7. Touch Sensitivity - degree of sensitivity to touch.
8. Sound Sensitivity - degree of sensitivity to sound, such as loud noises or thunderstorms.
9. Sight Sensitivity - degree of response to a moving object, such as chasing bicycles, children or squirrels.
10. Stability - degree of startle response to a strange object.

During the testing make a note of the heart rate of the pup, which is an indication of how it deals with stress, as well as its energy level. Puppies come with high, medium or low energy levels. You have to decide for yourself which suits your lifestyle. Dogs with high energy levels need a great deal of exercise, and will get into mischief if this energy is not channeled into the right direction.

Finally, look at the overall structure of the puppy. You see what you get at 49 days age. If the pup has strong and straight front and back legs, with all four feet pointing in the same direction, it will grow up that way, provided you give it the proper diet and environment in which to grow. If you notice something out of the ordinary at this age, it will stay with puppy for the rest of its life. He will not grow out of it.

How to Test

Here are the ground rules for performing the test:

The Volhard Puppy Aptitude Test

The testing is done in a location unfamiliar to the puppies. This does not mean they have to be taken away from home. A 10-foot-square area is perfectly adequate, such as a room in the house where the puppies have not been.

The puppies are tested one at a time.

There are no other dogs or people, except the scorer and the tester, in the testing area.

The puppies do not know the tester.

The scorer is a disinterested third party and not the person interested in selling you a puppy.

The scorer is unobtrusive and positions him or herself so he or she can observe the puppies' responses without having to move.

The puppies are tested before they are fed.

The puppies are tested when they are at their liveliest.

Do not try to test a puppy that is not feeling well.

Puppies should not be tested the day of or the day after being vaccinated.

Only the first response counts.

During testing maintain a positive, upbeat and friendly attitude toward the puppies. Try to get each puppy to interact with you to bring out the best in him or her. Make the test a pleasant experience for the puppy.

1. Social attraction - the owner or caretaker of the puppies places it in the test area about four feet from the tester and then leaves the test area. The tester kneels down and coaxes the puppy to come to him or her by encouragingly and gently clapping hands and calling. The tester must coax the puppy in the opposite direction from where it entered the test area. Hint: Lean backward, sitting on your heels instead of leaning forward toward the puppy. Keep your hands close to your body encouraging the puppy to come to you instead of trying to reach for the puppy.

2. Following - the tester stands up and slowly walks away encouraging the puppy to follow. Hint: Make sure the puppy sees you walk away and get the puppy to focus on you by lightly clapping your hands and using verbal encouragement to get the puppy to follow you. Do not lean over the puppy.

3. Restraint - the tester crouches down and gently rolls the puppy on its back and holds it on its back for 30 seconds. Hint: Hold the puppy down without applying too much

The Volhard Puppy Aptitude Test (*Continued*)

pressure. The object is not to keep it on its back but to test its response to being placed in that position.

4. Social Dominance - let the puppy stand up or sit and gently stroke it from the head to the back while you crouch beside it. See if it will lick your face, an indication of a forgiving nature. Continue stroking until you see a behavior you can score. Hint: When you crouch next to the puppy avoid leaning or hovering over the puppy. Have the puppy at your side with both of you facing in the same direction.

5. Elevation Dominance - the tester cradles the puppy with both hands, supporting the puppy under its chest and gently lifts it two feet off the ground and holds it there for 30 seconds.

6. Retrieving - the tester crouches beside the puppy and attracts its attention with a crumpled up piece of paper. When the puppy shows some interest, the tester throws the paper no more than four feet in front of the puppy encouraging it to retrieve the paper.

7. Touch Sensitivity - the tester locates the webbing of one the puppy's front paws and presses it lightly between his index finger and thumb. The tester gradually increases pressure while counting to ten and stops when the puppy pulls away or shows signs of discomfort.

8. Sound Sensitivity - the puppy is placed in the center of the testing area and an assistant stationed at the perimeter makes a sharp noise, such as banging a metal spoon on the bottom of a metal pan.

9. Sight Sensitivity - the puppy is placed in the center of the testing area. The tester ties a string around a bath towel and jerks it across the floor, two feet away from the puppy.

10. Stability - an umbrella is opened about five feet from the puppy and gently placed on the ground.

Scoring the Results

Following are the responses you will see and the score assigned to each particular response. You will see some variations and will have to make a judgment on what score to give them.

Test	Response	Score
Social Attraction	Came readily, tail up, jumped, bit at hands	1
	Came readily, tail up, pawed, licked at hands	2
	Came readily, tail up	3
	Came readily, tail down	4
	Came hesitantly, tail down	5

The Volhard Puppy Aptitude Test (*Continued*)

	Didn't come at all	6

Following	Followed readily, tail up, got underfoot, bit at feet	1
	Followed readily, tail up, got underfoot	2
	Followed readily, tail up	3
	Followed readily, tail down	4
	Followed hesitantly, tail down	5
	Did not follow or went away	6

Restraint	Struggled fiercely, flailed, bit	1
	Struggled fiercely, flailed	2
	Settled, struggled, settled with some eye contact	3
	Struggled, then settled	4
	No struggle	5
	No struggle, strained to avoid eye contact	6

Social Dominance	Jumped, pawed, bit, growled	1
	Jumped, pawed	2
	Cuddled up to tester and tried to lick face	3
	Squirmed, licked at hands	4
	Rolled over, licked at hands	5
	Went away and stayed away	6

Elevation Dominance	Struggled fiercely, tried to bite	1
	Struggled fiercely	2
	Struggled, settled, struggled, settled	3
	No struggle, relaxed	4
	No struggle, body stiff	5
	No struggle, froze	6

Retrieving	Chased object, picked it up and ran away	1
	Chased object, stood over it and did not return	2
	Chased object, picked it up and returned with it to tester	3
	Chased object and returned without it to tester	4
	Started to chase object, lost interest	5

The Volhard Puppy Aptitude Test (*Continued*)

	Does not chase object	6

Touch Sensitivity	8-10 count before response	1
	6-8 count before response	2
	5-6 count before response	3
	3-5 count before response	4
	2-3 count before response	5
	1-2 count before response	6

Sound Sensitivity	Listened, located sound and ran toward it barking	1
	Listened, located sound and walked slowly toward it	2
	Listened, located sound and showed curiosity	3
	Listened and located sound	4
	Cringed, backed off and hid behind tester	5
	Ignored sound and showed no curiosity	6

Sight Sensitivity	Looked, attacked and bit object	1
	Looked and put feet on object and put mouth on it	2
	Looked with curiosity and attempted to investigate, tail up	3
	Looked with curiosity, tail down	4
	Ran away or hid behind tester	5
	Hid behind tester	6

Stability	Looked and ran to the umbrella, mouthing or biting it	1
	Looked and walked to the umbrella, smelling it cautiously	2
	Looked and went to investigate	3
	Sat and looked, but did not move toward the umbrella	3
	Showed little or no interest	4
	Ran away from the umbrella	5
	Showed no interest	6

What the Scores Mean

The scores are interpreted as follows:

The Volhard Puppy Aptitude Test (*Continued*)

Mostly 1's -

- Strong desire to be pack leader and is not shy about bucking for a promotion
- Has a predisposition to be aggressive to people and other dogs and will bite
- Should only be placed into a very experienced home where the dog will be trained and worked on a regular basis

Mostly 2's -

- Also has leadership aspirations
- May be hard to manage and has the capacity to bite
- Has lots of self-confidence
- Should not be placed into an inexperienced home
- Too unruly to be good with children and elderly people, or other animals
- Needs strict schedule, loads of exercise and lots of training
- Has the potential to be a great show dog with someone who understands dog behavior

Stay away from the puppy with a lot of 1's or 2's. It has lots of leadership aspirations and may be difficult to manage. This puppy needs an experienced home. Not good with children.

Mostly 3's -

- Can be a high energy dog and may need lots of exercise
- Good with people and other animals
- Can be a bit of a handful to live with
- Needs training, does very well at it and learns quickly
- Great dog for second-time owner

Mostly 4's -

- The kind of dog that makes the perfect pet
- Best choice for the first-time owner.
- Rarely will buck for a promotion in the family
- Easy to train, and rather quiet
- Good with elderly people, children, although may need protection from the children
- Choose this pup, take it to obedience classes, and you'll be the star, without having to do too much work!

The puppy with mostly 3's and 4's can be quite a handful, but should be good with children and does well with training. Energy needs to be dispersed with plenty of exercise.

Mostly 5's -

The Volhard Puppy Aptitude Test (*Continued*)

- Fearful, shy and needs special handling
- Will run away at the slightest stress in its life
- Strange people, strange places, different floor or ground surfaces may upset it
- Often afraid of loud noises and terrified of thunder storms
- When you greet it upon your return, may submissively urinate
- Needs a very special home where the environment doesn't change too much and where there are no children
- Best for a quiet, elderly couple
- If cornered and cannot get away, has a tendency to bite

Mostly 6's -

- So independent that he doesn't need you or other people
- Doesn't care if he is trained or not - he is his own person
- Unlikely to bond to you, since he doesn't need you
- A great guard dog for gas stations!
- Do not take this puppy and think you can change him into a lovable bundle - you can't, so leave well enough alone

Interpreting the Scores

Few puppies will test with all 2's or all 3's - there will be a mixture of scores.

For that first-time, wonderfully easy to train, potential star, look for a puppy that has quite a few 4's and 3's. Don't worry about the score on Touch Sensitivity - you can compensate for that with the right training equipment.

Avoid the puppy with a score of 1 on the Restraint and Elevation tests. This puppy will be too much for the first-time owner.

It's hard not to become emotional when picking a puppy - they are all so cute, soft and cuddly. Remind yourself that this dog is going to be with you for 8 to 16 years. Don't hesitate to step back a little to contemplate your decision. Sleep on it and review it in the light of day.

It's a lot more fun to have a good dog, one that is easy to train, one you can live with and one you can be proud of, than one that is a constant struggle.

The Volhard Puppy Aptitude Test (*Continued*)

These candidates may be ready to nap. They'll appear sluggish, lazy, or unresponsive. An hour later, these same puppies may reveal completely different results. When possible, evaluate a litter a few times before making a decision. Determine as much as possible the good and bad qualities of both parents, as these things could reflect on the puppies and may aid in making your decision. When you're buying a puppy sight unseen, convey your goals for the puppy and your training ability to the breeder to assist the breeder's choice.

Do you want a male or a female or does this even matter? There are generalizations to consider and you've probably heard them all. Male puppies tend to progress slower but they do catch up to their faster-maturing sisters in time! As a result, however, females within a litter may look sportier than the males when young, and it pays to keep this in mind.

Males also tend to be hardheaded, while females are renowned for being sensitive and moody. Females will be sidelined once or twice yearly during heat cycles of approximately twenty-one days. The majority of females used to come into heat every six months, but nowadays many females have one cycle yearly. There are two ways to prevent heat cycles from interfering with hunting season: birth control can be effective but troublesome, or you can spay your female, thus providing a permanent and irreversible solution. Be certain that puppies won't ever cross your mind before electing to spay your female. A third scenario does exist—Lady Luck may intervene and regulate your female's cycles apart from hunting season.

Males won't have heat cycles, but often act like they're "in heat." Some males seem more interested in urinating on bushes and smelling for females than hunting. However, if actual hunting experience and training don't funnel the dog's instincts toward his job, he may be a dog with such low desire that you ought to consider a replacement. Sometimes that is an option, sometimes it's not. Most males are pretty bold and assertive overall. Intact males have a tendency to roam but today's control laws keep that in check. Bottom line? Both males and females are wonderful choices for lifelong hunting and family companions. Consider your options and make your choice.

Finally, you should become familiar with various physical deformities that could be problematic. "Dentally speaking" a bad bite—where the upper and lower teeth mesh, or not—reveals normal, overshot, or undershot jaws; abnormalities might be a disqualifying fault in some breeds and is hereditary. Therefore, this problem could hamper breeding or showing. It won't usually affect the dog's ability to hunt but could hinder proper chewing of food, possibly causing health problems.

Certain reproductive aspects should be considered. Are both testicles descended of the male puppy you like? Sometimes this is tough to determine in a seven-week-old puppy, but if you see or feel just one testicle there could be trouble ahead. The second testicle may be retained (cryptorchidism) in the abdominal cavity. This may or may not cause any problems in and of itself, but a retained testicle could become cancerous in years to come. If there is but one testicle the dog is a monorchid, which *may* be hereditary (the jury is mixed). A female should be checked for a normally formed vulva; some females have inverted vulvas. This condition may pose sanitary problems and might escalate to health or breeding concerns. Often, however, this is corrected naturally during the occurrence of a heat cycle.

Check a puppy over for other odd-looking places. Is the umbilical cord area on the abdomen healed normally or is there a bump or inverted area? This could signify a hernia, perhaps umbilical or inguinal, often requiring corrective surgery. Failure to do so might present a life-threatening situation down the road.

Look for eyelashes or eyelids that turn in or out; this condition can provide endless discomfort and the only permanent solution is surgery. How is the overall coat? It should appear healthy and shiny, without bare spots or dullness.

Once you take your puppy home, most breeders provide a twenty-four- to seventy-two-hour grace period for veterinary examination. During this time if any health or physical problems are uncovered, the breeder will provide an adjustment, exchange, or refund, depending on the problem. Most contracts contain this jargon, but if you find a physical problem that concerns you and you still want to take the puppy home, openly discuss the situation and any recourse with the seller. Should the contract not cover this, you may want the seller to add this provision before you buy the puppy. These same conditions usually apply when a puppy has been shipped by air. Ultimately, it pays to have any new puppy—or dog—checked by your veterinarian upon receipt.

Perhaps the Started Dog

When considering a new hunting dog, other choices besides a puppy exist. You might want to buy an older puppy, perhaps one "started" in training, which means the puppy has had introductory training and socialization.

Certainly the biggest drawback to buying a started dog is the missed opportunity to develop the bond that would have developed had you begun with a seven-week-old puppy. You'll resign yourself to the fact that you played no part in his early socialization; you have no knowledge of what did or didn't take place during that important period of mental development. This *might* be a factor in your dog's overall opportunities to realize his potential.

However, positive points abound when buying the started dog. You'll know more closely what he'll look like as an adult, and many—if not all—of the early puppy responsibilities are history. Your started dog may be already house trained or kennel savvy. His puppy vaccinations should be completed and you can begin his training. This option therefore becomes attractive to people with time constraints. Started dogs are often available at different stages of training. Advancement and level of ability are reflected in price.

Often started dogs are bought on a trial period from one week to a month. This is often commensurate with the buyer's experience and the dog's level of training. In the presence of inexperience, a decision to grant a trial by the seller may hinge on whether a professional or skilled amateur trainer will assist the buyer in the evaluation and decision-making process. Absence of this security blanket could understandably stymie any potential trial period. A thorough health checkup should be done during any trial or grace period.

Fully Trained Dogs

Your next viable option is to skip the puppy business altogether and purchase a fully trained dog. There are many advantages on your side with price being the biggest drawback. A completely trained dog will require little more from you than a "learning curve" as you familiarize yourself with your new hunting companion, and your dog in turn becomes accustomed to your idiosyncrasies. You know exactly what you're buying. What you see is what you get.

Your fully trained gundog should come with all health clearances. Dogs over two years old should have hip clearance and pertinent health certifications. In the absence of these things, you should insist on a full examination and X-rays when appropriate before you part with hard-earned cash. Once these precautions are secured, you can begin training, hunting, and enjoying your new fully trained companion right away.

Purebred versus Crossbred

Are you dead set on a purebred dog—which usually means registered with papers—or do you just want a good, solid hunting companion? Does crossbreeding matter? (Certain registries, such as the Professional Kennel Club [PKC], register crossbreds.)

A purebred dog has lineage strictly from within his breed that has been recorded for generations. Occasionally, purebred dogs do not come with papers; be certain of your purchase. Dogs without registration papers usually can't compete in organized field events (except PKC). This may not concern you when you get your puppy, but it might be a factor down the road. Without those papers your ship will be sunk.

Crossbred dogs *may* have known lineage on each side, but since the puppy is a product of two different breeds he cannot be registered as one or the other. Examples would include a golden retriever/pointer mix, or a field spaniel/Labrador mix. Although pedigrees may be available for both sire and dam, the resulting offspring are not purebred. The bottom line? You must determine what you want in your new dog. If you know that you will never wish to compete with your dog, perhaps the crossbred or mixed-breed dog is for you. Initial investment would be lower since most crossbred puppies cost far less, often with no charge. Some of the best hunting dogs ever to grace this earth heralded from mixed parentage. Let's face it—the dogs in the field know not whether they have papers—performance is job one. Weigh your options before you make this hefty decision.

Registration papers come in different varieties. Do your homework. Know exactly what you are buying and what rights your dog's papers give you as his owner. The AKC has limited and full registration. If you purchase a puppy with limited registration, you can't breed that dog unless you can persuade the breeder to change your dog's papered status from limited to full registration, even though you own the dog. Some breeders have good reasons for selling on limited registration, such as wanting to responsibly protect their breeding stock by withholding full registration until the dog reaches breeding age, procures all health clearances, and demonstrates the potential to improve the breed. Other puppies may have disqualifying faults and shouldn't be bred, but can live productive lives. Other breeders use limited registration to keep their breeding stock exclusive, making it impossible for a buyer who purchases their bloodline to breed the dog—even though the puppy owner not only paid for but also raised and certainly owns the dog.

Buying and Selling

When looking for a new puppy, find reputable breeders for considering prospective litters. The same theory applies when looking for a started or trained dog—look for creditable trainers that sell sound, well-adjusted hunting companions. How can you find these folks?

It helps to contact local dog clubs for suggestions. Seek out respected trainers and hunters in your area who will recommend kennels for your search. You should seek individuals and establishments that keep accurate records and clean facilities. These things reflect how animals are cared for and how decisions are made. Be prepared to ask legitimate questions about the sire and dam of prospective litters or dogs, and ask for photos or if the parents are on the premises. Determine field accomplishments and hunting experience as well as trainability, temperament, and personality. Do research on parentage of any puppies you're considering; these clues will reflect the overall character of your new companion.

PUPPY HIP and EYE GUARANTEE

All puppies are guaranteed to be sound for intended use for a period of 28 months. This guarantee Does not cover accident, death or communicable diseases and specifically covers the following:

The Puppy is guaranteed to be free of hip or elbow dysplasia until the age of 28 months (2 years and 4 months). This includes any severe elbow dysplasia and/or OFA moderate or severe hip evaluations. Pup is also guaranteed free of PRA (progressive retinal atrophy) for life. PRA is genetic and results from a recessive gene. Any other inheritable disease rendering the Puppy unusable for his intended purpose is also covered.

Should the Puppy develop any of the aforementioned health problems within the time given, the Buyer will have the following options:

1) The Buyer must provide proof of spay/neuter or euthanasia and due to said functional unsound condition, Breeder will give full refund of purchase price, or if available, replace the Puppy with another puppy of equal value when one becomes available (or within 12 months) or such other compensation as the parties may agree to; however, in the event a full refund is given, said refund is limited to purchase price only.
THIS GUARANTEE IS VOID IF PUPPY HAS BEEN BRED OR IF BREEDER'S KENNEL NAME, _____, HAS NOT BEEN INCLUDED IN THE DOG'S REGISTERED NAME.

2) The Breeder reserves the right to have the Puppy checked by a veterinarian of the Breeder's choice, at the Buyer's expense, for the purpose of a second opinion prior to taking any of the remedies above. If any dispute arises as to the cause or validity of the diagnosis, both parties agree to select a third mutually agreed upon veterinarian specialist in the diagnosed problem, or the Orthopedic Foundation for Animals in the case of hip dysplasia to resolve the dispute. Expenses for such specialist consultation will be split evenly between Breeder and Buyer. Breeder is not responsible for injuries or problems due to feeding, type of feed use, overweight conditions and subsequent physical repercussions of said conditions, or injuries or problems from training, biting, children or environment. The Buyer pays all shipping costs for a replacement. This guarantee is not transferable should the dog be sold or given away by the Buyer.

THIS PUPPY IS SOLD ON FULL REGISTRATION and Buyer agrees not to breed the dog prior to age two to allow for proper health hip and eye clearances in obtaining OFA or PennHip evaluations of good or better on hips, and a CERF eye clearance number on eyes. **IF DOG IS BRED PRIOR TO AGE TWO or without obtaining OFA and CERF numbers, the aforementioned guarantee does not apply.**

This agreement is made for the mutual benefit and protection of Buyer and Seller, for the protection of the dog, and for the protection and preservation of the _____ breed.

AGREED TO on this _____ day of _____, year _____, by

_____ (Seller), and

_____ (Buyer)

_____ (Buyer)

Puppy Hip and Eye Guarantee

PUPPY CONTRACT OF PURCHASE

This agreement is made this ___ day of _____, year _____, by and between:
John Doe of SmithDoe Kennel, 555 First Lane, Smith City, WA 55555
Telephone 555-555-5555, email Johndoe@ internet.com (hereinafter **Breeder** or **Seller**)
and **Buyer**:_____
at address:_____
_____
_____

Phone number:_____, hereinafter, **Buyer**
It is agreed by and between **Seller** and **Buyer** as follows:
This puppy is sold for the sum of $_____ and certain other good and valuable
considerations, including but not limited to the following:
Description of puppy sold under this contract:
Breed:
Sex:
Color:
Date of Birth:
Sire:
Dam:
Litter#:

Date:_____
Buyer's Printed Name:_____
Buyer's Complete Address:_____
_____

Buyer's Phone Number(s):_____
_____

Buyer's Email Address:_____

Puppy Guarantee
Puppy is guaranteed to be in good general health and free of communicable diseases. Buyer
agrees to have the vet of his choice examine the puppy within 72 hours of purchase. If any
Problems are detected in this exam, the puppy may be returned for a replacement puppy (if
available), or a refund, excluding shipping costs. Buyer is responsible for the initial visit
Costs and any immunization shots, if given at that visit. Buyer agrees that if the puppy is not
seen by a vet within the 72 hour limit it will not be covered under these terms except as Seller
determines.
Breeder has had dew claws removed, puppy has been wormed and given applicable shots,
_____, given on _____.
Buyer agrees to provide this puppy with proper care as needed including follow-up vaccinations
at proper intervals and routine health care including vaccinations, worming, and heartworm
preventative. Buyer agrees the pup will become a family member. The dog shall be subject to
repossession by Seller without refund of purchase price in the event buyer is charged or convicted
of cruelty or neglect to the dog.

In addition, this puppy may be returned to Breeder/Seller if Buyer is unable to keep it at any time,
for any reason, including but not limited to family, health problems, allergies of the Buyer or said
family member, divorce, moving, birth of a child, death, or any other unforeseen problem. In the
event that Buyer wishes to resell or place this dog, the Breeder/Seller has the first right of refusal.
This dog is under no circumstances to be surrendered to an animal shelter or rescue organization
without prior written permission from Seller. The Seller is always a safety net for the lifetime of
each puppy sold, no matter the circumstances or age of said puppy or dog. Should the puppy or
adult dog be returned to the Seller for any reason, this will be done at no expense or cost to the
Seller. Buyer will pay any and all actual expenses for return of this puppy or adult dog to the
Seller.
We encourage Buyers to furnish Seller with periodic updates and photographs of the dog and
Buyer agrees to notify Seller of any change of address or phone number in a timely fashion.

AGREED TO on this _____ day of _____, year _____, by:

_____, Seller, and

_____, Buyer

_____, Buyer

Puppy Contract of Purchase

Note the condition of dogs at places you visit. Ask for health re-cords reflecting worming and the vaccination history of puppies; these should be readily available. Inquire about guarantees and contracts and registration papers. Be assertive and ask questions about anything you don't fully understand—you are spending your hard-earned money on a new member of your family. It's up to you to be fully versed on everything you buy.

Many breeders, whether they're recreational (the occasional litter) or commercial (several litters a year), will proudly provide volumes of material on their litters. However, bills of sale and registration papers should be minimum requirements. Be aware that not all guarantees contain the protection you expect; some of them aren't worth the paper they're printed on. Take the time to clearly read everything you'll sign before doing so—just as you would in any business deal involving money—and when in doubt, ask.

Sometimes installment payments are arranged with registration papers withheld until the puppy is paid in full. Be sure that you and the seller are aware of any agreements and what recourse you may have if something goes wrong.

You have many choices to make when looking for that new puppy or gundog you're bringing into your life. Remember that the initial expendi-ture you make will be small potatoes compared to the amount of train-ing, health care, and love you'll invest in your canine companion. Treat these decisions seriously and do your homework. This will be time well spent—and will ultimately bring you ownership of the companion you'll build cherished memories with for the next decade or so.

CHAPTER
FOUR

What's In a Name?

When it comes to researching backgrounds of dogs within favorite breeds, the pedigrees of those dogs can be helpful in revealing clues about the abilities of ancestors of dogs you might be considering. In short, this pedigree is the paperwork that documents your dog's ancestry. It may be filled with intimidating-looking letters and fancy names, but those things could help you determine more about the traits and characteristics that your puppy or dog may have and might indicate the talent that's flowing through his veins. Depending on the source of the pedigree, it could have three to seven generations for review.

When inspecting a pedigree, you'll quickly see that it pays to know something about the types of titles that can be earned by your breed. You'll see that each dog has a name, but some of them have different letters either before and/or after that name. Those letters (prefixes and suffixes) will be Greek to you unless you're well versed in field and show titles.

A little homework will provide you with the knowledge on what these prefixes and suffixes mean. Note that to earn these letters a dog must be trained to a certain level of prowess, must have been campaigned, and must have satisfactorily completed a number of events to fulfill the requirements of any title or accomplishment. Once you understand how coveted some of these titles are in field dog sports, you may want them in your pup's parentage. However, the absence of titles doesn't necessarily signify lack of talent, but may mean either a lack of financial means or the desire to campaign the dog. It will be up to you to determine what's what in the pedigree game.

Let's examine the brass tacks. When you look at a pedigree, the middle and far left-hand entry on the paper will have something like "your puppy" or it will be the name of the dog you are buying or that of his sire or dam. Indented a bit to the right of this entry and a substantial distance above and below it will be two more names. These are the sire

THE ULTIMATE HUNTING DOG REFERENCE BOOK

(above) and dam (below) of the pedigreed dog. These immediate parents of the dog should have the most genetic influence.

Further indented to the right and above and below the names of the sire and dam are two more names for each. As you view the full page you'll notice that each set of names runs in a column on the page. This next recorded group of names relates to the dog's sire and dam and are *their* parents—the dog's grandparents. The names above and below the sire of the dog are *his* sire and dam; likewise the names above and below the name of the dog's mother are *her* sire and dam. The dog will have four grandparents. This generation of grandparents will have the next degree of influence over your dog's inherited traits.

Names of each dog's sire and dam will continue to progress to the right of the paper with the sire's name above and the dam's underneath for each entry. You've probably recognized that this isn't unlike some human genealogy papers you've seen. Directly to the right of the grandparents' names are the eight great-grandparents' names. These great-grandparents represent the third generation of your dog's heritage. Many experts feel this is the final generation that may influence your dog since genetic strength is quite watered down by that level. However, some pedigrees go back seven generations; this information is invaluable in determining how breeds have advanced over time. Some of the dogs' traits and physical characteristics still seem to reappear readily in some lines of dogs, and old-timers swear that prepotent sires and dams will carry their influence many times down the line.

Back to the name game and what it may mean to your new puppy or dog. Take a look at the pedigree sample for better understanding. You may notice that some pedigrees have recurring names of dogs, reflecting linebred or inbred crosses, while others have no related dogs at all, usually indicating an outcross. Breeders use pedigrees to help make decisions about positive points and strong characteristics that dogs have but also to determine the presence of certain faults or health problems that a dog might harbor within his line. (These issues are covered in detail in chapter 12.)

Several different registries record meticulous inheritance records of dogs. Examples include the AKC, UKC, Field Dog Stud Book (FDSB), Canadian Kennel Club (CKC), and PKC. Determine which registries pertain to your breed.(Note that some registries only register certain breeds, and not every breed is recognized by every registry.)

A Pedigree Sample through Four Generations

Puppy	Parents	Grandparents	Great-Grandparents
			Chief's Chosen Son, CDX (m) +
		AFC Honorable Justice Can-Do (m) _____	
			Jezebel Quake Addict (f)
	Sire: FC Blade Too Much MH		
			CH Marten's Master Latch (m) +
		Black Bess of Nettle Creek MH (f) _____	
			HR Cannonball Queen (f)
Your Puppy			
			Mister Eveready (m) +
		Jake the Knife III MH (m) _____	
			Queenie of Reddy Lake (f)
	Dam: CH Marguerite the Great IV		
			FC-AFC Incredible Luke (m) +
		HR Yellow Rose Blue (f) _____	
			CH Off the Charts (f)

Let's look at a *partial* list of letters that are found associated with the registered names of hunting dogs and determine what some of these letters mean. Some of these letters occur as prefixes—in front of the dog's name—and some occur afterward, as suffixes. Become knowledgeable to what these things represent. With retrievers, AKC puts Field Champion, Amateur Field Champion, Bench Champion, or certain obedience-based titles as prefixes to a name while all other accomplishments, such as the majority of obedience titles and also hunt test titles, are added as suffixes. In addition, an AKC-generated pedigree will only reflect AKC-recognized titles. In order for a pedigree to reflect titles from multiple registries it must be generated from an independent pedigree-building outfit. Some pedigrees highlight dogs with certain titles in colors different from untitled dogs. National Champions might be in red while Field Champions might be in blue and other dogs are listed in black text. Remember, these are partial lists.

Field-Related Titles/Accomplishments:

WC	Working Certificate	UH	Upland Hunter (UKC)
WCX	Working Certificate Excellent	***	Three asterisks as a suffix means
JH	Junior Hunter (AKC)		Qualified All-Age (AKC)
SH	Senior Hunter (AKC)	CH	Field Champion in FDSB—Field
MH	Master Hunter (AKC)		Dog Stud Book/American Field
GDSC	Gun Dog Stake Champion (AKC)	AFTCH	Amateur Field Champion (CKC)
RGDSC	Retrieving Gun Dog Stake Cham-	FTCH	Field Champion (CKC)
	pion (AKC)	AFC	Amateur Field Champion (AKC)
NGDC	National Gun Dog Champion (AKC)	NAFC	National Amateur Field Champion
NOGDC	National Open Gun Dog Cham-		(AKC)
	pion (AKC)	FC	Field Champion (AKC)
HR	Hunting Retriever (UKC)	NFC	National Field Champion (NFC)
HRCH	Hunting Retriever Champion (UKC)		

Nite Hunt and Coonhound Related:

NtCH	Nite Champion (UKC)	CNC	Nite Champion (AKC)
GrNtCH	Grand Nite Champion (UKC)	CGN	Grand Nite Champion (AKC)
CH	Champion level night events in	CSGF	Supreme Grand Field Champion
	PKC only		(AKC)
SCH	Silver Champion (PKC)	CGW	Grand Water Race Champion
GCH	Gold Champion (PKC)		(AKC)
PCH	Platinum Champion (PKC)	WNC	World Nite Champion (AKC)

Obedience-Agility Titles/Accomplishments:

AX	Agility Excellent	UDX	Utility Dog Excellent (AKC)
CD	Companion Dog (AKC)	TD	Tracking Dog (AKC)
CDX	Companion Dog Excellent (AKC)	TDX	Tracking Dog Excellent (AKC)
NA	Novice Agility	VST	Variable Surface Tracking (AKC)
OA	Open Agility	OTCH	Obedience Trial Champion (AKC)
UD	Utility Dog (AKC)		

Bench Show-Related Titles/Accomplishments:

CH	Champion—Bench (Show) Title	BOS	Best of Show
	(AKC & UKC)	GrCH	Grand Champion
BOB	Best of Breed		

Combined Bench and Field-Related Titles:

DC	Dual Champion—Bench &
	Field Titled (AKC)

Pedigrees may have information regarding health clearances with some or all of the names therein. Examples of these health clearances include hip rating numbers from the Orthopedic Foundation for Animals (OFA) as well as eye clearance numbers from the Canine Eye Registration Foundation (CERF). Coat colors may also be listed by dog.

By now you may be tempted to ask a valid question: does all this fancy stuff really mean anything to your bottom line and the puppy you hope to find? In today's market, do elaborate field-trial-based titles or nite-hunt achievements really have anything to do with the potential hunting ability of the puppy you're considering for purchase? Not long ago, many folks might have answered with a resounding *no*, but that tide is turning as breeding practices become more advanced and titled stud dogs are more readily available for breeding.

Overall, dogs are bred for physical soundness, pleasing temperament, intelligence, and trainability. Arguably, titles reflect those qualities. These same things that make a superior hunting dog are what make a trainable performance dog. Beyond the obvious, take the time to discover which lines within a breed are known for specific qualities you want in your dog. If you're viewing a pedigree without titles, try to establish the hunting abilities of the named dogs and whether they harbor any detrimental physical or mental problems.

While the presence of titles will probably increase the price of a puppy, those same blue-blooded dogs will make prospective breeding plans of your dog more profitable. Generations of health clearances in pedigrees reveal sound stock. Titles and health clearances of siblings, sometimes named in pedigrees, can reveal a predisposition to the success and potential reproductive ability of the dogs in question.

What is the bottom line? While pedigrees may look intimidating at first, you can quickly become well versed on deciphering their content, what everything means, and how that information might affect your pending decision. Buying a new dog is a sizable investment on your part; it behooves you to use everything at your disposal to make the right decision. The Name Game is one of those things!

CHAPTER
FIVE

Sound for Life

By now you may be wondering what you've gotten yourself into with this dog business. You just wanted a suitable canine buddy to team up with over hill and dale and through swamps and fields and marshes. But therein lies the key to this chapter. There is much to this business of training and hunting, and you want a dog that will hold up to the rigors of the job for a decade or more. Beauty is more than skin deep—let's take a look.

Physical Aspects

Eyes

The better to see you with, my dear. Truer words are hard to find. Eyes are the windows to your dog's world; he needs a pair with good vision and no impairments until old age takes its toll. There are many eye diseases and problems, but take heart, for the means exists to check for many of them with simple exams. Some of the more common eye maladies are covered here.

The Canine Eye Registration Foundation (CERF) was founded by concerned purebred dog enthusiasts to record and track hereditary eye defects. Board-certified veterinary ophthalmologists perform tests on canine eyes; results are recorded at a central registry. Thus, breeders have the means to track some eye problems in the hopes of eliminating them within breeds.

Diseases of the internal eye include retinal dysplasia (RD), progressive retinal atrophy (PRA), and cataracts. Eye maladies involving the eyelid include ectropion, entropion, and distichiasis.

Retinal dysplasia occurs when folds develop within the retina. Although the problem is often genetic, it can be caused by trauma or in the unborn puppy if the mother experiences suspect viral diseases such as herpes or parvovirus while puppies are in utero.

The canine retina is composed of six layers. When these layers separate either partially or completely from the choroid membrane, folds can result. Atrophy can occur in these membranes, causing vision problems or blindness. Folds can occur without detachment, however. RD can range from mild dysplasia, where only minor effects on vision are noticed, to severe dysplasia, where blindness results. There are two forms of RD that affect some gundog breeds. One is an autosomal recessive gene that strictly affects vision; the other is an incompletely dominant trait, or autosomal dominant gene, that can affect vision and has recessive affects on skeletal/limb development, causing dwarfism. Some of the affected breeds include beagles, English springer spaniels, Labrador retrievers, American cocker spaniels, and golden retrievers. RD can be diagnosed between six to eight weeks of age; however, it's not only possible to miss folds at that time, but also mild cases of RD diagnosed this young may disappear by four months of age.

Progressive retinal atrophy also affects the retina. It occurs because of a reduction of retinal blood cells and the subsequent atrophy of retinal vital receptor cells. Cells at the back of the retina degenerate and die. Generalized PRA, occurring in both eyes, is progressive and will worsen with age. Dogs with this condition can only see things directly in front of them and experience tunnel vision and night blindness. This usually becomes apparent by two to three years of age. In contrast, centralized PRA, although also progressive, doesn't cripple vision as severely; dogs usually retain peripheral vision for several years while the central vision is affected. Centralized PRA occurs in dogs aged four years and up. Some susceptible breeds include American cocker spaniels, Nova Scotia duck tolling retrievers, Labrador retrievers, golden retrievers, English cocker spaniels, Chesapeake Bay retrievers, and Portuguese water dogs. Presence of progressive rod-cone degeneration (PRCD), PRA, or generalized PRA can be diagnosed by a company called Optigen that analyzes DNA from a small blood sample taken by a veterinarian. This method provides a means to track the insidious retinal disease and provide breeders with more information about dogs within certain lines. *PRA can sometimes be misdiagnosed as the culprit of retinal problems.*

Cataracts occur in the lens of the eye as opacities. They're catego-rized by congenital, juvenile, or senile cataracts. Although often genetic, cataracts can be caused by injury, malnutrition, or inflammation. *Congenital cataracts* are present at birth but may be genetic or influenced by outside factors. *Juvenile* cataracts, often occurring in five-year-old or six-year-old dogs, are usually small and don't affect overall vision. *Developmental cataracts* may be inherited or influenced by trauma, diabetes, or infection, and occur early in age. *Mature* cataracts usually cause com-plete blindness. Some of the breeds that can be affected by cataracts include the standard poodle, beagle, curly-coated retriever, black and tan coonhound, Gordon setter, Irish setter, flat-coated retriever, Amer-ican cocker spaniel, Chesapeake Bay retriever, golden retriever, Welsh springer spaniel, and Labrador retriever. Surgery is the only means of treatment for severe cataracts. Some dogs respond to topical treatment of immature cataracts.

Entropion occurs when either or both upper or lower eyelids are rolled inward toward the eyeball. The eyelashes then rub on the eye. This painful condition can trigger squinting, tearing, conjunctivitis, and injuries like corneal ulcers and scarring. Surgical treatment can repair affected eyelids. *Ectropion* occurs when the lower eyelid rolls *away* from the eye, exposing the delicate conjunctiva. Sometimes topical ointment treatments help; corrective surgery is usually recommended. *Distichiasis* is a condition where extra eyelashes are present on the inside of the eyelid.

Elbows and Shoulders

The recognition of elbow dysplasia (ED) is a relatively new field and is evaluated and recorded by the OFA just since 1990. ED is still being researched but is generally accepted as a polygenic (caused by more than one gene pair) disorder of the elbow joint, causing instability in the joint. Lameness is the primary symptom and may be subtle for a while. There is no particular age when onset is first noticed. Three grades of ED, including Grades I, II, and III, are evaluations of the condition. When OFA deems a dog's elbows are ED-free, no grades are given.

Another skeletal disease of the dog is osteochondrosis dessicans (OCD) of the shoulder, an ossification of the cartilage mold beneath the articular cartilage of the shoulder joint. Eventually, the area collapses and a fracture of that cartilage results. OCD can occur in the shoulder, elbow, stifle, hock, or spine, and usually occurs before age one. Males are more frequently affected than females. OCD is considered genetic, but the mode of inheritance is unknown. Many of the larger breeds of gundogs can be affected by either OCD or ED.

Hips

The important hip joints propel your dog through physical exertion. Hip dysplasia is a serious and potentially crippling disease that can be found in many sporting breeds. Basically when canine hip dysplasia (CHD) is present, the hip joint has an abnormality or looseness that affects movement in varying degrees. Puppies with severe cases show symptoms early on, while other dogs may not exhibit signs for years when arthritis sets in. Some dogs manage well with CHD, while others cannot maintain simple movement without terrible pain. Virtually all large breeds of dogs are susceptible to the incidence of CHD.

Until recently, OFA was the only record-keeping organization that evaluated and rated hip X-rays. A panel of board-certified veterinary experts examines X-rays taken by clinical veterinarians of the dog with his rear legs extended and parallel to each other (dorsal recumbency). Anesthesia is usually recommended for proper positioning. (Another method of rating hip-extension X-rays is called the Norberg Angle Method.)

The University of Pennsylvania Hip Improvement Program (PennHIP) has been accepted by serious dog enthusiasts and veterinary experts for evaluation of the hip joint and the potential for development of DJD (degenerative joint disease) of the hip. PennHIP approaches evaluation in a different manner than OFA, by employing two additional views, distraction and compression. The sedated dog's legs are extended toward the ceiling during this radiographic process. PennHIP's database continues to expand as more veterinarians become certified and licensed for this process.

Both methods provide information on CHD. Of importance within any breed is the depth of CHD occurrence in generations of the pedigree, and also within specific litters in those pedigrees. However, it is true that two CHD-clear parents can produce one or more affected puppies. It's currently recognized that environmental factors, diet, exercise, and potential injury can also influence the incidence of CHD.

Heart

What organ is more necessary than the heart itself? Aortic stenosis, or subarterial or subvalvular aortic stenosis (SAS), is an inherited heart disease prevalent in some larger breeds of dogs, and is noticeably high in the golden retriever. What is it? Aortic stenosis is a condition in which the passageways for blood *from* the heart are narrowed. When this occurs beneath the aortic valve of the heart's left ventricle (and it usually does) it's called SAS. Symptoms can be as mild as a heart murmur or they can be severe enough to cause exercise intolerance, heart failure, infection, and sudden death. When a dog's heart has to compensate for obstructed blood flow by working harder to produce what's needed, the heart muscle will thicken over time. This, too, leads to life-threatening conditions.

A puppy with a heart murmur or symptoms including difficulty breathing, coughing, fainting, or exercise intolerance should undergo additional tests to determine heart soundness. Failure to follow up on these warning signs, particularly with goldens, could lead to a tragic, unexpected result while out training or hunting. Tests include an EKG and/or an echocardiogram (heart ultrasound) with Doppler and possibly a chest X-ray. Generally speaking, a puppy or dog without a heart murmur doesn't require additional tests.

Once a heart condition is diagnosed, steps can be taken to ensure the dog's welfare. Dogs with heart problems must have restricted exercise, which eliminates them from hunting—with exceptions granted to dogs with mild heart murmurs.

Other Concerns

Some breed-specific health conditions exist; it pays to do research on any breed you are considering so that you're aware of any problems. Some examples include canine von Willebrand's Disease, a blood disease similar to hemophilia in humans found in some goldens; hypo- or hyperthyroidism, seen in many breeds of hunting dogs, which can affect many things including skin, temperament, and reproduction; swallowing disorders; immune or autoimmune deficiency problems; allergies; epilepsy; narcolepsy; muscular myopathy, or centronuclear myopathy (CNM), which is covered in chapter 13; and deafness. Other health concerns can be found in chapter 12.

Mental Aptitude

Temperament and Intelligence

Let's face it—dogs, while not like people, do have corresponding attributes. Take temperament and intelligence, for example. Some dogs have pleasing temperaments while others are prone to sulking. Certain dogs are smarter than others. The type of your dog's temperament could affect his health. If very nervous and high-strung, the dog could be prone to kennel pacing or to separation anxiety. Either of these undesirable behaviors can promote problems with weight maintenance and cleanliness, skin problems, and lack of energy for hunting or training. (Take my advice—if you've never had a dog in this category, you don't want one.)

Intelligence in your dog will make you look like a great or gifted trainer in spite of your mistakes. It's much more rewarding to train a smart dog than one intellectually challenged.

Drive and Desire

These qualities can accentuate the talent and ability of your hunting dog. Always remember the old adage: you can take it out, but you can't put it back in. Harsh training methods and poorly timed corrections can be negatively received by your dog and can remove his starch or his drive. Dogs with drive and desire shouldn't be confused with those wild, bug-eyed maniacs we've all seen that cannot be controlled under any circumstances. Rather, drive and desire complement intelligence and biddability as top qualities you should seek in your new gundog.

The Well-Rounded Package

Your new puppy should be sound of limb and body so that he can fulfill his potential without maladies along the way. Absence of problems means an abundance of quality time spent with you; it is that simple. Your dog should possess the characteristics necessary to make a talented hunting dog and a good companion so that he can work for you over the next ten years and double as your buddy, ever at the ready. That's what it's all about!

CHAPTER
SIX

Social Status

The Importance of Bonding

There's something special about the bond that develops between humans and dogs. This bond isn't something on automatic pilot that suddenly appears by divine intervention. To complicate matters further, there are many definitions of this word *bond*. Perhaps the very mention of it intimidates people because it's a four-letter word. B-o-n-d. It can be quite misunderstood. Yet, when you've had the privilege of seeing this bond between a dog and his owner at its finest, you know you've witnessed something special and you yearn for it as well. This desire may be the catalyst that prompts you to bite the bullet and take that plunge to get your own dog.

Is this bond easy to develop or is it nearly unattainable? The shroud of mystery surrounding this word can rapidly be blown away and boils down to a few simple things. When a meaningful bond is missing, quite often a key link hasn't been forged from the beginning of the association between the owner and the dog.

Let me explain. One of the questions most frequently asked of me over the years from new and old dog owners alike is: "How can I get my dog to buddy up to me?" This is asked innocently enough and an unequivocal answer is expected, as if a magic spell can be cast over the dog to produce the "buddy" aspect, or more specifically, to create the bond. But when this question is posed, it's almost certain that the owner and the dog are running on disconnect, plain and simple.

What is a frustrated dog owner to do? The answer, in a nutshell, lies within another four-letter word. *Time.* The first prerequisite to a special bond with your dog is the commitment to spend quality time with him from the beginning. Let your dog know that you think he is tops in your world and that you truly enjoy his company.

This is accomplished by taking advantage of any time you have each day for your new puppy or dog. Since a puppy should be fed two or three times daily, depending on age, this can become an event between the two of you. Always greet your puppy. Say his name with enthusiasm—the way you would welcome a dear friend. After all, that's what you want in return from your puppy, isn't it? Convey this message when you have the opportunity. Let your pup know it! The same attitude applies during walks and play or puppy training sessions. Use your pal's name without *overusing* it so that he knows it. Food for thought—how many puppies grow up thinking their name is "No"?

Give your puppy chances to "drink" the tone of your voice and to appreciate the feel of your touch. Practice "laying of the hands" by stroking your puppy all over, on his back, the smooth skin of his tummy, under his chin. *(Do these things with any age dog.)*

From the very beginning, be fair with your new dog. Teach him that you're someone he can count on for everything. You'll provide for him and give him companionship, and above all you will treat him fairly. What does that last word mean? You'll never discipline your dog for something he doesn't understand. It means you'll teach him rules to live by so the dog knows how to respond and knows you'll be firm about those rules— you won't expect him to obey the rules one day and not the next. Doing so would foster an unproductive guessing game that would undermine training more quickly than anything else. It means that you won't lose your temper and you won't take frustrations out on your dog. Be consistent and patiently teach him right from wrong.

If you abide by these rules—and we'll go into greater detail as we go along—two things will result. Your new dog will develop a deep *respect* for you, and this translates into a *bond* of *love* that cannot be defied or denied. It's as complicated and as simple as that.

Socialization and Exposure

Enough cannot be said about the importance of socialization and exposure for the new puppy. As important as this is with a puppy, *it's also vital for any age dog,* and more so for one that has been starved for attention and handling early in life. For our purposes, socialization applies to the introduction of your new friend to other people and dogs, while exposure pertains to the introduction of experiences, places, and things. Time is once again a factor as you set out to accomplish these lessons of life. From the beginning, make the concept of time an ally for all things relating to your dog.

Plenty of ink has been given to the subject of Master and Dog and the premise that one person/one dog rules. However, you could build a ticking time bomb with that kind of attitude, which could be difficult to deprogram.

While it's a good idea to personally take care of your puppy's needs so that he looks to you as his leader, don't miss out on including others in the pack. If you have children and a spouse, take advantage of the contributions they can make by allowing them to play with the dog at times. Don't worry about the fallout that may seem possible from "many bosses." Contrary to what you may have read countless times before, *the key to balance lies within you.* If you remain consistent with your puppy every time you feed, work, and play with him, he will learn—and very quickly—that no matter what happens with other members of your family, he knows you're the kingpin of his world.

Canine interaction is nearly as important as people socialization for your puppy. Why, you ask, does that matter? The answer is once again quite simple, as you'll find with most things pertaining to this dog business. If you ever plan to hunt with a buddy who also has dogs, you'll expect yours to be well behaved and not wild and vicious. Also, if at any point in the future you become interested, never mind addicted, to any of the dog sports, your dog will need to demonstrate a certain decorum around his fellow competitors.

Seek and take advantage of opportunities to safely introduce your puppy to other youngsters and older dogs. This does not mean that you should go to the local park when you've missed your puppy's second vaccination appointment, no matter how much you're hankering to show off your new puppy. You could be unwittingly taking your dog into a dangerous deathtrap riddled with sickness because you don't know anything about the other dogs that have recently been to that park or those present when you arrive. Be wise!

The importance of exposing your puppy to experiences, places, and things cannot be overemphasized. Strange and sometimes loud noises, big, scary objects, and strange sights and smells are all things that might initially rock your puppy's boat. Expose your dog; he cannot learn about any of these things while sitting in a kennel. All groundwork you invest to develop your dog's senses in a well-rounded manner will pay off in the months and years to come.

Citizenship should always be encouraged. It's much easier to build good habits than to break bad ones, never mind that the former is more pleasant than the latter, for both you and your dog. Certain commands can be taught early on and certain behaviors can be encouraged while others are discouraged. "Come" (or "Here") and "Sit" or "Stand" are two important lessons that should be taught as early as possible because either one could save your puppy's life in a dangerous or life-threatening situation. Walking on a lead is pretty handy, too, and is necessary in lots of places. One word of caution—if you have a bird dog puppy, you may not want to teach him to heel at your side just yet. Doing so could impede your efforts to teach quartering on a checkcord, if you opt to use that method. Give this appropriate thought. You can get around this, however, by using a flexi-type leash to keep your puppy under control while not specifically at heel. Note that this decision—to heel or not—is personal preference.

Discourage frustrating puppy behaviors such as jumping up, biting, and chewing. (Details on how to achieve this are in chapter 22.) On the other hand, don't be a drill sergeant. Give your puppy a certain measure of play time for good mental development. Also, allow him to become acquainted with the dog bed in your den or family room.

Balance is one of the most important keys to successful dog training—indeed, it will be stressed often in these pages—and at no time is this more important than when you are first becoming acquainted with your new canine pal. In the process, you are also stimulating perhaps the most important lesson your new puppy can absorb—you are teaching him to "learn how to learn."

Read through this chapter again and you will quickly realize how many simple, yet important, ingredients have been disclosed that are necessary in a foundation meant to build a meaningful relationship with your dog. It only gets better.

CHAPTER
SEVEN

Be Prepared

Take a breath and push farther back in that favorite easy chair of yours for a few moments. Thus far we've covered quite a bit of material, and we're nearly to the point where you'll be taking your new puppy out of the world he's been accustomed to and transplanting him into your own. This is a big deal. By now it should come as no surprise that a certain amount of planning can make the experience less traumatic for your puppy and more rewarding for you. This premise is why you should read all these pages from cover to cover before you get started—because the underlying theme of this book is one you've most likely already picked up on: everything ties together in creating the whole package for you and your dog.

The Trip Home

First things first. If there's any way you can get your new puppy or dog at the beginning of a long weekend or when you'll have several consecutive days to get acquainted with him, I'd urge you to do just that. Those initial days will set the tone for things to come; an initial investment of time will be priceless.

Be prepared. That means you'll have purchased, in advance, the same food your puppy has been eating to facilitate a smooth transition from one place to another. An abrupt change in diet can be very traumatic to the digestive tract and a bad way to start a new life. (If you ultimately choose to feed your puppy something else, buy a small bag of the first brand and mix it with your own choice until your puppy has successfully changed over.) You'll also have purchased bowls for food and water and perhaps a jug of distilled water to minimize the possibility of digestive or intestinal upset; you can gradually mix your own tap water with the bottled water to ease the adjustment. Finally, you should have a suitable crate or other sleeping quarters ready for your puppy.

Whether your new arrival comes by air, land, or spaceship, you will need to pick him up from somewhere. That might be a busy commercial kennel, or someone's cozy home, or a noisy, bustling airport terminal. If you're departing from a kennel or home, chances are the puppy has already "aired out" by the time you get to your vehicle. However, if he's been on a jet for several hours he'll be most grateful for a few minutes on Mother Earth's green grass to take care of essential duties, and may appreciate a drink of water. Most air cargo terminals have a small, fenced area for just this purpose; ask airline personnel while you are completing necessary paperwork. Note: If your puppy has been shipped by air, take a supply of towels along with a tub of unscented baby wipes and some old newspaper for crate bedding, just in case you'll need to clean either your puppy, or the crate, or both, in the event an accident occurs en route.

Once you deem that you're ready to get under way, how or where will your puppy ride out the trip? Are you going to relegate him to exile in the puppy crate in the bed of your truck? Or will you give in and let him ride on your lap? If you've brought along a driver so that you can safely sit in the passenger seat, your puppy will probably choose to sit with you. On the other hand, if you're doing the driving, the dog's wiggling and moving around may distract your attention when you need it most. A safer alternative is an open box that can be situated on the passenger seat next to you and seat-belted into place. This way, you can reach inside when necessary to comfort your new puppy. If you have a long road trip, plan a few pit stops to let your puppy stretch and "air" along the way.

Outdoor versus Indoor Dog—
The Myth Uncovered

While many new puppies spend their first nights, if not weeks or months, in the house, there seems to be more opposition to this practice from owners of gundog breeds than all others combined. Invariably, hunters want to put their new puppy outside in a kennel, elaborate or otherwise. Why is this and is it warranted?

There has always existed a myth about the housing of hunting dogs. Despite plenty of evidence to the contrary, many folks still believe that a hunting dog will be ruined if kept in the house. He'll be spoiled and thus unwilling to work in the field. Not true, of course, but it "seems" like a plausible explanation for keeping a dog outside.

Please don't believe it for a minute. While there may be plenty of good reasons to keep dogs outside, particularly at certain times of the year and because of circumstance, the myth alone should not be the straw that breaks the camel's back. If you can keep your new puppy inside at first, please do so. This will create work for you, but it will also mean that you'll spend more time with your new dog. The two of you will begin the process of getting to know each other—through exposure—right from the start. You can employ necessary crate training (see chapter 8) while your puppy is young and vulnerable to new habits, and this alone will come in handy throughout your dog's entire life.

Dogs that are raised indoors have a good, solid grip on life and seem extremely well socialized. This is not surprising, by virtue of the time necessary from you, the owner, to make the arrangement work. And again, no well-bred hunting dog worth his salt will have a diminished hunting or prey drive from living indoors.

One argument for outside housing that has merit, aside from the previously mentioned circumstances, is climate. In particularly cold or hot weather when a dog is expected to hunt, he will be better acclimated to either extreme, therefore more able to perform if he spends the majority of his time in that environment. Obviously, care must be taken to protect any animal from extremes of heat or cold no matter how well conditioned he may seem.

Some dogs do well in outdoor kennels after having spent vital time raised indoors in a home atmosphere. Other dogs spend part of the day in a kennel and the remainder of time indoors. It remains a fact that quality indoor time during the formative phase of your puppy's growth can be invaluable to your dog's well-being and overall adjustment to his new home.

Speaking of the Home Front

Have you done your homework around the house? If you're planning to keep your little guy indoors, he'll be romping around at least part of the time; it's nearly impossible to keep your eye on a puppy every second. A household with a new puppy or dog should be "proofed" much the same way you'd prepare for a new child.

Some examples: hide extension and power cords. Lamps can come crashing down with one or two tugs of an attractive cord within reach. If your puppy chews on a power cord the result could be tragic. Tablecloths hanging temptingly within reach should be removed. Become familiar with household poisons and toxins that are harmful to dogs (see chapter 12), and put them out of reach or hide them from view. Remove any plants that might be hazardous to your puppy's health. Pick up any shoes, favorite shirts, or blankets that you don't want destroyed because your buddy will view them as fair game for his entertainment.

The best rule of thumb when preparing to bring your new puppy home is to begin cultivating a practice that will—get ready—prepare you for the dog training that lies ahead. Work on this one: think like a dog . . . walk in his paws. Not only will this jump-start you to think of little things that will help make the trip home and subsequent introduction to your home as smooth and seamless as possible for your puppy, it will put you a step ahead of "all things dog."

PART TWO

Maintenance, Health, and Care

CHAPTER
EIGHT

Home Sweet Home

When it comes to dogs and their care and training, there are many different opinions concerning everything from equipment and gear to dog food to training methods to types of housing. Indeed, on this latter topic, sentiments can run hot regarding most of the items that go into comfortable setups for your dog. We'll take a look at the different options available for your circumstances and your dog, and you can weigh the pros and cons of each and make your own educated decision on what works best for you.

Housing Options—Outdoor Dog

A number of considerations should be taken into account once the decision is reached to fabricate an outside kennel. At least a few different fence panel types are available; also, kennel flooring and the doghouse type must be chosen. Additional options would include shade or kennel covers and a small kennel building.

The first choice for the outside or indoor/outdoor dog is whether to build a kennel or to use a chain-and-house system. The traditional doghouse with a chain is frowned upon by many, but numerous kennels and individuals use this setup with good results. A number of commercial kennels have used the "tied-out" option that this presents.

Positive aspects include the economical cost and ease of arrangement. Some people have the space to move the setup to various areas of the yard, thus keeping the dog on fresh ground. Without that option, care must be taken to keep the immediate area clean, although some dog owners prefer to let the chain break down stool matter and they consider this a positive point. Others prefer a suspended runner chain for additional exercise potential. From a training standpoint, there are certain situations, with a shy dog, for example, where the chain can work in a positive way, such as allowing the trainer to be able to always reach the dog.

Drawbacks, however, are many. A dog on a chain could get tangled. Chains are more apt to conduct electricity during a lightning strike. The chain's snap will wear with time, as will links of the chain, and without regular inspections either of these could break, thus freeing the dog. Intact females kept on chains will need alternative quarters during heat cycles unless the area is secure. Dirt can become mud during inclement weather and can be tough to clean and to keep free of parasites. The area should be treated regularly with a borax solution; this will kill grass but will effectively eradicate parasites and worm eggs. (Note: Check regulations in your state as some have restrictions for tethering dogs beyond a few days.)

Many chain types are available, but the commercially packaged version is usually too fragile for active dogs. It's better to buy stout chain and hardware from a building supply store. Use a sturdy brass "swivel" snap—to prevent the chain from kinking—along with a strong link between the snap and chain. Experiment to find the best chain and assume all responsibility for its use as well as any potential malfunction from hardware or connections between the doghouse and your dog.

A doghouse should be of good construction with a slightly pitched roof. It should be well insulated with the door situated away from prevailing winds. Ventilation options may be needed during warm temperatures. Place the setup in an area with shade during hot weather—or provide artificial shade—and supply a wind/snow barrier (and possibly a door flap) during inclement weather. Slight ground clearance aids in keeping the area under the house clean and protects the house from wet, cold, or hot earth.

Another alternative to the ground kennel is the elevated pen, which is fully enclosed and raised off the ground about three feet, usually supported by treated 4 x 4 sturdy "legs." One end is dedicated for housing and made from plywood in a square 3 x 3 or 4 x 4 foot size; the "run" area of the kennel extends out between eight to twelve feet, or longer. Flooring can include wooden 2 x 4s or reinforced hardware cloth. Sides are made from various types of wire or mesh in sizes of 2 x 2 or 2 x 4. Droppings and urine fall through hardware cloth but must be washed from the wood; this is sometimes difficult. Wood may splinter as well. Kits are

A basic design for an off-the-ground kennel. (Author photo)

also available for these kennels. These elevated pens are becoming more popular for smaller breeds and for raising litters of puppies.

The most popular choice, also considered the safest, is a kennel run. Properly constructed ground kennels are impossible for dogs to dig under, chew out, or climb out of with proper constraints and can also be locked. Various sizes such as square enclosures or long "run" configurations that allow for exercise are options. Most kennels measure 4 x 6 feet and 10 or more feet long. Ultimately this is a matter of personal preference. Variations of kennel runs, building attachments, and materials used are almost endless.

Galvanized chain link has always been the standard for kennel runs and enclosures and will last a lifetime with proper maintenance and care. Prefabricated kennels are available with prestretched chain link, eliminating some steps in constructing safe enclosures. Regarding chain link—it comes in different gauges with low-numbered gauges being more durable, albeit more expensive and difficult to find. Specialty fence companies carry stout fencing.

Standard chain link in weaker gauges can be damaged by any destructive, bored dog; two-inch mesh is harder to grab. Fence alternatives include a new type of coated, welded wire or horse panel fencing; check

Welded wire and a sloped floor leading to a drain makes for a good on-the-ground kennel. (Author photo)

your local building or farm supply stores for options. Six-foot heights are usually preferred with optional kennel covers available.

Kennels may be free-standing or in side-by-side run configurations. In the latter, an additional option is to construct concrete block walls of two- to three-foot heights to prevent waste from entering neighboring runs and cut down on face barking between kennels; chain link or mesh completes each "wall." Concrete block is also an economical option for housing.

The top choice for flooring is concrete, usually completed with a fine broom or smooth finish. Concrete is easily cleaned and disinfected and resists odors. However, it's porous and not indestructible; cracks can harbor worm eggs. A concrete sealer is recommended, particularly when daily disinfection isn't practical. Some dog enthusiasts feel that concrete may be hard on the feet and joints of working dogs. Raised platforms or kennel-deck material provide additional comfort for kenneled dogs.

When planning a concrete pad for your kennels, you may want to add extra feet around the circumference to allow room for maneuvering and/or to provide for placing houses on the outside of the enclosure.

A slope should be included for ease of cleaning and draining, and a trough or drain added to transport waste.

Other flooring options include the second most popular choice of pea gravel, followed by dirt, wood, kennel-deck material, and rubber mats. Some regard pea gravel as more comfortable on the feet of dogs (it's a personal preference), while another plus is that stools and urine will seep through gravel. Without proper building precautions gravel may be difficult to maintain. Firm stools should be removed daily. This same cleaning policy should apply to all flooring options, most of which are more difficult to keep clean than concrete. They are, however, less expensive to provide, with the possible exception of properly laid pea gravel, which requires forms similar to concrete.

Where will the doghouse be placed? Some people prefer the house on one end with the door on the other. My personal preference places the house on the same end as the door—any dog is more inclined to move away from his sleeping area to do his business, and thus uses the far end of the kennel to "air" while keeping the surface near the house and door clean. Of course, any run not kept hosed can be "messed" by the occasional pacing dog. Some dogs have higher cleanliness standards than others.

Another consideration is whether to place the house inside the enclosure or attach it outside the run. Housing inside the run offers more security since the door can be locked, but this positioning will mean that you'll need to enter the run to clean or maintain the house. A house with a removable end or lid that's outside the run can be easily accessed.

Housing Options—Indoor Dog

What should be considered for the indoor dog? A young puppy should be kept in a crate overnight for safe keeping; this practice will assist in the housebreaking procedure and will help teach the puppy a sense of "home." Crate training will transfer the sense of place for your dog to less-confined areas of your home, such as a dog bed in your library or family room. A properly used crate becomes a safe haven for the new puppy instead of a prison, and can double as a home away from home

Griffon, German shorthaired pointer, and cat in harmony. Dogs and cats can get along fine when introduced and integrated properly. (Jennifer Zwicker)

when you're traveling with your dog. (See information on crate training and housebreaking in chapter 22.) Some dogs become bedroom buddies. This isn't all bad as long as you maintain your position of leadership. You can be your dog's pal—and you should be—but you should always remain the boss.

Indoor dogs must be regularly walked to assist in elimination needs and for exercise, unless a safe turnout area is available. "Doggie doors" provide an option for the inside dog to go outside at will.

Housing Options—Combination Dog

The combination indoor/outdoor setup is often the best solution for many dogs and their owners. Some folks prefer to leave one or two dogs loose in a fenced yard as opposed to putting them in a kennel. Strict attention should be paid to gates and the fence line to ensure there is no potential for escape. Others opt for an "invisible/underground fence" to help police the boundaries of the yard. Before buying one, do your homework. Some are more effective than others.

This indoor/outdoor arrangement works especially well for dog owners who work. An outdoor kennel gives you peace of mind that your dog is well provided for until you return home, and it eliminates worrying about what your dog might be doing for entertainment in the house during work hours. When you arrive home, you can train, exercise, or play with your dog and finally bring him in at night.

Kennel Placement and Considerations

There are additional decisions when constructing an outdoor kennel arrangement. Where will you place it in relation to the house? You may not want it so close to interfere with regular family activities, but yet neither so far from the house that it is out of sight, out of mind. An optimal location is one where you can see your dog and he can see you.

Position your kennel so that prevailing winds aren't blowing into the door of the doghouse. Consider a roof if you live where snow is a threat, or provide some kind of a barrier to protect from blowing snow or rain. You may wish to construct a small building for storage and/or for sheltered housing within its confines, with the run positioned outside. A portion of your garage might work for this purpose. Would a pole-barn type of shelter be sufficient?

Consider running water and electricity. If you'd like these conveniences, you may not want to stick your kennel out in the back forty of your property, unless you can easily overcome the obvious technical difficulties. Will you use self-feeders or watering systems that are activated when your pet takes a lick? Will you install a sprinkler system to cool the air during hot summer months? Do you want an airing/exercise enclosure?

Many commercial doghouses are available, some insulated and others not, while homemade doghouses or barrels can be equally suitable. Your decision should be based on budget, climate, and your dog's comfort and safety. Check with other kennels or dog owners to learn what works best for them and also review the paragraph earlier in this chapter on doghouses for additional considerations. Bone up on state regulations, and you might want to check with the Department of Agriculture.

Additional Facilities and Accessories

Helpful tips: A commercial cleaning system, such as a Wysiwash, attaches to your kennel hose with a chlorine tablet inside for ease of kennel disinfection and avoids the mess of bleach that can spill from the container onto your clothes. Hydrated lime can be sprinkled around kennels and on gravel to cut down on odor. One pound of baking soda in a five-gallon bucket of water can be a great neutralizer. Commercial disinfectants are also good odor eliminators.

If you live in a cold climate, you may consider commercial water bucket heaters or deicers to prevent having to break ice for daily fresh water during freezing weather. You may also want to consider heated concrete. If you position your kennel under trees, you may need to protect drains from falling leaves.

Have you planned for waste disposal? If you have a concrete surface, did you include drain provisions? Where will the waste go? Your options include a septic system, a lagoon-type pit, or a drain field. A Doggie Dooley waste elimination system works well if you have just a few dogs. Check local regulations for any required specifications. You may need certain permits to comply with local laws.

Building regulations should be checked before you construct a kennel, particularly if you have several dogs, to ensure that you're within the law before you spend much money. Laws pertaining to animals are increasingly under fire in these changing political times; make certain you're within legal boundaries.

Beyond that, take a careful assessment of the options available for the outside dog before you decide on what works best for you. Consider your circumstances and the seasonal changes where you live. Take advantage of experienced advice; visit nearby kennels and view outdoor kennel facilities of trusted friends. Ask plenty of questions; what you learn will contribute to your optimal kennel setup.

CHAPTER
NINE

Picture of Health

From the time you commit to the prospect of a long-term relationship with a hunting dog companion, you should also view him as a canine athlete. Your dog will be expected to perform in various types of environments and conditions over a period of ten years or more. It makes sense to treat your dog like the athlete he is. You should begin during puppyhood to establish good habits for you and your dog. This realization will help you make sound decisions pertaining to his lifelong care.

The first step toward this care is a strict maintenance schedule that should include a vaccine regime, worming protocol, and certain preventive programs. Other items pertaining to your canine athlete are covered in the next three chapters, but first things first.

Health Maintenance Program

Diseases Covered by Vaccines

From the beginning, a sound vaccination program is mandatory. There are many diseases in the wild world that will infect unprotected animals—and our dogs—but fortunately, because of widespread vaccination protocol, most of them are seldom seen in these modern times. However, they're out there. Complacency has no place in a vaccination program for our dogs.

Puppies are born with maternal antibodies that initially protect them from such woes. How much protection they receive will depend on the mother's active titer level. It's important that any brood female be up to date on all shots before any breeding occurs. As puppies grow, maternal protection wears off and puppy immunizations are necessary to keep antibody protection high. The catch is that it's impossible to tell when maternal protection wears thin. Thus, puppies are given several shots, each three to four weeks apart (consult your veterinarian) over a certain period of time.

Vaccine protocol is undergoing changes, and some experts now feel that yearly boosters aren't necessary once a dog receives adult vaccinations at over a year of age. This is not written in stone, and most veterinarians still recommend the commonly accepted practice of yearly or twice-yearly boosters (depending on the vaccine). Check with your vet for updates on this matter.

Changes have been initiated with puppy vaccinations. Not long ago, puppies received combination boosters that included leptospirosis, but current data advises against this practice. Recent studies reveal that inclusion of leptospirosis in puppy vaccines may interfere with maternal antibody protection while also altering the protection of other portions of the vaccine, thus instilling more risk for some of the very diseases these boosters should protect against. Also, lepto is responsible for more adverse reactions to vaccines in puppies and dogs. This reaction potential is sufficiently high that in parts of the world where leptospirosis is not considered high risk, many veterinarians choose to use a combination vaccine without lepto. Puppy shots should include distemper, hepatitis, parainfluenza, and parvovirus and coronavirus (DHPP) protection. In the meantime, in some areas lepto incidence has been on the rise. This is found in areas where dogs are exposed to wild animals and livestock, particularly cattle. Do you train or hunt on land that has cattle or is used as pasture?

New strains of lepto have been seen as well. Currently, one manufactured vaccine will protect from these new variations of lepto. It's now recommended that all hunting breeds working outdoors should receive a vaccine containing all available strains of leptospirosis in combination with other coverage (DHLPP) during the final puppy booster and yearly after that.

Leptospirosis

This bacterial infection has the potential to be fatal. Generally, it's contracted through contact with an infected animal's urine, but can be passed via a bite wound or by ingestion of infected matter.

Without getting too technical, there are two species of lepto: *Leptospira interrogans* most commonly affects dogs. Until recently, this species had two strains, but four threatening strains now exist. Again, currently just one vaccine protects against all four. This vaccine also reduces the risk of adverse reactions because of new manufacturing technology.

Leptospira infection seems most prevalent during moderate seasons of spring and fall. Infections occur in many ways, by drinking water contaminated with "lepto urine" or by direct urine contact, or via a bite, or by eating infected tissue. Lepto is found around cattle. Other culprits are raccoon, opossums, skunks, and rats. Once infected, a dog becomes a host as the lepto settles in his kidneys. In time it sheds bacteria to potentially affect other dogs.

The infected dog experiences fever, decreased appetite, conjunctivitis (an inner eyelid condition), vomiting, lethargy, and overall pain. These symptoms occur within four to twelve days. After onset, the fever could drop while the dog becomes thirsty. Urine color may change to deep orange. Frequent urination can cause dehydration, but decreased urination can occur. Jaundice might set in. Eventually, the dog's appetite will worsen and the dog will be depressed. Breathing will be difficult; muscle spasms, abdominal pain, and bouts of bloody vomit and stools could occur. There could be liver compromise and renal failure.

Diagnosis requires certain tests. Laboratory results can reveal changes in blood chemistry, a spike in liver enzymes, and other problems. Several serologic tests are available; some have greater likelihood for false negative or false positive results. Treatment includes a strong course of antibiotics during the onset of lepto, which can shorten the duration that lepto is contagious and decrease the potential for liver and kidney damage. Action may be needed to reverse kidney failure. Blood transfusions may be required. During this time urine and waste from an infected dog must be treated as hazardous so that others aren't infected. Living areas should be cleansed with an iodine-based solution. Following potential recovery, a dog may shed lepto for three additional months and should be quarantined.

Some dogs will die within weeks, but this percentage is low. More dogs will die in subsequent years because of complications in liver and kidney function caused by the disease. It is also wise to note that a recovered dog, while protected from the strain of lepto he has contracted, will still be susceptible to other strains.

Distemper

Canine distemper is a viral disease once feared worldwide. Sound vaccination practices have helped reduce its threat to young puppies and older dogs. It's highly contagious and spread by airborne infected respiratory secretions. It affects the central nervous system and the respiratory and gastrointestinal systems. Most dangerous to young un-vaccinated puppies, distemper quickly strikes unprotected adult dogs, too. Symptoms include characteristic eye "gunk" from drainage and/or eye swelling, spiked fever, listlessness, and depression. The disease progresses to a messy eye and nasal discharge, additional fever, lack of appetite, diarrhea, vomiting, pneumonia, convulsions, and finally to neurological complications. Up to 80 percent of infected puppies die; those that survive often have lifelong problems including partial paraly-sis or trouble with hearing, sight, and smell. This disease strikes people, but anyone who has had a measles vaccination is protected.

Hepatitis

Early symptoms mimic distemper but can include a sore throat and cough, although this seems contraindicative since hepatitis is a viral disease that affects the liver. Bluish corneas, increased thirst, bleeding, seizures, bruising, and abdominal pain may be evident.

Canine infectious hepatitis is spread through respiratory secretions and infected urine. Hepatitis is caused by adenovirus type 1. Modern vac-cines contain either adenovirus type 1 or type 2 (producing the cough); either one protects against both. There is no actual treatment. Support-ive therapy can result in recovery, although a recovered dog is contagious for another nine months.

Cough

We'll examine several types of cough. Most any cough is labeled "kennel cough"—otherwise known as bronchitis, tracheobronchitis, or bordetella—and can stem from several viruses and/or bacteria acting in concert or alone. Primary culprits include parainfluenza and *Bordetella bronchiseptica*, airborne viruses that are highly contagious. Kennel cough involves inflammation of the windpipe and bronchi, or the air passages to the lungs. Initial symptoms include inflamed nasal passages and/or discharge, eye redness, and a dry hacking cough often followed by a gagging sound that becomes worse with exertion.

Kennel cough can be very debilitating for the working dog and is a particular threat when hunting trips or field events draw near, since any activity can exacerbate the condition and affected dogs aren't welcome where healthy dogs congregate. In its mild form, kennel cough may last as few as six days; more serious cases—which can appear three days following exposure—might encompass ten or more days. Kennel cough will go away without treatment as the disease runs its course, but occasionally progresses to pneumonia and certain life-threatening problems.

If your dog contracts the disease, you should monitor him closely and watch for symptoms like a productive cough, fever, or pneumonia that require veterinary care. Isolate your dog from other dogs and keep him quiet until he recovers. That means no hunting or training. Exercise induces coughing, which further irritates the respiratory tract and will hinder recovery. Note that once your dog recovers he is capable of spreading the virus for up to fourteen weeks.

Combination vaccines contain some protection against bronchitis, and a bordetella vaccine is available for supplemental protection.

Parvovirus and Coronavirus

First appearing in the late 1970s, "parvo" has been brought under control to a degree but remains a threat, particularly to puppies. This viral disease can kill puppies and young dogs quickly following onset of symptoms. A similar disease called canine coronavirus, not quite as severe, offers similar symptoms and can also be life threatening.

Highly contagious, this viral intestinal disease is most debilitating to young puppies and older dogs. The virus is shed in feces of infected dogs and can be spread by visiting flies or people that make contact with contaminated feces and bring it home. Initially, debilitating vomiting and diarrhea occur rapidly. Diarrhea is frequent and harbors a foul, distinctive odor. The stool is watery and bloody or may be an unusual gray or whitish color. (A serious cardiac form of parvovirus sometimes strikes young puppies and usually causes sudden death.) An affected dog's white-blood cell count will drop severely along with body temperature.

Depression is immediate. Dehydration is life threatening. Treatment includes appropriate fluid therapy, provision of dry bedding, and warmth.

Parvovirus can exist in the environment for six to nine months. Hypochlorite, or bleach, will kill the virus and should be applied to any affected areas and sprayed on housing and anywhere a sick puppy or dog has been. All bedding and towels should be washed with bleach.

Young puppies initially receive antibodies from their mother, but they should receive aggressive vaccination beginning at age six to eight weeks as recommended by your veterinarian until sixteen weeks or older. Parvovirus is included in most combination vaccines, but can also be purchased as a stand-alone vaccine or in combination with coronavirus.

Rabies

Rabies is a serious threat to our hunting dogs. Because your dog may encounter potentially rabid wild animals while hunting, you should never take your dog to the woods if he has not been vaccinated against rabies.

All states require current rabies vaccinations for dogs. Check with your veterinarian for your state's regulations; some states require yearly boosters while others have two- and three-year boosters. Laws have changed governing who administers rabies vaccine. Not long ago, dog owners routinely gave their own rabies shots to their dogs. New laws mandate that veterinarians administer rabies vaccination in most parts of the United States and worldwide. Keep current certificates readily available for travel and for events.

Lyme Disease

A vaccine has been developed to protect against Lyme disease, a tick-borne bacterial disease first recognized in the 1980s and more prevalent in some areas of the country than others. Lyme is caused by the bacteria known as *Borrelia burgdorferi* and is transmitted by blood-sucking ticks.

Symptoms include fever, lameness, loss of appetite, severe pain, and signs of arthritis. Other cases of possibly related tick fevers, such as Rocky Mountain spotted fever and ehrlichia, can mimic Lyme.

Quick onset of painful joints and lameness is indicative of Lyme, but dogs respond quickly to correct antibiotic treatment. Many dogs will relapse one or more times following initial treatment.

Some veterinarians don't recommend this vaccine unless you and your dogs live in a particularly high area of potential exposure. The vaccine could promote symptoms without tick exposure and require treatment. Others feel that tick maintenance programs, including topical or oral preventatives for ticks, and aggressive physical inspections to monitor tick presence and removal, may work better than the vaccine to prevent Lyme. Ticks removed within twelve hours shouldn't infect your dog with Lyme. When vaccination is recommended, it's usually initially administered with two shots up to four weeks apart and then is bolstered annually.

Giardia

Caused by a harmful protozoan parasite found in contaminated water sources, giardia is often found near beaver populations, hence the nickname "beaver fever," although any stagnant water may harbor *Giar- dia lamblia*. Hunting dogs are exposed to giardia because we hunt them in these types of places and it's a sure bet they'll satisfy their thirst while ranging in the woods by drinking nasty standing water.

Symptoms include weight loss, inability to gain weight, loss of appetite, vomiting, sporadic diarrhea, or chronic diarrhea. Giardia is difficult to diagnose as it seldom shows up during a fecal exam; doing a direct smear of fecal matter may help. Neither test is absolute. Treatment is often prescribed in the presence of undiagnosed symptoms with good success.

A new vaccine has been developed to prevent giardia. It can be given to puppies in two doses and then boostered one time the following year. Adult dogs are given two doses with no subsequent booster. Check with your veterinarian for changes to this protocol.

More on Vaccines

While changes to protocol for viral vaccine protection may occur, this may not apply to bacterial organisms such as bordetella, lepto, and

Lyme disease, and some recommendations for bacterial protection include vaccination within a twelve-month period, or sooner. Never assume—check with your veterinarian.

Combination vaccines may include distemper, hepatitis, leptospirosis, adeno type 1 or 2, parainfluenza, parvovirus, and coronavirus. Many combination vaccines are available. Remember that young puppies should receive a series of combination shots from six to eight weeks until they are about sixteen weeks of age—these shots are recommended at three to four week intervals. Most experts advise that initial puppy vaccines be given *without* leptospirosis, but the final shot in the series should indeed contain lepto.

Rabies vaccine should be given initially at about four months of age and then bolstered annually or as state law dictates. In areas where parvovirus is a problem, an early vaccine of parvo/corona is given at about six weeks of age and prior to the first puppy combination shot and sometimes repeated. Other vaccines to consider include a supplemental kennel cough vaccine (bordetella) and those for protection against Lyme disease and giardia. Consult your veterinarian for your dog's vaccination schedule. (Note: A vaccine for certain kinds of snakebite became available in 2005.)

Internal Parasites

Heartworms

The incidence of heartworm infestation in dogs has spread at an alarming rate to include most parts of the world that harbor mosquito populations, with most cases occurring in the United States, Canada, and southern Europe. Adult heartworms grow to be four to twelve inches long (males four to six inches and females ten to twelve inches), and one dog might have from one to thirty or more adult worms in the heart and lung area. Heartworms could severely affect the performance of your dog and can even kill him.

Your hunting dog needs his heart to do his job and to be your companion. If you have never seen a canine heart infested with heartworms, ask your veterinarian to show you the next time you stop by the office.

Once you see how these worms can strangle your dog's vital heart organ, you will have a deeper appreciation of the importance of giving your dog preventive medication on schedule.

Heartworm infection is spread by a bite from a mosquito that has previously fed on a heartworm-positive dog or other animal such as a coyote, wolf, or fox. The larvae will grow, migrate, mature, and reproduce, creating offspring (microfilaria) during a seven-month period. Adult worms aren't fully grown for about a year, and have a five- to seven-year life span.

Most blood tests check for microfilaria, but heartworms can be present without producing offspring. When single-sex heartworms are present a test could be false negative. New tests such as antigen and "occult" versions, radiographs, and ultrasounds can successfully detect heartworms.

Symptoms include a cough and exercise intolerance. Other symptoms seen when heartworm infection worsens include the inability to maintain weight, rapid heartbeat, enlarged liver, and a swollen abdomen due to fluid buildup. Dogs with moderate to severe disease often die without treatment, but note that any dog with just a mild case *could die* if an adult heartworm twists and obstructs the heart chambers and/or vessels, causing heart failure.

Treatment is costly and not without potential harm to the dog or residual effects, although newer methods are less debilitating. Usually, hospitalization of one to a few days is required along with laying off from exercise for an additional thirty to sixty days.

Medications are available to prevent heartworms but must be given regularly for effectiveness. Choices include daily or monthly doses with some experimentation on six-month medications being conducted. In some areas, prevention should be practiced year-round, while in colder climates it may be safe to use prevention when the mosquito season begins and for a few months afterward.

Puppies should be started on preventive heartworm medication when they are just six to eight weeks old in high-risk areas. Older dogs with a questionable history of heartworm medication should be checked for heartworms before a preventive schedule is begun to avoid potential complications.

Be sure to keep stagnant water to a minimum around your home. Avoid leaving jugs, used tires, or other receptacles for rainwater that might be breeding grounds for mosquitoes. Yard sprays and repellants are helpful in areas near swamps or in humid, mosquito-prone areas.

Intestinal Worms, Flukes, and Protozoa

Let's look at the most common intestinal afflictions caused by worms and protozoa, most undetectable with the naked eye, and better understand how these things can harm our dogs. Some of the details may surprise you.

Roundworms

The most common worm in puppies, roundworms are spread via the placenta and/or from larvae in the dam's milk. Puppies with an unhealthy pot-bellied look usually have roundworms. Other symptoms include poor growth, diarrhea, listlessness, and poor hair coat; roundworms absorb precious nutrients that puppies need to thrive and grow. They can sometimes be seen when passed in fecal matter, and they resemble thin spaghetti noodles.

Severe infestations of roundworms can kill young puppies. Pregnant females should be treated on a schedule recommended by your veterinarian, and puppies should begin a safe worming schedule as early as two weeks of age with regular worming intervals thereafter through three months of age.

Hookworms

This type of worm is common and dangerous to dogs and puppies. The hookworm attaches to the small intestine and sucks blood, causing anemia. Severe infestations of hookworms can be fatal to puppies but are a threat to adult dogs, too. Symptoms may include dark, almost black, diarrhea, weight loss, and poor condition.

Hooks can be passed in milk, by ingestion of infected matter or feces, or passed through the skin. Hookworms get into the soil and can penetrate the pads of your dog's feet, as well as your own—or your children's bare feet—which is a strong case against dirt pens. Dirt can, however, be treated with sodium borate (good old bleach), which will also kill grass. Stools suspected of containing hookworm eggs should be picked up and disposed of before their presence contaminates the earth.

Whipworms

Mild forms of whipworm aren't serious, but severe infestations of the large intestine can be life threatening. Symptoms include fresh blood in the stool, diarrhea, weight loss, abdominal pain, and anemia. Whipworms do not thrive well in sanitary conditions so this is your best means of defense against whips. If your veterinarian suspects whipworms it may take more than one fecal examination to find the culprits; they're difficult to find. Note, however, that not all worming medications are effective for whipworms.

Tapeworms

Have you ever seen worms in your dog's stool that look like grains of rice? These are segments from a tapeworm that inhabits your dog's small intestine. Tapeworms can cause weight loss, occasional diarrhea, vomiting, and abdominal sensitivity. Two primary tapeworm species affect dogs. These are very different in the ways they're contracted and sometimes in the medication choices for treatment.

One tapeworm species is from fleas, while the other comes from ingesting matter or dead flesh from infected rodents. The use of a good antiflea product will help prevent the first species of tapeworm, but hunting dogs often run across dead animals and sometimes sample the fare. Many prescription and over-the-counter medications are available; some are less effective and more potentially harmful to your dog than others. Use caution in making the right choice.

A Weird-Looking Worm

Occasionally, a worm may show up in your dog's stool that looks like something from outer space. It is white, wrinkled, and fairly large in size. This creature comes with the long technical name of *Macracanthorhynchus ingens* and is a parasite harbored by raccoon. There are no real symptoms and there is no treatment, but it's mentioned here in case you ever see one.

Flukes

Perhaps you've heard of salmon poisoning disease where a dog gets sick from eating raw fish. This is found primarily in the northwestern United States as well as southwestern Canada and Siberia. Infected salmon, trout, or pacific salamander tissue harbors a fluke from eating a snail that in turn hosts a deadly bacteria that makes the dog sick; symptoms target the gastrointestinal tract and mimic parvovirus. Without treatment the disease can be fatal. However, treatment with antibiotics and often supportive fluid therapy is quite effective and usually successful when started in time.

In other parts of the world, similar flukes can cause problems in dogs but are also treatable. For instance, in the Western Hemisphere, Europe, Australia, and Japan a snail again acts as the first host by penetrating tadpoles, which are consumed by frogs, snakes, and mice, which can be eaten by dogs. A similar fish experience is known in certain North African and Asian countries. There is also a hepatic fluke found in eastern Europe and parts of Asia that can cause problems in the bile duct, pancreatic duct, and small intestine of dogs, and when untreated, is thought to sometimes progress to cancer; again, the snail and fish connection is present.

Coccidia

Certain protozoa cause coccidiosis in many mammals, which is characterized by diarrhea (sometimes bloody), weight loss, anemia, fever, and even death. Because coccidia oocysts are not shed daily in the stool, it can be difficult to diagnose without a series of stool sample checks. Coccidia are known as opportunistic pathogens, which means essentially that symptoms can appear during times of stress, including those associated with weaning, shipping, and diet changes. Although coccidiosis can be self-limiting without reinfection, treatment is used to address the symptoms. Without treatment severe dehydration and anemia could occur requiring possible fluid therapy and even blood transfusions. Often associated with poor sanitary conditions or overcrowding, coccidia can occur in the one-dog home as well, or in clean kennels. Prompt treatment as well as good sanitary practices and reduction of stress factors will prevent coccidia from becoming a more serious problem.

Giardia

Although giardia was mentioned in the section on vaccines, it warrants another discussion here since it falls under the protozoan category and because it occurs worldwide. Diarrhea can occur in spurts or remain constant and may contain mucous. An infected dog may be unable to gain weight or maintain its condition. A few drugs remove giardia cysts from feces. Your veterinarian should be consulted for treatment.

Lung Flukes and Lungworms

Although rare, lung flukes occur in dogs. This condition isn't often suspected by veterinarians but it is seen in hunting dogs (and people) in North America, Southeast Asia, and China. Snails are the first host, with crayfish and crabs being the second. Dogs can become infected through contact with raw crayfish or crabs, or with animals that have eaten them. Flukes can penetrate your dog's intestinal wall and eventually set up shop in the lungs. Symptoms include a nasty cough, listlessness, and pronounced weakness as the lungs become compromised. When caught in time the condition can be treated.

Lungworms are spread from the saliva or feces of an infected dog and eventually settle in the respiratory tract. Symptoms include a cough from mild to insistent, respiratory distress, pneumonia, and respiratory failure. Diagnosis can sometimes be made through a fecal exam but is most successful through a tracheal wash. Prolonged treatment may be successful if this disease is caught in time.

External Parasites

Fleas

Fleas need no introduction. They're hardy, irritating little pests that feed on the blood of your dog, causing discomfort and itching. A severe flea infestation promotes anemia while a single flea can create serious skin irritation in a dog with a flea allergy. When fleas are ingested (during the dog's personal grooming or in efforts to relieve itching) they also are responsible for tapeworm.

Flea control is the first line of defense. Keep your dog's environment flea free by treating your yard, kennel, and home with proper applications. If fleas are already a problem, your dog and all his favorite haunts will have to be treated at least twice to disrupt the flea's reproductive cycle. Topical treatments are now available that repel fleas from your pet. Various sprays and powders are available for immediate use, but most of these shouldn't be used on young puppies, or around children. Some repellant flea products are toxic to cats. Read all labels before using any pesticides on your pet.

Ticks

Ticks include deer ticks, brown dog ticks, and American dog ticks, and they spread Lyme disease, Rocky Mountain spotted fever, and other forms of tick paralysis. Most preventive medications available for fleas will work against ticks, although the time interval for giving or applying it may vary slightly. Use physical inspections to promptly remove ticks, but the treatment must be given over a prolonged period of time.

Ehrlichiosis

A relative newcomer to tick-borne diseases is ehrlichiosis. This organism can be passed to your dog by an infected tick bite and becomes a rickettsial blood disease that attacks your dog's immune system. Once your dog is bitten by a tick carrying *ehrlichia*, incubation will usually last anywhere from one to three weeks. Certain symptoms appear, alone or in concert, but many of these things suggest that something else is the cause. Coughing, red eyes, glassy eyes, excessive drinking, reduced energy level or activity (lethargy), weakness, fever that comes and goes, anemia, loss of appetite, mild reaction to vaccinations, loss of muscle tone, swollen lymph glands, discharge from eyes or nose, prolonged bleeding or nose bleeds, hemorrhages under the skin or in the gum area, rash, seizures, difficulty walking, pneumonia, neck and back pain, bruising, and swollen joints are all symptoms. However, a few other things can tip your vet off to ehrlichiosis; for example, an enlarged liver and/or spleen as well as enlarged lymph nodes. Another consideration is thrombocytopenia, a disorder with low platelets and possible abnormal bleeding. Also your dog could have low red or white blood cell counts, and (potentially irreversible) bone marrow suppression.

This disease can linger for years. In the first stage of ehrlichiosis, called the acute stage, it's possible for the dog's system to progress rapidly to a serious condition where he could possibly die without treatment. You'll know something is wrong. In the absence of this, however, symptoms may vanish and you could conclude that your dog has recovered on his own. Then, ehrlichiosis progresses to the subclinical stage, which could last for years. Some dogs can "clear" this organism from their systems without treatment during this phase. Any number of stimuli can trigger the body to launch the disease into the final chronic stage where your dog can die without treatment. If this condition is treated early enough a full recovery can be expected in 98 percent of cases, but you've got to get your dog to the vet and on proper medications. Many times, ehrlichiosis is misdiagnosed as Lyme disease, and if the treatment prescribed for Lyme is amoxicillin, this antibiotic won't cure ehrlichiosis. However, it could hold any secondary infection in check. Sometimes, doxycycline is prescribed for Lyme and this would also treat ehrlichia if given in the correct dose and for the right length of time. Certain dogs will also require hospitalization, fluid therapy, and/or blood replacement (transfusion) to gain control of the disease.

If you find a tick on your dog or on yourself, use the proper procedure to remove it. Use tweezers and pull gently until the tick dislodges from your dog's skin; don't pull quickly or a portion may remain. Once you've removed the tick, dispose of it or drown it in rubbing alcohol. Don't burn the tick or step on it; this could spread bacteria.

Mange

Mange mites cause unsightly skin problems that can become life threatening when left untreated. Two types of mange are demodectic and sarcoptic mange. Demodectic (red) mange is believed to be related to autoimmune problems and is hereditary. Most experts feel that this type of mange is not contagious. Conversely, sarcoptic mange is highly contagious. Since sarcoptic (scabies) mange can become inflamed and progress rapidly, it's often mistakenly referred to as "red mange"—which it's not—and the treatment for the two differs.

Sarcoptic mange causes intense itching in the dog and often shows up initially at the base of the ears or around the elbow area, but this is not always the case. Note that cases of sarcoptic mange are less frequent since ivermectin, a heartworm preventive medicine, is one form of treatment. Also topical dips kill the mites, but normally a minimum of two dips is needed to cure the problem. The sarcoptic mange mite is round and difficult to detect with a skin scraping.

Demodectic mange is called "red mange" because of the areas of skin that become leathery, coarse, dry, and reddened from the irritation and from blood. The demodex mite is cigar shaped. Usually but not always hair loss is first noticed on the head, often around the eyes and mouth. Localized and generalized demodex occur. Either type usually shows up in fairly young puppies. Localized is much easier to treat, and some veterinarians choose to let this form run its course. Demodectic mange is often linked with an inadequate immune system. It's accepted that most dogs harbor the demodex mite on their skin, but pups with poor immune systems seem to exhibit symptoms. It's seen from three to eighteen months of age with recurrence possible during that time. Beyond eighteen months the immune system will eventually mature. However, older dogs could get demodex when under severe stress that further compromises the immune system.

Identification

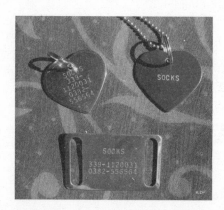

Different tags for different methods of attachment: around the neck on a chain (top) or fitted to a collar band. (Rossella Di Palma)

Many identification choices, such as ink tattoos, freeze branding, identification tags with a centralized phone number, and imbedded microchips are available to identify your dog. With the last two methods, use the provided data bank by registering your dog. Any of these methods could prove helpful to recover your dog should he ever become lost or stolen.

Take lots of photographs of your dog; they could be useful if you must go to a court of law to prove ownership. While it's more difficult to identify a black Lab from a photograph than a uniquely marked treeing Walker coonhound, there are often many identifying characteristics present in photos that can be seen when necessary, particularly when you have photos depicting various positions.

Grooming and Inspections

Your dog will be a companion and family member for many years and will need a certain amount of grooming and physical care, just as you do. The time to accustom your pet to these procedures is when the dog is young and less able to object to your wishes. When properly introduced, grooming can be pleasant to your dog.

Some dogs wear their toenails down during activity, but others have a propensity for growing long nails no matter what. Would you like to walk around on your fingernails or toenails? Of course not—and neither does your dog—which is why toenails must be regularly monitored to

One method of grooming after an inspection. (Rossella Di Palma)

make sure they are an appropriate length. You'll need to trim overly long toenails with a nail clipper or trimmer, available at most pet supply stores. Puppies introduced to this procedure at a young age, with a minimum of fanfare, quickly adapt. Note that the simple act of nail trimming can become a battle royal for improperly introduced dogs. Your dog may need to have a broken toenail doctored, or a cut pad medicated, and it pays for the dog to be comfortable with having his feet handled.

Regular maintenance of the ears, eyes, teeth, and body will pay big dividends during times when treatment of these areas is necessary. Accustom your dog to baths, washings, dips, and being brushed. If the dog's coat is medium to long, you'll sometimes need to remove mats, briars, and cockleburs. Check the ears, clean them regularly, and watch for a discharge or abnormal odor. Observe the healthy appearance of your dog's eyes so you can quickly detect something amiss. Inspect your dog's teeth regularly and watch for plaque buildup, which can cause serious problems and lead to infections that may spread to other parts of the body. Dental problems can also lead to impaired sense of smell—and that is one of your hunting dog's most valuable assets. Protect it!

Inspections of your dog may reveal problems in their infancy, before they become injurious. Keep in tune with your dog's normal body condition. If something seems out of the ordinary, make book and take note; you'll likely want to plan a trip to your veterinarian for a checkup. It's always better to be safe than sorry. If you live in an area that has not seen many cases of ehrlichiosis, but you have been hunting in other places or states—indeed, even if you've just been hunting around your home—you may need to suggest the possibility to your vet, who can make a thorough check. This disease can easily be misdiagnosed for other conditions or ailments, and that is what makes it potentially deadly to your dog.

Finally, remember that you know your dog better than anyone. If the dog "just doesn't seem quite right" to you, chances are he is not. It's up to you to monitor your dog's health. We will look at more health concerns in chapter 12. Proper adherence to such things as vaccination protection from diseases, as well as heartworm prevention and external and internal parasite removal, will help keep your dog in the picture of health.

CHAPTER
TEN

What's for Supper?

We arrive at another loaded question. There are as many opinions regarding types and brands of dog food as there are breeds of dogs. Well, not quite, but you get the picture. In this chapter you'll be presented with helpful details to make an informed opinion regarding the best diet for your dog. You'll need to complement your choice of feed with sound feeding practices and good observation. Let's take a look.

Dog Food Choices

While some dog foods can only be bought from dealers or specialty stores, others can be purchased from farm supply outlets and still others can be obtained from—yes—the local grocery store. Today's market is flooded with dog food. In any grocery store you'll find a veritable smorgasbord of brands and flavors. Venture into a pet superstore and you'll find even more aisles, all stocked with dog food, than you ever thought possible. Another thing you'll notice is the range of prices. What makes one bag $10 and another of the same size $40? What do you need to know about all these options to make a good choice for your dog? How important are these things when you choose what you are going to feed your dog?

It's clear there are a number of things to consider when you look at the subject of dog food. Yes, there are many quality feeds to choose from as well as some less than adequate. With a little research you can make an informed choice that's right for your dog.

Evaluate your own dog's situation. Will he be hunted on a regular basis, perhaps several times a week? Does your dog stay in a kennel with only occasional bouts to the field or timber? What is the climate where you live? Does your dog stay inside or outside most of the time? The answers to these things will help your decision-making process.

Choose a high-quality food if your dog falls in the hard-working performance category. If you're hunting the dog hard or training and

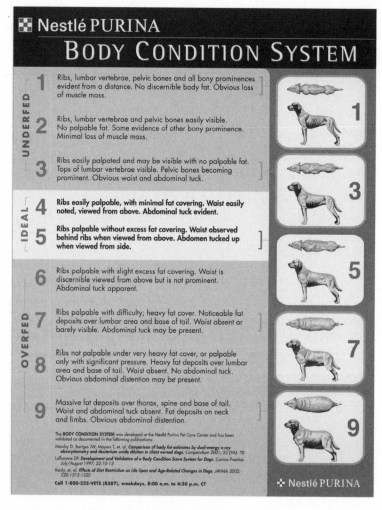

Purina body condition chart. (Nestlé PURINA)

perhaps competing in field events, you don't want your dog to let you down when it counts. Part of your dog's ability to work is directly related to what you put into his diet and nutrition. This is your dog's fuel. Dogs also need more calories during extremely cold weather just to maintain normal body temperature and weight. Add to that the extreme workouts that certain bird dogs, retrievers, coonhounds, and big-game hounds experience and you have dogs in need of excellent nutrition.

What constitutes a high-quality dog food? Quality ingredients are necessary and constitute an essential part of protein and fat availability in the food. High protein versus high fat—this always starts an argument. One myth that's been around forever is that high protein will burn up your dog's kidneys. *This isn't true for the average healthy dog of any age.* (Older dogs have more difficulty metabolizing protein and need more protein intake to maintain their protein reserves, necessary for optimal immune system function and protection.) Benefits of higher protein levels from quality sources are important to your dog's overall performance and well-being, such as helping your dog ward off infection and disease. He'll be better able to deal with stress, and recovery time from muscle fatigue and injury will be quicker.

Many dog foods may claim 26 percent or 28 percent or 30 percent protein but may actually have very different amounts that can be used by your dog. This is why protein source is very important to a good dog food. Shoe leather is high in protein but won't do much for your dog. Make sure that the food you've chosen gets its protein content from quality sources, which include meat (chicken, beef, etc.), meat meal (such as lamb or beef), beef and bone meal (quality varies greatly depending on the source), poultry by-product meal, soybean meal, and corn gluten meal. Poor or inadequate protein levels and digestibility are indicated by a dull, lifeless hair coat, poor growth, reproductive problems, weight loss, and decreased appetite.

All feeds are not created equally. While two different bags say 27 percent protein, protein from one bag might come from real poultry and the protein in the other bag might come from animal by-products, or worse. Sometimes a 21 percent protein feed may have more usable protein for your dog than one that claims 27 percent protein. Whether your dog can actually process the protein in his food is more important than the percentage of protein or the price tag on the bag. Can your dog get the most from the protein in the food he eats, or will much of it be eliminated, unused?

What about carbohydrates and fat levels? When you read a food label, you usually see the ratio of protein to fat. For example, the bag might read 26/18 or 25/15 or 30/20 or 21/10 (first number = protein, second number = fat). We've just reviewed the benefits of protein levels from quality sources. What actually does higher fat do as opposed to lower fat? How will this affect your dog?

You've possibly seen dogs—or had personal experience with your own dogs—when they've suddenly appeared to "run out of gas" and can't go any farther or hunt much longer. These symptoms can come from nutrition imbalances or shortcomings where your dog must depend on carbohydrate bursts of short-term energy to do his work because his diet doesn't provide enough fat for long-term energy. The amount of fat in a diet suddenly can become very important to the performance dog because of energy requirements. This is often extremely misunderstood.

What happens during the off-season or during warmer seasons to the choice of diet for the hard-working performance dog? Should the feed's nutritional content be reduced because of higher temperatures and reduced activity? Maybe, but then again, maybe not. Reducing protein and fat intake during summer months and periods of inactivity can sometimes make the rebound time for peak conditioning take longer than when diet isn't altered. This isn't a blanket statement; the amount of layoff time and factors like temperature extremes would need evaluation. Some dogs fare better on slightly reduced protein/fat diets in the warmer months, and you'll have to experiment with your own dog to find the best situation that works for you.

Protein—its balance of amino acids—is vital to the growth and maintenance of most tissues in the body, including muscle, bone, hair coat, and organs that dictate your dog's health. When your dog eats, the protein content is broken down into amino acids by digestion and then distributed in the bloodstream to cells that rebuild these amino acids into body protein. In short, high-quality protein in adequate levels will help your dog's system to function.

Fat has been recognized for its importance to the working dog. Fats contribute to the overall taste of the food but also supply fatty acids and certain fat-soluble vitamins. They contain more than twice as much usable energy than found in the same amount of protein or carbohydrate sources. It's been proven that diets high in fat are instrumental in providing long-term energy for dogs that work for lengthy periods of time. Diets with high fat content also have a high caloric density, however, so a high-fat diet should not be fed in excess to a sedentary dog. Fat sources include beef tallow and chicken fat.

Carbohydrates, a source of energy and fiber, come from grains such as ground corn, ground wheat, rice flour, corn flour, wheat flour, rice, and oats. Other sources of fiber come from beet pulp and soybean hulls. Fiber provides the "full" feeling necessary to calorie-restricted diets.

When you decide on a brand and formula of dog food, choose a brand/company with good quality control. It's reassuring to know that the ingredients going into your dog's food are safe. You want to know that the food will be properly cooked and processed so that your dog gets optimal nutrition out of every bag. Some companies check ingredients to determine that they do not contain harmful additives, spoilage, or dangerous fungus growths, while others don't check or check only sporadically for such things. Dog food companies without these quality controls have had serious problems with dangers like aflatoxin (a corn fungus) that end up being processed into the feed, then consumed by dogs eating the feed. Aflatoxin poisoning can be lethal to dogs at certain doses over a period of time. All these things are reflected in the price tag.

You want to choose a reputable dog food company that has a history of manufacturing safe food, and you want to feel confident that you can count on consistent quality in each bag you open. Where does your dog food's manufacturer buy the many ingredients used? Is it the same source each time, or do sources change as the market changes? Does the actual formula of the feed change as ingredients become more costly during certain times of year? Some dog food companies change formulas—does yours? Are you comfortable with that? Who is responsible for quality control of these ingredients?

Another thought about dog food. If you have several dogs you may qualify for one of the kennel programs available from some leading manufacturers to help customers with multiple dogs save money buying in bulk. Check with your company to see if such a program is offered. Another option you may want to consider is a homemade ration such as BARF (Biologically Appropriate Raw Food).

Treats and Supplements

We all want to give our dogs treats at one time or another. These might include the Milk-Bone, rawhide bones, knuckle bones, pig ears, cow hooves, liver pieces, hot dogs, and a host of popular treats. Beware. While the Milk-Bone brand and other biscuit-type bones made by reputable companies are fine, sometimes cow hooves, pig ears, and certain chewable toys can fragment and make your dog very sick, possibly even requiring surgery to remove an obstruction. Or worse. Liver pieces are OK in moderation, and hot dog pieces are fine and a favorite treat of mine, but most commercial treats should be approached with caution. Observe your dog when he's chewing rawhide to make sure that he doesn't swallow huge chunks. When buying rawhide, make sure it's from U.S. cows and that it's been processed and produced in the United States. Rawhide from other countries is often treated with dangerous chemicals. Know what you are giving your dog!

Should you offer supplements? Most quality commercial diets are formulated with proper balances of vitamins and minerals to make the diet complete. If you are feeding a premium food, your dog shouldn't need supplementation with vitamins, particularly the average working dog. You could rock the boat and end up with too much of a good thing. Over time, your dog might pay the price.

However, certain instances for high-stress, hard-working dogs may warrant supplementation. Examples include exceptionally hard-working bird dogs, retrievers, sled dogs, or hounds, and also lactating females with disproportionately large litters of puppies. The best supplement in this case would be the addition of meat or meat by-products.

Table scraps are OK if they make up less than 10 percent of the total diet. Scraps shouldn't include any cooked bones. Many foods are toxic to dogs and should never be fed to them. See chapter 12 for a helpful list of foods dangerous to your dog. Avoid feeding from the table (unless you don't mind the begging and finicky eating that usually follows) and realize that the addition of table scraps to your dog's diet may create a picky eater.

Also, do not feed your dog raw eggs. This relatively common practice is done in good faith—the folks that do it feel they are contributing to the diet to make a shiny coat—but nothing could be farther from the truth. While adding an occasional raw egg won't cause harm, raw eggs interfere with biotin breakdown, causing a deficiency in biotin. What can stem from this? Skin problems, hair loss, and poor growth are the main factors. If you want to add eggs on a regular basis, please cook them first.

Feed Schedules

The importance of a consistent feed schedule cannot be overstressed. Young puppies should be fed three times daily, while older puppies thrive on twice-daily feedings. Try to feed your dog at the same time every day and maintain this schedule throughout his life. It'll be one of those constants your dog can count on as his system thrives on regularity.

Certain other decisions go into the feed process that should be given careful thought. Do you want to use a self-feeder? If not, should you feed your dog once or twice daily, and should you use the feed dry or add water to the feed? What about other additives, such as gravy or canned food?

The biggest drawback to the self-feeder is that you don't have the ability to monitor your dog's feed intake. You might not know if your dog suddenly goes off his feed, which could indicate the beginning of a health problem. This is the primary reason I don't use self-feeders. I want to know that my dogs are eating properly and that they're thriving on their food. I also want twice-daily contact from the feeding procedure itself. Some dogs, however, do seem to manage their weight and feed intake better on self-feeders. Be vigilant about the amount and substance of your dog's stool if you use a self-feeder because you don't have that just-mentioned ability to closely watch his feed intake. A sudden decline in your dog's normal stool volume could clue you in to the fact that he's off his feed; a change in stool, such as mucous or blood, might tip you off to developing problems.

Some people believe that twice-daily feedings can reduce overall intake volume, and this is often true when regular schedules are followed. You end up feeding less for the same condition and weight result in your dog. Using this schedule may be more trouble than many folks can invest. But feeding twice daily will keep overall bulk feed volume to a minimum; this could help to prevent other potential problems, such as bloat. (See chapter 12.)

Should you use a moistened dry ration or should you offer it to your dog in its original state? Once again, the experts are divided on this issue. While feeding dry kibble may help keep your dog's teeth clean, adding a small amount of water to the ration just prior to feeding can help even out water intake, particularly when you are traveling. If you don't let it soak, the kibble will still retain teeth-cleaning properties. Still others choose to soak the feed or to add canned dog food. This last practice is not a recommendation of mine unless you want to develop a finicky eater.

Along with any good feed program it is important to provide fresh, clean water, which is necessary for proper digestion and your dog's over-all health. Provide water at all times. This may require additional effort for certain climates as detailed in chapter 8, and a regular schedule when traveling—see chapter 14.

As you give proper thought into the feed and water availability for your dog, also make sure that your dog is in the proper condition (see next chapter) to be hunted. It is unfair to expect your dog to suddenly perform several days a week at top levels or for an entire weekend, when he's been kept in a kennel for several months with inadequate exercise or poor diet. Please keep in mind that our hunting dogs are athletes; they require proper nutrition and adequate physical conditioning to perform under any conditions.

Supplies

Your dog should have his own food and water bowls or dishes. Stainless steel versions are the top choice as they're unbreakable, will last for-ever, and are easy to disinfect. They come in all sizes and shapes. Other choices include the crock/pottery style, glass, and plastic. (Note: Con-tinued use of plastic dishes can sometimes cause inflamed, reddened skin of the muzzle and lips. Discontinue using plastic bowls and this condition will likely disappear.)

When you go shopping for pans and buckets you'll find several types of one-dog feeders that are elevated in a benchlike fashion with two holes for dishes, one for food and one for water. These are marketed toward larger breeds of dogs so they don't have to reach to the floor to eat or drink. Some studies have suggested this arrangement may be safer for the larger breeds and might reduce the incidence of bloat, while other studies indicate that raised feed bowls may compound that potential problem. Be aware of these considerations and speak with your veterinarian before you make your choice.

An opened bag of dog food should be stored in a pestproof container. Some companies make durable plastic pails sized appropriately for their bags of food, which can be found in pet superstores. Other options include plastic or galvanized trashcans with tight-fitting lids to keep out rain, insects, bugs, and rodents.

If you have several dogs it may be more economical and time efficient to buy multiple bags of feed at once. Store your extra bags in a clean, dry place. Elevate them from the floor surface on raised pallets or other suitable material to keep the feed dry. This also reduces the incidence of rodent or bug problems. Some kennels store their feed in old, unplugged chest freezers as the freezer walls work well to keep all unwelcome intruders out.

Finally, if you need a hose to supply your dog's drinking water, be choosy about the hose you buy. Read the label, as most garden-variety hoses are marked as unsafe for drinking water. It's possible to find hoses that are safe, but they often must be specially ordered.

Details. Details. They seem to never end, but attention to details pays big dividends, whether we are caring for our dogs, feeding them, training them, or making plans for special hunting trips, or . . . The list is endless.

CHAPTER
ELEVEN

Tip-Top Shape

L et's take a look at some principles of care and maintenance with regard to your dog's well-being and overall level of conditioning. By the time you buy a puppy and raise him to an age where you can begin serious hunting and training, you've already invested much time and money. These costs will continue to mount through the lifetime of your dog, so it makes sense to consider a sound health program for your dog in a similar fashion that you would for yourself. Good health can repel or minimize injury and sickness recovery. It's well worth your time to consider some valuable points in your dog's care and maintenance.

The bottom line is that your dog is learning to count on you for his needs just as he will count on you to be fair in training. Here is where the bread gets buttered on both sides. The flip side to all this is that you'll count on your dog as well. When you make that long drive on a hunting trip you expect your dog to get out and perform at his best. If he doesn't, you feel let down. Ask yourself if you've done everything to ensure that your dog performs his best "when the truck stops and the tailgate drops."

If your dog is obviously not up to par, why might that be? Yes, just maybe, your dog has dropped the ball. After all, he's a dog, and dogs will be dogs. They'll do things that you least expect and when you least expect them. When you proudly tell your fellow hunters that your dog won't run a deer, chances are the moment you turn him loose he will scorch one out of there, proving you wrong, much to your surprise and chagrin. That is just how it is with dogs.

It's possible, however, that when your dog doesn't perform well it's not because he's being a dog, but perhaps because *you* dropped the ball. Let's take a closer look at what can go wrong. Many things go into the care of a sporting dog. He is an athlete. There's that word again, but it cannot be overstressed. The dog is expected to perform. You train your dog—or you bought him trained—and you expect him to deliver his best every time you take him hunting. What should go into this equation from your side of the fence?

As with many things, proper care begins at home. Your dog should have clean, dry housing and comfortable quarters. When your dog is not out exerting himself for you, he should be able to obtain quality rest. (You should also provide a comfortable dog carrying box for transporting your dog to and from training areas and on hunting trips, for all the same reasons.)

We've just seen that dog food choice is always highly debated among hunters, while the fact remains that all dog foods aren't created equally. If you have high performance expectations of your dog and if you are working that dog hard, he should have a good diet. This bare-bones fact becomes one of the most important things you can do to contribute to your athlete's care and well-being. If you skimp on the quality of food you feed your dog, his system will be forced to compensate. Often the end result translates into something less than top performance. It's as simple as that.

Another tip that helps keep your dog in top condition is a consistent feeding schedule. For example, if you plan to feed your dog twice a day, try to make it the same time every day. A dog's system will thrive on your attention to detail. And the same thing applies if you choose to feed the dog just once a day. As also mentioned in the previous chapter, fresh, clean water should be given on a daily basis. If your situation makes it difficult to tend to this you might want to consider an automatic watering system.

Consideration of the climate that you live in should be reflected in the choice you make for your dog's housing. Monitor extremes of temperature just the same as you would for yourself. This isn't to suggest that you build an air-conditioned doghouse, but make sure that the dog is warm enough in the winter and cool enough during summer. If you've chosen to make your dog an inside dog, keep in mind that during extremes of the seasons, he may not be able to handle long periods of time outdoors.

We discussed the importance of vaccinations in chapter 9. Puppies need a scheduled series of different vaccines. Give special attention to kennel cough vaccines so that your dog won't lose hunting time because of a pesky cough. Use everything in your arsenal to protect your dog, such as heartworm, flea, and tick preventive medications.

Take note of your dog's daily habits. How much does he eat and drink? If you have a dog go off his feed, even a little bit, it could be an early indication of a health problem that is beginning to surface. The same applies to drinking—increased or excessive thirst could give you early signals to some serious internal problems.

Sometimes ears can be difficult to maintain and keep clean. Problem ears can affect your dog's performance, and this becomes more serious if you have a tree dog because infected ears can create discomfort when your dog barks. Therefore it's critical to maintain your dog's ears. Floppy-eared and droopy-eared dogs (almost all breeds of hunting dogs fall into this category) that spend time in the water are susceptible to otitis externa, an infection caused by any number of things that love a moist environment, such as mites, bacteria, or yeast. While a hound with ear problems might not tree as hard, all hunting dogs may have balance or equilibrium problems, just like people, when ear problems are present.

Another thing: keep your dog's teeth clean! Your dog's olfactory network is directly related to the mouth area. An infected tooth, or tooth decay, could directly affect a dog's sense of smell. Tonsils can also cause problems—some dogs are more prone to tonsillitis than others and this can affect both voice and sense of smell.

Some breeds of hunting dogs are prone to chew on sticks. If you see your dog pawing at his mouth, not wanting to eat, or if he's having difficulty trying to eat, check the roof of the mouth. A broken-off piece of stick may be lodged between the upper molars. If left there, the stick will begin to decay and can cause an infection in the roof of the mouth.

It's a good idea to make a quick, overall inspection when you finish hunting each night. That brief once-over might reveal an imbedded thorn, a cut, or something that needs attention. Early treatment can often help avoid costly long-term problems.

During road trips, maintain the same attention to care that you do at home. Try to keep your dog's feeding schedule as close to normal as possible. Be sure to bring food with you, and start out with a six-gallon jug of water from home that you can gradually mix with water from the road, which will minimize digestive upset. You can also buy distilled water in gallon jugs along the way. (See chapter 14.)

Finally, conditioning is as important as anything you can do for your dog. You want the dog to stay the course when the going gets tough. How many days or nights in a row do you think your dog can hunt and still be on top of his game? You don't want the dog to quit just when you need him most. Your hound needs to be in shape the same way that you do, and it's your responsibility to see that the job gets done.

You can do this a number of ways. Some hunters simply prefer to train or hunt their dogs hard and on a regular basis. Other methods include the use of a treadmill or dog walker, swimming in a pond, roading with an all-terrain vehicle (ATV), and pulling with a harness. Moderation is key to any type of exercise, just as with people. Start your dog at a reasonable pace and distance, and gradually increase these things as he becomes able. Swimming, roading, and pulling are probably the most popular means of conditioning, but any of these exercise routines should begin gradually. Swim your dog behind or beside a boat for just ten minutes to start, and build up to thirty or more stress-free swimming minutes.

Roading is most popularly done with an ATV (four-wheeler), although a vehicle can be used with caution. To do this properly the dog should wear a harness and be allowed to run alongside the vehicle. Many a dog will initially resist, but if you patiently show him what you want, he'll probably grow to love this exercise. Every one of my dogs loves to road, and some of them become upset when they don't get to run. You should

English coonhounds on a dog walker. (Berton Oney)

Vizslas in sled harness. (Jeff Malone)

start out with a distance of a mile at five to ten miles per hour, but you'll be surprised how quickly the average dog increases distance to five miles. Watch your dog throughout the run as he may need to stop and "empty out," and also watch for any changes in his attention or focus that could bring him into the path of the four-wheeler or vehicle. The safety of this procedure ultimately rests with you as you are the one driving. When you begin roading, your dog's tail should be carried in a happy position; use this telltale sign as the main clue when your dog is beginning to tire. As exhaustion sets in the tail will begin to drop and sag. When this happens it's time to halt the session.

Pulling is also terrific exercise and can be done as simply as pulling children on a sled in the wintertime to pulling chains in the summertime. Proper harness fit is important and moderation is key. Just as you have to build up weight resistance when you begin an exercise program, so does your dog.

If you only hunt your dog during season, you'll be way ahead of the game to keep him in shape the rest of the year. This way, when season opens you'll be ready to go and you won't have to spend several important weeks of season getting your dog ready to spend a full day on the go.

It's easy to spot a sound, physically fit dog: clear, sharp, intelligent eyes; a healthy, vibrant coat; and good muscle tone and weight. But, as I strongly feel, when you take good care of your dog, he knows it! And that is an important part of your give-and-take relationship. In fact, it's the biggest part.

CHAPTER
TWELVE

Is the Doctor In?

Your veterinarian should be someone you trust implicitly in the care of your dog. Just like medical doctors, not all veterinarians are specialized in every field—some are experts in large-animal care, some concentrate on equine practice, some are best with pets, while others are top-notch with sporting dogs—and time is well spent to find the veterinarian that best complements your dog and his needs. Your ideal veterinarian should be someone you are comfortable with who has a working knowledge of the potential problems unique to hunting dogs.

Knowledge of your dog's normal habits and close observation on your part for any subtle changes to his daily patterns can often supply you with helpful information that can give your veterinarian potential clues for successful diagnosis of pending problems. Also, build an awareness to things that can threaten your dog's well-being and safety. Learn how to recognize an emergency and what to do if you're presented with one. All of this will all help you contribute to the long life of your dog.

Know Your Pal

Learn to observe the little things about your dog. How long does it normally take your dog to eat meals? How often does he drink? Sometimes the first clues about pending trouble relate to eating and drinking habits. If your dog suddenly starts to pick at his food, or perhaps begins to drink excessively, take note. These could be significant warning signs.

What is the normal appearance of the eyes? You'll be able to tell when the slightest amount of redness develops, which could indicate any number of ailments just beginning to show, such as ehrlichiosis (see chapter 9). Anything unique to your dog and his personal habits should be noted regularly and monitored for changes that might occur, however slight. What may seem insignificant to you could be very helpful to your veterinarian in the event he's called upon to solve the mysteries of your dog's problem. Your vigilance may pay off in spades.

Be Observant

Develop an awareness of the surroundings where you train and the types of places you regularly hunt as well as new locations that you may have visited just once or twice. You might find submerged wire, cut tin, a dangerous cliff, or hidden hole. Many accidents can be avoided.

One such hazard you may encounter when you are out training or hunting occurs in the most innocent of settings—it's found in some ponds throughout the country and seems most prevalent during the hot, sunny days of late summer and early fall. Blue-green algae bloom is toxic to animals and is almost immediately fatal to your dog. There are several types of poisonous algae. Nothing can save your dog if he takes in water tainted with the stuff. When dogs ingest water that's poisoned with toxic algae bloom, symptoms appear quickly and include tremors and severe abdominal pain. (Note: Not all toxic algae is bluish green in color. Other colors can be poisonous and, conversely, not all algae blooms are fatal.)

Before you allow your dog to romp in a strange pond or body of water that has algae, check the leeward side of the pond where the wind blows the bulk of algae to see if you find any dead animals there, including mice. Even without such evidence, if the pond raises your suspicions, keep your dog out for safety's sake. Once thought to be limited to the Northeast and Midwest, these algae threats have been found throughout North America, including the Southwest, West, and Canada.

Another threat to dogs found primarily in the western states is foxtail. At certain times of the year, the seed head from this plant can be inhaled or lodged in ear tissue, the hair coat, and between the toes of your dog's paws. This seed head works its way in but cannot work its way back out. Muscle movements or breathing can propel the seed head, allowing it to migrate, piercing and burrowing through tissue and organs. Foxtail can ultimately cause pneumonia, severe illness, or death. If you live in or visit western states during the summer and fall when the seed heads are dry and dangerous, learn to recognize the offensive grasses (foxtail, rip-gut grass, cheatgrass, and others) and keep your dog out of them. In the event your dog does venture into grasses resembling foxtail, groom him carefully as soon as possible. Inspect your dog thoroughly and use saline solution to flush seed heads from nostrils. See your veterinarian at once if necessary.

Foxtail, a troublesome weed to the field dog. (Dr. J. Curtis Clark)

Valley fever is harmful to humans and dogs. This deadly fungus lives in the soil of the Southwest, Mexico, and Central and South America. Without treatment, valley fever can progress to pneumonia, meningitis, and death.

First-Aid Kits

Suppose your dog cuts his foot pad deeply and you are miles from the nearest veterinarian and it's after midnight during a special hunting weekend or critical hunt. This injury needs attention and unless cared for may nix the remainder of your trip. Alas. Although you recently learned that sometimes superglue can close a wound of this type, you never bought any and have none in your truck. You don't have anything whatsoever to help repair the injury and your whole weekend is on the line, not to mention the well-being of your dog's paw. You vow to be prepared next time and make a solemn promise to yourself to get a first-aid kit for your dog that you'll keep in your truck forevermore. It helps to be versed in emergency procedures as well; a little preparation often goes a long way.

We're all human and most of us don't attend to simple things that can help us be more prepared in an emergency. We're aware that we constantly put our dogs in harm's way, and we know at any given moment they may be injured while hunting. Therefore, take steps to be prepared should you need to stabilize your dog to get through a weekend or a trip to the veterinarian.

Carry first-aid kits for yourself and for your dog when afield. Be prepared for emergencies; this could mean the difference between life and death if an accident or injury should befall your dog while hunting or traveling.

You can build a first-aid kit from various materials, or you can buy one already equipped with most of the important items you may need in the event of an emergency. It may seem like a daunting task to put together a kit. We'll look at various items you should consider for inclusion.

Besides medications, cleansers, and bandages, you should include a number of instruments. You can add items as necessary to the following list:

hydrogen peroxide
eye wash
ear wash
iodine solution
iodine scrub
antibiotic wash
saline solution
scrub brush
syringe, 6, 10, or 12 cc
pill gun
rectal thermometer
skin staple gun
superglue
gauze, 2 x 2 inches and 4 x 4 inches
alcohol prep pads

stretch gauze material
Vet Wrap self-cling wrap
triple antibiotic ointment
hydrocortisone cream
Benadryl capsules, nondrowsy formula
buffered aspirin
Kaopectate tablets
Pepto-Bismol tablets
Vaseline or petroleum jelly
burn relief gel pack
insect sting relief pads
snake antivenin
tweezers
scissors
forceps
antiseptic wipes
cotton balls
Q-Tips or cotton swabs
styptic pencil or powder—silver nitrate to cauterize a cut
2-inch elastic bandage
1/2-inch adhesive tape
vinyl or rubber gloves
cold pack
splint material
tourniquet
muzzle
ziplock bags
three-ply towels

Consider other items specific to your dog or hunting area:

Nutri-Cal
calorie bar or vet-recommended emergency nutrition for hypoglycemia
   (low blood sugar)
epileptic/seizure medication
certain antibiotics
dexamethazone (anti-inflammatory for stinging nettle, etc.)
poison antidotes
good first-aid book

The last item is possibly the most important one. Get a good canine first-aid book and read it as soon as you can after you buy it. Gadgets and items in your first-aid kit won't be any good if you don't know when, why, and where to use them when the need arises. If you have to take time to read an entire section when you should be doctoring your dog, precious moments can be lost. You don't have to become an instant expert on emergency first aid, but if you take the time to read the book you will at least be familiar with some procedures and you will also know about where to look when you need information quickly.

We've included forceps or tweezers to assist in removing thorns, fishhooks, and porcupine quills, among other things. A syringe can be used to rinse certain wounds with betadine (iodine) or antibiotic wash. Scissors are used to clip hair from a wounded area and to cut adhesive tape and bandages. If you have a staple gun or a tourniquet, be sure you know how, when, and why you should use either one as they can be misused. A thermometer can give you vital information on your dog's elevated or decreased body temperature, helping you to quickly assess potential shock, heatstroke, and hypothermia. A pill gun can help administer antibiotics or aspirin to an unwilling patient. The addition of a muzzle might be helpful if your dog is seriously injured and tries to bite while you are attempting to stabilize him.

Gauze pads, gauze bandage, adhesive tape, cling bandage, cotton balls, cotton swabs—all are helpful in dressing and preparing wounds. The various washes listed are also used for these purposes, while eye and ear washes are self-explanatory.

Other first-aid items: Kaopectate is handy should diarrhea suddenly afflict your dog. Buffered aspirin can help your dog overcome mild arthritis or a hard night of hunting. (Note: Never use regular aspirin or Tylenol.) Benadryl can help in the event your dog gets stung by a bee or bitten by a spider. Snake antivenin can save your dog's life—if anything will—in a severe snakebite emergency, but know that sometimes all the antivenin in the world won't reverse certain snakebites, and that antivenin is very expensive. Ask your veterinarian if the newly developed snakebite vaccine is advisable for your dog.

Consult your veterinarian for any further recommendations for additions to your first-aid kit. There are at least a few commercially available first-aid kits you can buy that are already equipped with many of the items on my list. My favorites to recommend are made by Creative Pet Products (see Resources section) and packaged in convenient, durable, water-resistant bags.

Whenever you travel to unfamiliar areas, be one step ahead—research phone numbers and locations of veterinarians so they're handy in case of emergency. This small investment of time could prove priceless. Keep an index card in your first-aid kit for important numbers such as these, and include your regular veterinarian's office and emergency numbers. Leave additional spaces for numbers when traveling. Another number that should be at your fingertips when poison might be involved with your dog is the ASPCA Animal Poison Control Center at 888-426-4435; however, be forewarned that this agency may charge you a $50 consultation fee.

Emergency Procedures

Certain emergency procedures may stabilize your dog until you can get to a veterinarian for further treatment in the event of severe trauma or injury. There is no question that when precious minutes mean the difference between life and death, knowing how to respond might save your dog's life.

Anytime an emergency occurs you must immediately assess the situation and make quick decisions. Almost always it's important to remove your dog from further danger and then it's usually necessary to administer some type of first aid. Next, it's vital to get to a veterinarian as soon as possible.

What do you do if your dog has been hit by a car or has injured himself? Assess the injury or the nature of the emergency. In many cases your dog is in danger of lapsing into shock, a life-threatening situation. You'll need to keep your dog warm to combat shock, and you must get to a veterinarian immediately so that fluids and supportive therapy can be administered while injuries or treatment is being evaluated.

With any injured dog, be cautious of involuntary retaliation when you try to help. He may try to bite any hand that comes near, and you may need to restrain him or put a makeshift muzzle on the dog before you try anything further. Use caution.

You must determine whether your dog is breathing, or if breathing is compromised. Check his airways to make sure nothing is in the way; clear debris from the mouth and throat. Pull the tongue forward to assist in clearing the airway. Also, just like with people, mouth-to-mouth resuscitation might be necessary and could make the difference in saving your dog. Hold the jaws shut and breathe through the dog's nostrils just as you would breathe into a person's mouth during mouth-to-mouth. Any injured dog should be transported with as little compromise to the back, neck, and head as possible. Try to stabilize the dog and limit movement during the trip to the veterinary hospital.

With uncontrolled bleeding you'll need to do something to stop it, such as applying direct pressure to an open wound with a bandage or dressing. Blood flow must be arrested.

In the case of near drowning, turn the dog upside down if you can and swing him back and forth, not unlike the procedure used to resuscitate newborn puppies, to help dislodge water in the chest cavity. This emergency situation is critical, and the dog should be taken to a veterinarian as soon as possible, even if the dog appears to recover. Pneumonia and other issues can arise that can cause death without treatment.

Seizures are frightening and regarded as emergencies by many people, especially those not experienced with them. If your dog has a seizure, contact your veterinarian immediately and explain the situation. Some types of seizures require veterinary attention immediately while others respond to quiet time. An inexperienced person cannot accurately make this assessment. Read about the seriousness and gravity of seizures. They can be caused by a number of things including but not limited to hypoglycemia and epilepsy, as well as tick-borne diseases such as ehrlichiosis and babesiosis, hypothyroidism, reaction to vaccine, and cardiac problems.

Poison is life threatening. A number of poisons can threaten your dog's well-being, including ingestion of antifreeze, contact with certain chemicals, ingestion of rat poison, and even too much chocolate or grapes. If you suspect any of these culprits, call your veterinarian immediately and follow instructions. Sometimes vomiting can be induced, but other times this will further compromise your dog's chances for survival. You may need to take your dog straight to the veterinarian for antidotal treatment and follow-up. Some poisonings happen too quickly for you to respond in any fashion.

If your dog fractures a limb or breaks or injures any other part of his body, do your best to immobilize and stabilize your dog. Get to the vet as soon as possible. If a break exists below the hock (rear leg) or elbow (front leg), a makeshift brace can be made with a magazine or newspaper tied in place to immobilize the limb.

Bloat from ingestion of air or food constitutes a life-threatening emergency with the danger of gastric dilatation-volvulus (GDV) where the stomach turns and twists. Should this happen, shock will set in, and lack of circulation will set many things into motion as your dog's system shuts down. The sooner you can get to an attending veterinarian, the better your chances are of saving your dog. If your dog's stomach actually twists, doing nothing will result in death. Signs of bloat include a distended abdomen that occurs in a rapid time frame and sounds of discomfort from your dog, as well as distressed activity. (For more information on GDV, see the section "Bloat or Torsion" on p. 160).

If your dog has a penetrating wound, don't remove the object. Removing an object from your dog—such as an arrow, for an example— might cause your dog to bleed to death in a matter of minutes. Instead, do what you can to keep the object from rotating or moving and get to the veterinarian immediately. Snakebite is critical and often nothing can be done by the time you get back to a vehicle and to the vet. Sometimes, a poisonous snake does not discharge enough venom to kill a dog, but enough to make him ill. Haste in getting to a vet is the most important thing you can do. Recent research has shown this is better than trying to use electric shock or to drain venom via a cut. Just get to the vet—as soon as possible.

Heatstroke is serious and you should counteract this situation as soon as possible. It's important to bring your dog's body temperature down without doing so too quickly. Alcohol can be applied to the pads of the feet, ice packs can be applied to the top of the head and under the elbow areas as well as under the flank areas, and the dog can be submerged in cool (not cold—too quick and traumatic) water for brief periods. Do not let the dog drink more than a tiny amount at a time. Even if you appear to have succeeded in bringing heatstroke under control, seek attention from your veterinarian as soon as possible. Other serious health issues can result from heatstroke and if not treated, your dog can die days later from these complications. Dogs are also prone to frostbite and can suffer from too much cold.

Bite wounds often involve compromised trachea and other internal injuries beyond external cuts and wounds. Again, stabilize your dog en route to the veterinary clinic.

A cooldown is essential after hot workouts. (Author photo)

Certain things play a factor in the treatment of any emergency, including the severity of the condition or trauma, how much blood or fluid is lost, the age of the dog and other underlying or previous health problems, and the amount of lapsed time from the onset of injury or accident until treatment. Certain things must occur in a timely fashion in emergencies for the dog to have a chance at survival. Emergency situations dogs die from include excessive blood loss, shock, internal or external hemorrhaging, heat prostration, extensive diarrhea, ruptured/prolapsed organs, cardiac arrest, and airway obstruction.

Ultimately, it helps to keep a cool head in the face of any emergency. Determine what needs to be done to help stabilize your dog and keep his life signs operating until you can get him to a vet.

Some Hunting Dog Maladies

While not intended to be a complete discourse on health, this section will highlight some of the more commonly seen problems that affect hunting dogs. This information may help you recognize symptoms of serious problems or give you pointers for your veterinarian. Always seek professional help when you have concerns about the health and welfare of your dog.

Limber Tail Syndrome

This affliction happens to hunting dog breeds, including Labs, bird dogs, and hounds. While it is also called "cold water tail" or "wet tail" and the symptoms are often attributed to an affliction from excessive swimming in cold water, this can happen in pointing breeds with *no* water activity. It's very alarming, especially the first time you see it, since the tail hangs down limply from a place just beyond its base. Many an owner immediately jumps to the conclusion that the dog has broken his tail. While this is certainly a possibility, it's not as likely as limber tail.

Usually occurring after periods of lengthy activity, it has also appeared following just thirty minutes of exercise. While very cold-water or warm-water swimming may be involved, it can also occur after working on land in cold or wet weather. The tail hangs down from the base or extends out three or four inches from the base and then hangs limply; the affected dog cannot wag his tail and considerable pain is present.

Studies have shown other contributing factors, such as inadequate nutrition, poor physical condition coupled with work that is too strenuous, overtraining, and a high tail set. Limber tail may occur more frequently in males than females. Veterinary examination may reveal an elevated level of the enzyme creatine kinase (CK) during the first few days, but body temperature and radiographs will be normal. While dogs from six months to nine years can suffer from limber tail, it seems most prevalent in the two-year-old range than any other.

All dogs will recover when rested, usually within two weeks, without further treatment. Anti-inflammatory medications or Rimadyl-type drugs may hasten recovery and relieve the pain. Some dogs will have reoccurrences.

Exercise Induced Collapse (EIC)

A condition currently being studied involves serious compromise to the dog's limbs and motor function after short bursts of exercise. The affected dog may lose his ability and function of one leg, which usually quickly progresses to all four legs and the dog "collapses" and cannot get up or move. The dog will appear alert and agitated during this time. He will recover in most cases when allowed to rest. Some fatalities have occurred from this condition. Not much is known regarding treatment or diagnosis at this writing.

Bloat or Torsion

What is a twisted stomach? You've probably heard the dreaded words or you have just read them under "Emergency Procedures" in this chapter. Bloat refers to the distended abdomen that occurs prior to the "twist" of the stomach. A twist of 180 degrees or less is called "torsion" while a twist of more than 180 degrees is termed "volvulus."

Seen in most large breeds of hunting dogs, GDV develops rapidly and should be considered an emergency that can kill your dog. Symptoms include a distended abdomen (bloat) accompanied by distress, difficulty in breathing and in maintaining a comfortable resting position of any kind, whining, groaning, pacing, pale gums, unsuccessful attempts to throw up or eliminate, excessive salivation, and glassy eyes. When your dog is so uncomfortable that he wants to lie down on his front end with paws and chest on the ground and hindquarters elevated, the situation is critical. This should not be confused with playing. It will be obvious your dog is in distress.

Learning to recognize early symptoms of this condition and to immediately seek emergency treatment could save your dog's life. Lack of treatment will result in death. Healthy dogs found dead in their kennels often suffered from GDV and died before being found. Treatment is no guarantee for survival, however, since half of all treated animals will still die from GDV or succumb to related difficulties, often within a week's time.

Once your dog's stomach bloats, the dog can go immediately into shock. Many things happen very quickly. Tissues and organs lack oxygen, and toxins build up in the abdominal cavity. Once toxins are absorbed in the bloodstream, disseminated intravascular coagulation (DIC)—often referred to as "death is coming"—sets in. This usually spells disaster and may not be reversed.

Two things must happen almost immediately if there is any hope of overcoming GDV. Both shock and the pressure caused by the condition itself must be treated by a veterinarian. Radiographs confirm the condition's severity. During surgery an attempt is made to return the stomach to its proper position, and the stomach is inspected to determine if any portions have suffered tissue damage.

Surgical options include tacking down the stomach (gastroplexy) in an effort to prevent future torsion, or the stomach can be anchored to the abdominal wall or attached to a rib. Your dog's heart must be monitored. Abnormalities may arise during and after surgery that can cause death, and other internal organs could be severely damaged from lack of oxygen and toxin buildup when the heart is compromised.

In the event your dog survives surgery, expect no quick miracles. Overall recovery is gradual at best. I don't want to paint a bleak or hopeless picture because if treatment has been introduced quickly enough after the onset of GDV, there is definite hope for as much as a full return to an active, productive life.

What are the leading theories regarding GDV? The most popular is that since the stomach is suspended by ligaments, over a period of time food bulk in the stomach produces weight that eventually stretches these ligaments, therefore providing more room for the stomach to twist. In addition, it is thought that the stomach may become "paralyzed" in a sense, where for whatever reason digestion and activity stops, putting pressure on vital abdominal veins and creating buildup of gases. Considering the fact that most cases of GDV occur in dogs above four years of age, this theory remains the most popular. Exhaustive studies have been done with contradictory results, and little is known.

If you've never had a dog that suffered from GDV, you may not give this subject much thought. But, the experts stress that performance dogs should be fed on a strict, consistent schedule that includes no activity at least one hour before and one hour after feeding. Two smaller feedings are preferred over one large feeding. Water consumption should be monitored, especially when dogs have become overheated or when they have worked exceptionally hard. Efforts should be employed to change the habits of dogs prone to gulping food or water. Stress in the life of any susceptible dog should be kept to a minimum. Keep a close watch on your dog, particularly after periods of exercise and after eating and drinking. Your quick actions—in the event a problem arises—could save your dog's life.

Blastomycosis

Often called "blasto," this deadly disease primarily affects male dogs from two to four years of age, although females can contract it and they have greater chance of recurrence. Disease percentages appear to increase in late summer and early fall. Sometimes confused with histoplasmosis, blasto is primarily located in North America, while histo is a worldwide problem.

Blastomyces dermatitidis is a fungal organism found in various parts of the country, but it's most prevalent in the river valleys such as those surrounding the Missouri, Tennessee, Ohio, and Mississippi Rivers and the St. Lawrence waterway. It's found in North America from the northern Midwest to southern Canada, in upstate New York and down to the southeastern states. Areas with watersheds such as the Great Lakes in Wisconsin, Minnesota, and Michigan, and the eastern coastal states are also hotbeds for the fungus. It can also be found elsewhere.

This fungus exists in the soil and can be picked up in several ways. Usually spores are inhaled by the dog and they settle in the lungs where a pulmonary infection develops, or the dog absorbs the spores through an open wound. Once in the body, the spores transform into a yeast state since the dog's body temperature is higher than soil. Upon diagnosis, blasto has progressed to a generalized stage from the lungs to other organs of the body, including the skin, lymph nodes, subcutaneous tissues, eyes, brain, and urogenital systems as well as to bone.

What are some of the symptoms of blasto? They may be indicative of many things, thus making diagnosis difficult, including coughing, fever that doesn't respond to medication, depression, anorexia (not eating), subsequent weight loss, difficulty breathing, eye problems, exercise intolerance, enlarged lymph nodes, lameness, and/or skin lesions with pus or bloody drainage.

Pulmonary blastomycosis may be limited to the lungs, pleura, and overall chest area. Usually there is an infection coupled with a bad cough that could be dry or may produce phlegm; this often progresses to respiratory distress syndrome. Blasto can also insidiously affect many different parts of the body.

How does your vet determine that your dog actually has blasto and not some other disease? He'll do a blood profile. Often the white blood cell count is elevated, as are calcium levels. Radiographs should be taken for accurate prognosis. Many veterinarians miss this diagnosis if the dog lives in an area of low incidence without being aware that the dog may have been hunted in areas with much higher concentrations of blasto spores. Definitive diagnosis can be made by culture, needle aspiration, or biopsy. Pulmonary blasto or blasto that infects genital areas is sometimes mistaken for tuberculosis, and blasto manifested in skin lesions is sometimes mistaken as skin cancer.

Treatment in dogs can be lengthy and costly and is not always effective. Untreated blasto almost always progresses to death. Because of treatment difficulty, some owners choose to put their dogs to sleep. If you decide to have your dog treated, understand that the best you can hope for is to keep the disease in check, although many dogs, as high as 65 percent, recover with expensive treatment.

Histoplasmosis

Histoplasmosis, a worldwide problem, is becoming more commonly diagnosed in sporting dogs. Often called "bird" or "bat" disease, it's spread by a fungus found in bird and/or bat droppings with high levels of nitrogen in areas that harbor large concentrations of certain birds or bats. While originally it was thought to be found primarily in moist, humid, subtropical areas, it's been found as far north as the Great Lakes states, possibly because of the large numbers of seagulls. Histo affects dogs and other mammals, including humans.

Histoplasmosis is contracted by inhaling *Histoplasma capsulatum* fungal spores from contaminated soil. Like blasto, the fungus transforms into yeast in the body. Histo is not contagious and in almost all cases is inhaled, although occasionally it is contracted through oral ingestion. From the point of inhalation, histo settles in the lungs and thoracic lymph nodes, creating pulmonary histoplasmosis. With disseminated histoplasmosis, organisms also enter the bloodstream and affect other parts of the body, including the eyes, small intestine, and other organs.

Pulmonary histoplasmosis may be present in the dog for an extended time with no warning symptoms except for sporadic coughing and abnormal lung function. Sometimes, high fever occurs with disseminated histoplasmosis and doesn't respond to normal antibiotic treatment. Weight loss, lethargy, and overall depression might be evident. Some dogs exhibit prolonged weight loss with a bad cough, diarrhea, fever, and clinical findings that include obstructive respiratory compromise. When histo becomes disseminated, weeping or ulcerated skin lesions and serious eye problems can occur.

Acute disseminated histoplasmosis can cause death in two to five weeks after the dog initially contracts the disease if left untreated. While the pulmonary form may be self-limiting, disseminated histo often resists treatment, thus requiring a long course of combined antibiotic and antifungal drug treatment. Small areas of infection may be treated with a 3 percent formalin solution. Generalized cases respond much more poorly to treatment, as do cases that have progressed without diagnosis, and these cases require additional steps to increase the odds of recovery from the disease. Any time symptoms are present that include respiratory distress and coughing, diarrhea and straining with fresh blood in the stool, enlarged lymph nodes in the bronchial area, or when pulmonary nodules are found, histo should be suspected.

Hypoglycemia

Many hunting dogs can have hypoglycemia, a condition that occurs when an abnormally low sugar level or blood glucose level manifests itself in the dog. When this happens out in the field, a dog might have seizures. The brain needs sugar to function properly, but in dogs with this disorder there is a limited ability to store this glucose. Blood glucose provides an important energy source and is governed by a complex interaction between hormones and other body functions. When hypoglycemia occurs, there's a malfunction in a dog's ability to convert glycogen to glucose fast enough to keep up with energy demands, leading to inadequate levels of available glucose.

Several conditions can cause hypoglycemia, including the presence of a tumor that affects insulin production, which then decreases blood sugar. This tumor is called an insulinoma and grows in insulin-producing cells in the pancreas. Another cause could be an overdose of insulin in a diabetic animal. Yet another cause, somewhat rare, is hypoandrenocorticism, otherwise known as Addison's disease, where the adrenal glands produce insufficient amounts of hormones.

Symptoms of hypoglycemia include lethargy, tremors, nervousness, seizures, and unconsciousness. In serious cases, glucose must be administered intravenously, otherwise this condition can be reversed by feeding the dog honey, jam, Karo syrup, or a honey bun so that sugar is quickly absorbed into the blood. This treatment is *just* to reverse a problem, however, as giving the dog these simple sugars can also cause a spike in blood sugar followed by an abrupt decline, which can lead to serious complications.

If you have a dog prone to hypoglycemia (common with bird dogs and hounds), the best prevention is to feed the dog a handful of high-quality performance food (such as one with a 30/20 protein/fat ratio) every couple of hours while working during periods of extended activity. Puppies have reduced ability to store glucose and therefore should be fed several times a day to prevent any hypoglycemic condition.

Pythiosis, Leptospirosis, and Giardiasis

Any of these diseases can be contracted when your dog drinks contaminated stagnant water. All are serious concerns; leptospirosis and giardia have been covered in chapter 9. Pythiosis in dogs has been recognized in just the last five or six years, and many people have never even heard of it. Often it is not high on the list of possibilities for diagnosing veterinarians, but it can cause serious problems including cutaneous and subcutaneous lesions on the legs, tail, and abdomen, and gastrointestinal compromise that prompts vomiting, diarrhea, and weight loss. Tumors develop and both skin and intestinal pythiosis progress rapidly requiring surgery to remove infected areas. No known drugs are effective against pythiosis.

Poisons and Toxins

Alcoholic beverages. Because alcohol can be fatal to dogs, no amount of an alcoholic beverage is safe, including beer.

Chocolate is toxic to canines. The darker the chocolate, the more harmful it can be. The methylxanthines (caffeine and theobromine) in chocolate can cause a dog to vomit, have diarrhea, and experience a rapid, irregular heartbeat, increased urination, and muscle tremors and seizures. The effects can be serious. Death from chocolate toxicity can occur within twenty-four hours.

Coffee, tea, and cola are people food. They contain caffeine, a methylxanthine also found in chocolate. The signs of toxicity include rapid heartbeat, hyperexcitability, tremors, and seizures.

Macadamia nuts can temporarily cause muscle weakness, often in the hind legs. Other adverse reactions include vomiting, fever, and abdominal pain. The mechanism of the toxicity is unknown. Affected dogs recover with no treatment and no long-term effects.

Onions and garlic have a chemical that damages red blood cells in dogs and can cause anemia. Even one small, whole onion can cause death. Use caution in disposing of leftovers that contain onions. The small amounts of onion and garlic powder used in pet foods is safe and well below the toxic levels.

Raisins and grapes can cause vomiting, diarrhea, and kidney failure. The minimum safe amount is not known, so keep these foods out of reach.

Sugarless gums and candies contain a sugar substitute called xylitol that can cause a rapid drop in your dog's blood sugar.

Moldy or spoiled food and garbage should stay safely in the trash. Multiple toxins may cause vomiting, diarrhea, and damage to internal organs.

Yeast dough from making bread or desserts expands. If swallowed by your dog it can expand and produce gas in the digestive system, causing pain and possibly a rupture of the stomach or intestines.

Ibuprofen, acetaminophen, and naproxen can be deadly to your dog. Keep all drugs safely out of your dog's reach. Never give your dog medication unless you are familiar with the situation and dosage or as directed by a vet.

Plants are pretty but possibly deadly for your dog. Many common yard and houseplants can be poisonous, including lily, daffodil, oleander, rhododendron, azalea, yew, foxglove, rhubarb leaves, and cycads.

CHAPTER
THIRTEEN

To Breed or Not to Breed?

Another serious decision lies on the horizon. Have you given thought to the prospect of breeding and, more important, do you know how you feel on this subject? Breeding is a serious responsibility and one that shouldn't be taken lightly. Many things are involved in the process. Once you study breeding you may want no part of it, but then again, you may.

Have you considered neutering your dog by spay (female) or castration (male)? While research indicates that these procedures may reduce the incidence of certain types of cancer in both sexes, there are benefits regarding personality changes in some dogs as well. Before you take the plunge, however, be certain that you don't want puppies even if your dog turns out to be a special asset to the breed. You cannot turn back the clock once you've done the deed. If you have the slightest doubt, hold off for now and see what the future brings. Many veterinarians recommend spaying a female before her first heat cycle and neutering a male before a year old, but if you're not ready to jump that hurdle, opt to wait.

Breeding Considerations

Most responsible breeders plan their litters with certain conditions in mind. A cross should potentially improve the breed and, ideally, prospective puppies should be presold or spoken for. These rules should be followed whether you're an experienced breeder or a first-time novice with a nice dog. If your dog possesses strong performance ability and qualities that will contribute to better dogs than those available today, don't be discouraged by naysayers. Understand that it's your responsibility to toe the line and complete a number of steps regarding health clearances before your dog can be considered sound breeding stock.

Preparation

Probably the first thing you'll hear is that you shouldn't breed your dog before he or she turns two years old. This is sound advice. By this age you'll know the potential of your dog. Hip and other clearances (from the OFA, CERF, et al.) can be obtained for a sound dog. Potential breeding animals should be physically sound, of good temperament and trainability, and possess excellent hunting qualities.

You'll likely need certification on your dog's eyes, and depending on the breed, you may need other areas checked, including elbows, heart, thyroid, and breed-specific problems. The Labrador breed now has a test available to determine a dog's carrier status of the gene for centronuclear myopathy (CNM), formerly known as muscular myopathy. It'll take time to get all clearances in order. Don't expect to accomplish them in a week. Allow a few months to have X-rays taken and submitted for evaluation and other tests done and certified. These considerations apply to both males and females.

Stud dog owners now have the option to collect frozen semen on their males that can be stored indefinitely in specialized facilities. Services are contracted with an accredited veterinary hospital, and appropriate fees are assessed for collection procedures and yearly storage. These facilities will assist in breeding arrangements.

The brood female should be current on vaccinations. This is vital so that she'll pass optimal maternal immunity to her puppies. She should be free of all intestinal worms, parasites, and external problems.

A brucellosis test to check for this canine sexually transmitted disease is performed on the female prior to breeding; this test is required by most stud dog owners to protect their valuable males. In the event of a positive brucellosis condition, an afflicted female could render a male sterile, which can destroy the virile stud dog's career. Brucellosis in the

STUD CONTRACT FOR:

_____
REGISTRATION #:
OFA OR PENNHIP:
CERF:
OWNED BY/ADDRESS:_____
PHONE/FAX/EMAIL:_____

TO BE BRED TO:

_____
REGISTRATION #:
OFA OR PENNHIP:
CERF:
OWNER/ADDRESS:_____
PHONE/FAX/EMAIL:_____

UNDER THE TERMS OF THIS AGREEMENT, THE UNDERSIGNED PARTIES OR AN AGENT APPOINTED BY THE SAME, AND_____OWNER(s) OF THE BITCH AGREE AS FOLLOWS:

1. THAT A STUD SERVICE WILL BE PROVIDED BY NATURAL MATING, OR BY ARTIFICIAL INSEMINATION (AI) UPON AGREEMENT WITH OWNER OF FEMALE;
2. THAT SAID STUD DOG WILL BE CURRENT ON ALL NECESSARY CLEARANCES: HIPS, ELBOWS, EYES;
3. THAT PRIOR TO BREEDING OF ANY KIND ALL CLEARANCES OF THE SAME ON THE BITCH WILL BE PROVIDED TO THE STUD DOG OWNER INCLUDING A NEGATIVE BRUCELLOSIS.
4. IF REQUESTED, THE STUD DOG OWNER WILL BOARD BITCH TO BE BRED DURING THE TIME OF THE MATING, AND EVERY EFFORT WILL BE MADE TO PROVIDE FOR A SAFE AND COMFORTABLE STAY, HOWEVER THE STUD DOG OWNER AND OR AGENT WILL NOT BE HELD LIABLE FOR DAMAGES, ILLNESS, OR LOSS DURING THE PERIOD THE BITCH IS IN THEIR CONTROL; BOARDING TIME WILL BE CHARGED AT $_____ DOLLARS PER DAY.
5. ANY VETERINARY EXPENSES WILL BE COVERED BY THE OWNERS OF THE BITCH, IE: PROGESTORONE TESTING , SMEARS, ARTIFICIAL INSEMINATIONS, HEALTH CERTIFICATES, OR ANY OTHER COSTS INCURRED FROM THIS BREEDING.
6. ANY AIRPORT COSTS/TRANSPORTATION FEES ARE THE RESPONSIBILITY OF THE OWNER OF THE BITCH. PICKUP OR DELIVERY TO THE AIRPORT IS $_____; NECESSARY PAPERWORK IS THE RESPONSIBILITY OF THE OWNER OF THE BITCH.
7. THE BITCH WILL BE GIVEN THE OPPORTUNITY OF A MINIMUM OF TWO NATURAL BREEDINGS, ANY AI'S WILL BE DISCUSSED PRIOR TO ATTEMPTING.
8. WHEN USING FROZEN SEMEN, a nonrefundable deposit of $_____(applied to stud fee) is required to be paid prior to shipping of semen; all expenses associated with semen, shipping, storage and veterinary services are the responsibility of the owner of the bitch being bred. Payment for these services will be made to the storage facility; frozen semen will be released after the above mentioned expenses have been paid. We are not responsible for frozen semen once it has been released from the storage facility.When using Frozen it is the responsibility of the owner of the bitch to make sure that he/she is dealing with a competent and experienced veterinarian. The veterinarian selected for frozen semen breeding must have extensive experience in surgical or transcervical A.I. procedures and should have on site storage equipment for the frozen semen. A minimum of three-business days notice is required for securing tank for shipping.
9. THIS BREEDING IS GUARANTEED FOR LIVE PUPPIES, LIVE PUPPIES IS CONSTITUTED BY 3 OR MORE LIVING PUPPIES AT THE AGE OF SEVEN DAYS. THERE WILL BE NO RETURN OF THE INITIAL DEPOSIT IF THERE ARE NO LIVE PUPPIES OR A PREGNANCY, HOWEVER THE BITCH (or mutually agreed upon replacement) MAY BE SENT ON HER NEXT SEASON FOR A REPEAT BREEDING; BALANCE PAID AS DETAILED BELOW.
10. CHILLED OR FROZEN SEMEN SHIPMENTS MUST BE PAID FOR BY OWNER OF THE BITCH AS WELL AS A NON-REFUNDABLE DEPOSIT OF HALF THE STUD FEE. PAYMENT CAN BE MADE BY CREDIT CARD OF CHECK OR CASHIERS CHECK, BUT WITH CHILLED OR FROZEN SEMEN BREEDINGS, MONIES MUST BE GUARANTEED BEFORE SHIPMENT IS SENT.
11. THE **STUD FEE** WILL BE _____, OR THE PRICE OF THE MOST EXPENSIVE PUPPY, WHICHEVER IS GREATER; STUD DOG OWNER RESERVES THE RIGHT TO SELECT A PUPPY IN LIEU OF STUD FEE; NONREFUNDABLE **DEPOSIT** OF_____ TO BE PAID PRIOR TO ANY BREEDINGS OR SHIPPING OF SEMEN, THE REMAINING FEE IS DUE WITHIN 30 DAYS OF LITTER WHELP AT WHICH TIME APPLICABLE LITTER REGISTRATION PAPERS WILL BE SIGNED.

SIGNED:

_____DATED_____
owner or agent of stud dog

_____DATED_____
owner or agent of bitch to be bred

BITCH BRED ON _____   _____   _____

Standard breeder contract

female also causes premature abortion of pups or stillborn litters. There is no reason to skip this step. An in-office rapid slide agglutination test is available that can provide prompt results during a veterinary visit. Otherwise, a blood sample must be sent to a laboratory for analysis. Results could take up to ten days. Most responsible stud dog owners have their males checked at least once yearly.

Once the stud dog is chosen, a number of options are available for the breeding procedure, including natural breeding, artificial insemination, or surgical implant of fresh chilled or frozen semen. The process can be further assisted with progesterone testing kits and vaginal cultures and smears. Veterinary clinics that specialize in reproductive issues are available for consultation or help with advanced problems.

All financial responsibilities regarding the mating should be understood up front. Some stud dog owners want payment at the time of service, while others accept a portion up front with the remainder due at birth. Still others want full payment only when the puppies are whelped. Any refund provision or return service in the event of no puppies, or few puppies, should be clearly stipulated. Everything should be discussed before the deed takes place.

[SEE CHARTS and EXAMPLE STUD DOG CONTRACT]

Gestation and Delivery

After the breeding, the pregnant bitch requires special care. With an average fifty-seven- to sixty-five-day gestation period, the female's nutritional intake should increase in the second month of her pregnancy. As her abdomen swells, she'll require smaller feedings in more frequency as puppies consume available abdominal space. (See http://www.upland birddog. com/dogcamp/whelp.html for a useful whelping chart.)

A suitable whelping box should be secured for the expectant female. Time of year should dictate outside or indoor facilities for the event. For example, an outdoor whelping area during summertime requires adequate ventilation, while winter conditions would mandate a heat lamp.

Whelping boxes with a lip all the way around the inside circumference will help to keep the female from lying on puppies. Bedding should be carefully considered. Cedar shavings are unacceptable because they can obstruct tiny nostrils and they can cause conjunctivitis under the

An outdoor puppy area. (Pamela Kadlec)

closed eyelids of newborn puppies. Hay and straw contain dust and possible mites. The best options are layered newspaper—which can be repeatedly changed—or tightly woven indoor/outdoor carpeting. A handy trick: Construct at least two interchangeable, fitted whelping box floorboards with carpet fastened to them; one can be in use while the other is removed for handy spray cleaning. Carpet gives puppies traction as they begin to move about.

Make contact with your veterinarian as your female's whelping date draws near. Discuss all potential scenarios and have contingency plans in place should any problems arise. Your veterinarian may suggest that you keep a small amount of oxytocin available, depending on your experience. Care should be used with this drug, which can be used to induce labor contractions or to stimulate milk drop down, which occurs approximately twenty-four hours after the puppies have been delivered. Prior to milk drop-down, colostrum is present and quantity seems inadequate.

Stock up on milk replacement and learn how to tube feed or nurse puppies before the fact in case you're presented with an emergency. If you're planning to have dewclaws removed or tails docked on your puppies, such procedures should be done within two to five days following birth. Arrange a tentative appointment with your vet. Become familiar with upcoming worming schedules for your female and the puppies.

When the female nears delivery, her body temperature will drop (normal temperature is near 102 degrees F) to around 100.5 degrees F, and it'll further drop to between 98 and 99.5 degrees F within twenty-four hours of whelp. Your female will likely go off her feed within twelve or so hours of delivery. If twenty-four hours pass once the temperature drops and no labor is evident, trouble could be afoot. You may need to call your vet.

When delivery begins, you should be present to monitor effective progress. Each puppy should have afterbirth associated with it. Keep track of details. If your female labors hard for over thirty minutes between puppies, you might call your veterinarian. Duration of an hour between puppies isn't necessarily a cause for alarm *unless hard labor* is present. Six hours of resting labor is too much when you know your female isn't finished whelping. Look for signs of trouble. Some bitches begin with normalcy and experience difficulties in midwhelp. Make sure that you're in close contact with your veterinarian should a cesarean section or medical intervention become necessary.

Birth to Seven Weeks

Umbilical cords will dry within hours and should fall off within a few days. Puppies should gain strength within the first several hours of birth and should actively seek colostrum from mom. Puppies that cry incessantly or feel cold may be in trouble. Another tip: Healthy puppies will rest nestled closely together when not nursing. A puppy that stays apart from the others at this early stage may have problems. Watch for anything out of the ordinary that might indicate fading puppy syndrome, a condition in which the puppies lose vitality and expire without known cause. If you're concerned, contact your veterinarian for help or solicit the advice of an experienced breeder.

Healthy puppies should have strong nursing, rooting, and righting (turning upright) reflexes. They should actively twitch and move during sleep. Take weights of newborn puppies and monitor their progress on a daily basis. Puppies should gain weight steadily; absence of this indicates problems. By the time the puppies are about a week old they should have doubled their birth weight.

Newborn puppies are blind and deaf. Eyes begin to open around ten to fourteen days and ears open a few days later. Newborns cannot eliminate wastes on their own until after two weeks of age and they rely on their mother to stimulate this function. She accomplishes this by licking her puppies. The gyp will meticulously keep things clean, thus if any fecal matter is found in the whelping area this could indicate possible diarrhea. In the event that puppies are orphaned, you'll have to manually stimulate the puppies to eliminate, and this is best done by massage with a warm, soft, wet cloth.

Observe the bitch frequently and make certain that milk drop down occurs within twenty-four hours. The female will need three good meals a day for optimal milk production. Provide an ample supply of easily accessible, clean, fresh water for her.

Stage one of the puppies' development process is the time from birth to twenty days. During this time most of the puppies' needs are met by the dam, including security, warmth, food, elimination stimulation, grooming, and rest. Senses are limited during this stage but the olfactory sense is blooming. Gentle handling of each puppy can be initiated at this time, dispelling the old myth of leaving puppies alone the first few weeks. The Monks of New Skete have published findings that regular daily handling of pups during this stage can positively increase minor stress levels, which in turn trigger reactions that will boost the puppies' resistance to interference and disease. Neurostimulation is currently in vogue and consists of a series of steps in handling puppies during this stage.

Stage two occurs between days twenty-one and twenty-eight. The senses rapidly develop and puppies begin to explore as they discover that they can see and hear in their little world. Maternal contact and continued human contact are important during this time.

Stage three extends from day twenty-nine to day forty-nine, and a multitude of important changes take place during this phase. Puppies respond to different voices and begin to recognize important people. During this time the puppies will be weaned from their mother.

Weaning requires much work from you, the breeder. You'll need to feed the puppies four times a day to start. A high-quality puppy food that's soaked and blended to an almost liquid gruel works well. Gradually you can begin to process the feed less until the puppies are eating kibbled puppy food. Fresh water should be present at all times.

Once you commit to the weaning process, the bitch should be removed from the puppies and relocated to a separate area where she cannot hear or smell her puppies and they cannot hear or smell their mother. If even one puppy suckles on the female once you've taken her away, this will impede her drying-up process. You should inspect her daily to make sure that she's not developing mastitis until she has dried up completely, which could take up to a month.

During stage three, the puppies begin to blossom mentally and will demonstrate differentiation between canine and human socialization.

Personalities begin to emerge. Puppies learn to play and develop social skills and pack order. They're aware of their environment. This is an optimal time to challenge and stimulate their senses with toys and safe obstacles, surfaces, and stimuli—a play yard is a good idea!

Puppy Placement

At forty-nine days the puppies go into stage four of development. This is widely considered an optimal time to send puppies to new homes, but this isn't written in stone. Some breeders prefer to keep puppies for up to another month so they may better determine unique characteristics and temperaments between puppies that will aid in placement decisions. At about eight weeks old, puppies might go through a brief timid stage. As a breeder, be cognizant of this possibility and discuss it with the puppy's new owner if shipping or pickup must occur during that time. If you are the buyer, you may want to broach this subject with your puppy's breeder if pickup spans this time frame.

Puppies that require shipping will handle the experience better if they've been introduced to shipping crates at least a week beforehand. Also, separating puppies for a few hours each day will help shorten their anxiety level when leaving the comfort of family and entering a strange new place. Good breeders attend to these details with their puppies.

Parting Thoughts

If you've concluded that this business of breeding and whelping puppies sounds like a lot of work, you're right, and we've just scratched the surface. We've not mentioned the considerable financial investment required, which is another side to the breeding picture that must be factored into your decision. Take heart. A number of good books cover the art of breeding, whelping, and raising puppies. You'll find references in the Resources section. I strongly suggest you obtain at least two titles on the subject and read them before deciding whether to tackle the prospect of raising puppies. The futures of the breeds we love rest within us, each and every one, and in the decisions we make.

CHAPTER
FOURTEEN

Traveling in Style

Hunting and training sessions often involve road trips, whether they're short or long. Of course, training sessions are necessarily spent getting your dog ready for hunting season. Sometimes trips involve air travel. Many precautions and items can help prepare your dog for a safe, uneventful trip to your destination. When flying, certain guidelines must be followed. Practical suggestions can help make travel trouble and stress free.

By Air

Get ready to toe the line when you fly your dog. A sturdy, airline-approved shipping crate (such as Pet Porter or Vari Kennel) is needed. The crate must meet proper size requirements for each dog. These specifics are predetermined per airline and accommodate the height and weight of the dog. You'd be wise to check regulations in advance to avoid problems once at the airport. There's nothing more frustrating after a long drive to the airport and a wait at air cargo than to be informed you can't ship your dog because your crate isn't properly sized. All the protests in the world won't change this regulation. Be prepared.

Certain weather conditions present problems when flying. Most airlines won't fly dogs during summer months because of the high temperatures while the planes are grounded. A temperature embargo is issued; sometimes arrangements are accepted on the day of shipment if the shipper can determine that at each ground location for your dog, the temperature won't rise above a preset limit (usually 85 degrees F). Another option is to take your dog in the airline cabin with you.

However, this only works with young puppies or small dogs that fall in line with size and weight requirements. The dog must fit in an approved soft-sided crate that you can stash under your seat. Winter months can cause temperature problems at the opposite extreme. Taking red-eye night flights during summer months when temperatures are coolest or daytime flights during winter months in warmer temperatures can sometimes overcome flight problems.

Reservations must be made in advance for your dog, just like your own, whether your pet is flying with you or in air cargo on a separate flight. Most airlines reserve space for one or two animals per flight, but these spaces fill quickly. Plan as far in advance as possible.

Necessary paperwork is part of the flight plan. Airline regulations state that your dog must have a current (usually within ten to fifteen days) health certificate from your veterinarian. Check with your airline for these specifics so that your paperwork is in order. Remember to schedule an appointment with your vet to secure the needed form. Vaccinations must be up to date.

Airlines require that two small plastic dishes be wired to the door of the crate for water and food. Special instructions about feeding and watering procedures should be taped to the top of the crate, along with a ziplock bag filled with a few cups of your dog's normal food ration. You never know what might go wrong. The crate must have absorbent material inside. Wood shavings or shredded newspaper are most commonly used.

Since everything will be hectic once you arrive at the airport, plan to adequately air your dog one last time before sending him down that conveyor belt. It could be a long trip for your dog. This may need to be done at some distance from the airport. Since your dog may be confined for a lengthy period of time, withhold food twelve hours prior to the flight, especially if your dog isn't seasoned at flying. Water should be given sparingly prior to the flight.

If your dog isn't crate trained, make the time over several days to accustom him to the confines of his crate. Some dogs become extremely agitated during flying and may require sedatives or tranquilizers, but this can only be determined through trial and error. Anything you can do to contribute to your dog's comfort will help make the trip go smoothly. Here's an excellent reason to have crate trained your dog as a puppy!

Once you arrive at your destination, your dog will probably need relief when you pick him up from air cargo or the baggage area. Get him outside as quickly as possible. If you'll need a rental vehicle, reserve one that can transport both of you comfortably, such as a truck or SUV.

Over the Road

Driving trips usually involve long hours in the vehicle. Simple guidelines will ensure the safety and well-being of your dog—the occasional horror story that occurs during travel need not happen to you. On any trip a variety of precautions can help your dog arrive safely and be ready to handle whatever looms ahead.

Certainly, the most important factor regarding your dog's comfort and safety is the means of transport. Where will the dog be situated? Will he be riding inside your vehicle? If so, you can make the trip more comfortable for your dog by preparing a secure area and covering it with an old blanket or cushion. A variety of commercially made seat covers are available for vehicles that are tailored specifically to meet dog owners'

A crate arrangement in a vehicle for transporting hunting dogs like this Drathaar. (Rossella Di Palma)

needs. Safety window and backseat barriers are available, as are ramps to assist older pets when entering and exiting vehicles. Most SUVs, station wagons, and vans can be equipped with shipping crates or small-dog boxes.

An obvious benefit to placing your dog inside the vehicle with you is that he is being transported in a temperature-controlled environment. Safety, however, might be a factor. You may be distracted by odor if your dog gets into foul-smelling mud or experiences digestive upset. When you park your vehicle, extra care must be taken to ensure proper ventilation (rolled-down windows).

The most popular mode of transportation is the dog box in your truck's bed. Never allow your dog to roam freely in the bed of your truck. Choices abound in dog box selection, and safe, well-built models are of paramount importance. A good dog box has adequate ventilation and insulation. Your dog should be cool in the summer yet warm in the winter.

The dog box should be secured so that it cannot shift during travel. A mat in the bottom of the box will increase your dog's comfort. Keep in mind that when you arrive at your destination and jump out, all ready to go, your dog will be prepared to join you if he's had a restful trip.

Goldens in a wagon. (Rossella Di Palma)

A homemade wooden dog trailer. (Author photo)

Dog boxes are manufactured from wood, fiberglass, diamond plate aluminum, and stainless steel. There are choices for every vehicle and need. Most will be at least two-dog models. On the high end, custom-made stainless and aluminum dog boxes that replace the bed of a pickup truck can be ordered. (See chapter 18.)

Another option is the dog trailer. Many units come with power fans or breezeways to assist in ventilation. They can be equipped with lights and other convenient features. Care should be taken to frequently inspect tires and the tongue-securing system of any dog trailer, however. Safety lights should be frequently monitored.

Other Items of Concern

As you plan to hit the road, consider your dog's water supply. Possibly no other factor—besides stress—contributes to digestive upset more than the abrupt change of the water source. An upset stomach can ruin any trip. Take a supply of water from home in as large a container as possible and refill it before it becomes empty so that new water can mix with old to ease any dramatic change.

Distilled water can be purchased on the road to further avoid stomach upset. Particularly during times of competition or during the trip of a lifetime when you don't want anything to go wrong, this relatively small additional investment could pay big dividends.

Be sure to bring your own dog food. If you can't do this, you'll run the risk of being unable to find your dog's particular brand of feed at your destination. Changing food in midstream can cause severe stress and digestive upset that will be unpleasant for you and your dog.

Use care when choosing suitable places to air your dog. Keep a vigilant eye on your dog while in strange areas. Watch out for garbage or discarded food that could sicken your dog. Likewise, don't let your dog drink from ditches or standing water. Puddles in parking lots might contain antifreeze. Keep your distance from anyone else exercising dogs. Do stop frequently as this important "stretch" time breaks up the trip for both you and your dog.

Bring along food and water bowls. Some people choose to feed their dogs on bare ground when traveling. Not only is this unpleasant for the dog, but also kernels of food can be left behind to spoil and affect some other unsuspecting dog. Discard any unconsumed food in appropriate trash cans.

When staying in motels, hotels, or cabins, observe regulations regarding pets. It's a fact that actions by all pet owners at these establishments will affect future rules regarding dogs. Look for locations that allow pets. Advance planning can eliminate disappointments in this regard. Some places require that pets be kept outside; others allow pets inside, often coupled with a deposit. If your dog will be kept outside in the parking area, be sure everything is locked and that your dog has adequate ventilation for the night. Do your part so that he won't bark. Try to secure a room that has a window overlooking your vehicle.

Finally, an often overlooked travel necessity is a proper vaccination schedule. When you travel, you'll be exposing your dog to strange areas, sights, and smells and other dogs and wildlife. Veterinarians and pro trainers alike suggest giving boosters—at six-month intervals instead of yearly—for dogs that will be on the road frequently and often exposed to different dogs. Important choices include bordetella (kennel cough), parvovirus/coronavirus, and the DHLPP combination shot. Rabies shots must be current. Carry all veterinary paperwork. You may also need a current health certificate for intrastate travel.

Some of our most coveted memories will be those shared with our favorite dogs on special trips. Let's face it: We love our dogs and enjoy doing things that include them. With a little planning and attention to detail, travel can be relatively uneventful and stress free.

Helpful Tips

- Check regulations pertaining to travel before you go.
- Spend time to acclimate your dog to his crate or dog box or your vehicle.
- Invest in a well-made dog box with safety features.
- Don't feed your dog several hours before departure by vehicle or plane.
- Bring your own initial water supply and refresh before empty, or purchase bottled water.
- Bring dog food.
- Travel with veterinary paperwork, including rabies certificate.
- Maintain current vaccinations.
- Be vigilant when airing dogs in strange places; be considerate of others.
- Stop frequently during road travel.
- Have a safe trip!

PART THREE

Training Prerequisites

CHAPTER
FIFTEEN

Training Philosophy

Get ready—get set—go! Well, almost. We've now reached the point where we can dig into the interesting stuff, the real honest-to-goodness business of how to approach dog training. Make no mistake about it, though—there is much work ahead. Aside from the drudgery associated with that word—work—note that the act of successfully training a dog into a talented hunting dog is rewarding and worth the time and effort you've invested. You'll discover this as you continue on your journey with your dog down this training path.

How does one find the secrets to dog training? What things should you know before you begin to train your dog? Do you have what it takes to do a good job? These are valid questions that indicate the proper, conscientious approach on your part to do well in the months and years ahead. You'll discover, however, that there aren't any secrets to dog training. Not unless you consider the golden rules of common sense and patience to be secrets. And patience may translate into years of working toward your goals with your dog.

What about prerequisites to dog training? Any prospective trainer should possess an even temperament, a genuine love for dogs, and the willingness to take the time to teach the dog what is expected of him. If you have a short fuse or display the tendency to take things out on your dog, you might be better off—and your dog much more so—by paying a professional dog trainer to do the job for you.

How Dogs Learn

This is an intentional short course on an in-depth subject. Talk about training dogs and you will find so many opinions and studies it will make your head spin. There are, however, many absolutes regarding how dogs learn that can make the process more understandable.

Dogs have the senses we do—sight, smell, taste, hearing, and touch—plus at least one more, a sixth sense encompassing one or several more senses, which we'll refer to from time to time. The sense most important and necessary to security and survival at birth is touch—indeed, sight and hearing are at that point "asleep"—and we do well to realize how powerful this sense of touch is to a new puppy or dog. We can use this sense of touch, along with other senses, to help our dogs learn, and we will discuss these forces in just a bit.

You've heard the saying dogs learn by repetition. And they do, quite like us, in fact. Patience and repetition can teach many desirable behaviors. The principles of classic conditioning and operant conditioning are at work in most learned behaviors—mentioned here because we're talking about how dogs learn—and these things are at work whether you recognize them or not. Indeed, classic conditioning happens constantly through no conscious effort of your own and includes behaviors you may not notice but that may affect your dog.

You most likely first heard of classic conditioning in junior high when you were introduced to Pavlov, the Russian physiologist. In Pavlov's experiments, dogs exhibited salivation when they heard a bell ring and expected to be fed. This principle applies to everyday things your dog experiences on a consistent basis. If you feed your dog canned food and keep him inside, he will soon learn that when he hears the can opener he is going to be fed and the dog will come running. This could then occur whenever your dog hears the can opener, even if it's being used to open soup for you. Note that your dog can be further conditioned via his "internal clock." The dog can be taught that the can opener will be used to give him food at 6 a.m. and 6 p.m. and that during other times the can opener is insignificant. When you housebreak your puppy, he learns that the smells and sights in your yard where you consistently take him to do his business mean that the pup is supposed to take care of his natural urges. When you pick up your car keys, it means your dog is going for a ride. When you grab the leash, it's time for a walk or to go training. When you get your gun out and pack your gear, a hunting trip is in the offing. Yet these last examples also converge on operant conditioning.

Operant conditioning refers to a number of variables applied during training to effect desired results. Dogs learn to increase or decrease their behaviors depending on the consequences. Consistency of timing and response by the handler can influence success in training behaviors to the dog.

There are four quadrants in the form of reinforcements and aversive stimuli that can be used to mold good behaviors or discourage bad ones. From these reinforcements different training methods and programs have evolved. Although this can get confusing, behaviorists use these terms based on mathematical principles (for every negative there is a positive) including: Positive reinforcement, R+ = Reward for a good behavior; Negative reinforcement, R- = Removal of an aversive (unpleasant) technique when a certain behavior occurs; Positive punishment, P+ = Negative behavior results in aversive technique; and Negative punishment, P- = Removal of something good as a result of a bad behavior. R+ occurs with P- and R- usually pairs with P+. Note: Operant conditioning and classical conditioning often happen concurrently. However, these forces often work simultaneously and without understanding or comprehending their dynamics, many trainers employ them either quite well or very poorly every day.

While many aspiring dog trainers have neither the desire nor the wherewithal to delve this deeply into canine behavioral science, recognition of the terms and how they interact with training will help you learn with your dog. You'll see how these things occur in training. Some of you will want to dig into this even deeper. (Check the Resources section for more help.) You'll apply these dynamics and others when you train your dog. You can also build certain behaviors and eliminate others with your approach and method.

Portions of these four quadrants are not the only learning principles in action when you train your dog, however. Often trainers proceed by trial and error, and without understanding what is causing the problem (at hand) they simply blame the dog as being hardheaded. Other behaviorial and learning principles at work may include successive approximations, chaining, and antecedent power. These are fascinating behavior principles and learning methods and procedures better saved for an in-depth behaviorial learning manual.

If you observe dogs in the wild, clearly they learn a lot by trial and error. As trainers we can make the training process much smoother by showing our dogs exactly what we want and by being consistent every single time so that they learn certain things are absolute, or black and white, instead of gray, meaning they are not exactly sure what's expected of them.

Dogs also sometimes learn by observation. Monkey see, monkey do. I can't resist telling a little story of my own regarding this phenomenon about a not-so-scientific result observed over the years with my own dogs. Much of the initial work with my retrievers and bird dogs, such as obedience and retrieving, is done at home near the kennel. My coonhounds watch this retrieving work—by now you've possibly guessed what I'm about to tell you—and these hounds have picked up the knack of retrieving! Invariably they'll show off this new talent when I release them for recess—they'll find a bumper (a rubber or foam object used as a training tool) in the training yard and scoop it up and bring it to me. Once this occurs I can then throw objects for them and they'll retrieve. It's an odd thing to see a bluetick or treeing Walker with a retrieving bumper in his mouth. I've noticed no difference within hound breeds— they all learn the art of retrieving bumpers and birds—and many of them will tote a raccoon out of the woods for me. This example provides food for thought about how we train our dogs and how we might be able to improve our methods!

When training your dog, you must first teach a behavior, then you must train that behavior to become reliable, then make the behavior consistent in different settings, and finally you must maintain the behavior over time. I'll use another coonhound training example. To effectively teach the here command to a headstrong breed with a strong prey chase drive, you must first convey what you want; in this case you will identify the here command. Next, you must consistently train that behavior for reliability; you teach your hound to come each time you give the here command in the yard. Next, you perfect the behavior by adding different distractions and locations so that your dog learns to comply no matter what or where, so here you build consistency; you want your dog to perform in various environments. Finally, you have a trained, reliable behavior that you'll maintain as your dog repeatedly complies over time; you've reached the maintenance phase and your dog knows what is expected.

Art of Speaking Canine

You've probably heard about "pack behavior" and how dogs respond to many experiences, stimuli, and situations based on this premise. It makes sense, when you think about it, that dogs should have a certain degree of communication and social hierarchy among themselves, stemming from the necessities of living as a unit and surviving in a hunting pack. However, in recent years many dog trainers refute this concept while stating they've never seen pack behavior in action (a pack of wolves) and they ask: "Have you?" This pack behavior is evident even when walking with several dogs at one time.

However, any observant study of dogs reveals a number of communication methods that dogs use, beginning with puppies in litters. Although young growing puppies in a litter don't qualify as pack behavior (this time is essential to puppies learning their "dog" boundaries), when the time draws near for the dam to wean them, she'll begin to nip and fuss at them when they overstep their bounds. She's saying "No!" or "Off limits" and puppies quickly learn what this means. The mother will move each puppy by picking the puppy up by the scruff of its neck, and she may discipline in this manner. This is why communication can be effective by using a scruff shake or grabbing the muzzle or sides of the face or picking a puppy off the ground by grasping it at the withers and the rump. As puppies get older and start to play among themselves, another hierarchy emerges, as some puppies are dominant over others within the litter. "Hands off my toy!" or "Follow me" are just a few of the things puppies seem to say. As puppies become adults and interact with other dogs, you see versions of the communication levels that they absorbed as puppies, such as "Stay out of my space!" or "Welcome to my parlor." I suppose you get the picture. All these things and more are there for any observant person to see and take in.

Watching how dogs communicate can help you do the same with them. Indeed, you can "talk" to dogs in any number of ways by using their methods. You can also talk down aggressive or fearful dogs, often by yawning or blinking at the right time. Trust me. For example, staring can mean attention but can also be interpreted as a challenge. If you are on the receiving end of a "challenge" from a strange dog, try blinking, yawning, or looking briefly away. You'll likely defuse the situation. Staring at your own dog can be an act of dominance and he'll often finally look away. Blinking is usually an indication of friendliness. Pay attention to dogs and apply what you learn.

Note that when the pupils of your dog's eyes are small, he's relaxed. Enlarged pupils signify excitement or alarm. From the standpoint of dog training beyond dog talk, cultivate good eye contact for attentiveness and communication between you and your dog. You'll discover this is easier said than done and close to impossible with some dogs.

Dogs discern much about you from signals you transmit. They quickly learn your body language and when you're happy or upset. They also use their sense of smell to evaluate you. Your sweat composition will reveal whether you're hot and perspiring naturally or whether you're anxious or fearful.

By the same token, body language will clue you in to many things concerning your dog. When the tail is held in a happy, jaunty position, the dog is fresh and full of vigor. Conversely, a wagging tail, while usually a pleasant greeting, may indicate nervousness and precede a fear-biting action. If the tail begins to drop during a workout, the dog is becoming tired. If the tail is up and bristled, whether or not the hackles are aroused,

The "smiling" demonstrated by this Chessie can be misinterpreted as a sign of aggression. (Julie Reardon)

the dog may be alarmed, cautious, or ready to fight. Head shaking may indicate an ear problem, but it could also mean your dog is nervous about what he's doing. Yawning may indicate apprehension and the need to become calm; rarely does it signify boredom or a need for oxygen.

Pinned-back ears may be a warning or a sign of fear or worry, or the dog may be ready to play. Ears pricked indicate attention, or possibly alarm. Even floppy-eared dogs have an attentive ear position. When you get to know your dog you'll recognize this attractive feature. The proverbial tail between the legs is never a good sign and indicates shyness, sensitivity to a correction, or fearfulness, among other things. Lips curled can mean anything from "Hello" to "Watch out" and one should never be mistaken for the other. Many Chesapeake Bay retrievers, as well as dogs from other breeds, tend to "smile" and when someone isn't accustomed to this behavior it could be misread for a snarl. There's a big difference between the two! Never discipline a dog for smiling. This is a good example of being in tune with your dog and walking in his paws. Learn what he's saying to you and learn to read your dog.

Teaching and Application

The most valuable lesson you can teach a young puppy—or a dog of any age for that matter—is to *learn how to learn*. This begins with the bonding process between you and your puppy and in his socialization to other people, places, and things. The communication methods you use, consciously and subconsciously, will be added to the things your puppy has already learned from his mother and littermates. Communication is the primary ingredient to a successful relationship between you and your dog.

I've often stated and written that each of us is endowed with strong medicine for dog training, and what I'm talking about are your magical powers of body language, voice, and touch. Learn to artfully apply these things to the process of dog training.

Body language is something you should become conscious of since your dog will be watching you closely. From day one your dog will observe you and in short order will know more about you than you do about him.

Your voice has the potential to provide as much power and communication or lack thereof as you let it. How meaningful or meaningless your voice actually becomes to your dog is entirely up to you. If you talk incessantly to your dog with much mindless chatter, you're reducing the power of your voice. Regular use of a loud or harsh voice will quickly negate the power of your voice. But if you use a calm tone during most "talk" your voice will become comforting to your dog. Your tone of voice will convey that all's OK in the world. Then, when you change this tone of voice to a "boss" version and give the dog a command, he'll know that it's time for work. A gruff tone will signify disapproval, while a praising lilt will be appreciated.

Tones of voice include matter-of-fact everyday tone, boss tone, disapproval tone, praise tone, and noises, including clucks and guttural sounds you'll use to communicate with your dog. Words aren't always necessary. You can "growl" just like Mom used to, and other sounds, such as whistles, clucks, and even "Sic 'em," which is often effective with hounds when you want them to go hunting, are quite useful.

One tone you should omit from your repertoire is the question. Asking a question of your dog may net a question in response. If you say "Sit?" your dog may respond with "Do you really mean it?" This is a common error with trainers, neophytes, and experienced alike. Always strive to put a period at the end of each command you give your dog. This can be difficult for many people because they don't realize the errors they are making and they think they are doing X when in actuality they are doing Y. Because of this, if you are having difficulty with some facet of training your dog, it may help to ask a knowledgeable trainer to observe your sessions and give you helpful advice.

The power of touch is immense and often misused or ignored in training. This power is at your fingertips, figuratively speaking, and can break through the shells of the most difficult canine training personalities, including shy, timid, and fearful dogs. When time is invested in quality touch with these dogs, for days or even weeks before any formal training is attempted, the results can be much more forthcoming. Conditioning these dogs to touch develops the necessity of human contact and builds trust, which is vital to a successful training relationship. (Note: Certain shy dogs and frightened dogs may attempt to "fear bite" during the touch-conditioning phase of training. Watch for this, and apply a muzzle if necessary, so that your movements are not misread as threatening

A reassuring hand on delivery reinforces the behavior. (Brian Schmidt)

gestures. Use calm, deliberate motions coupled with a soothing, not begging, voice.)

Beware of the dog that tries to manipulate you by climbing on you or trying to "hug" you; many people respond by using lavish praise and emotion when this is misplaced reinforcement to the dog for the wrong things. Remain in control and don't let your dog get the upper hand.

As you might expect, touch can be overdone with any dog. It's also unnecessary much of the time with certain alpha-type dogs. Yet, even these dogs respond well to touch applied at the right moment. Applying touch for praise during training can be very strong medicine, more so than voice, but like voice, if overdone it will lose its effectiveness. Touch should be administered sparingly and wisely. Touch can help win the hearts of some dogs. It can help others gain confidence through reassurance during a complicated training session, as you say "Yes! By golly that's it—you've got it!"

Learn your dog's favorite touch "places" where he's most receptive. This is different from dog to dog. Oddly enough, many dogs don't like being stroked on the head, while some love it. Favorite places for most dogs include just below the ears and along the backbone or rump. Try burying your fingers in the hair of your dog's coat just in front of his hips and make a circular motion—you'll likely be a big hit!

Reward, Praise, Correction, and Reinforcement of Behavior

What is praise? Or better yet, what comes to mind when you hear the word? Is it a pat on the head, an encouraging word, getting down on your knees and fondling your dog, some pleasing words with or without touch added? It can be in any or all of these forms and many others. Praise is a very powerful tool and often overlooked or improperly administered.

Is it the same as reward? Actually, dogs do not really know the difference, because they do not understand that you had any reward in mind before you issued a command. Reward is something you give as soon as your dog correctly performs a task. Immediate compliance with the sit command usually gets a click (from a clicker trainer) and/or a food tidbit. Eventually the food reward is replaced with "Good dog" and all these reinforcers are phased out excepting the occasional reward or praise to keep things interesting and sharp. Ultimately intermittent use of a reward produces the strongest and most reliable behavior. When used appropriately, praise can help train dogs of all temperaments, including timid, shy, sensitive, or hardheaded dogs. Praise has power when doled out with proper timing and amount, and should be eventually phased out, or randomized.

The most solid relationships between humans and dogs are those built upon respect and love, which evolve through a give-and-take affair. How is this achieved? You spend time with your buddy and teach him general obedience and rules of life that apply across the board. You use fair methods to teach and then reinforce commands. You'll use praise as a reward or for reassurance when a command is performed properly or when your dog grasps a new lesson. Let your dog know you think he has done well. It's easy to see how any relationship built in this manner will be solid for life, and it's even more evident in any dog that's been trained this way by observing the level of respect and love he has for his owner— you can see it in his eyes. Your dog learns that you will be fair with him.

What is the real deal or formula for this praise business? Always keep in mind that every dog is different and that various levels, doses, and methods of praise will be appropriate from one dog to the next. During the earliest stages of obedience training, such as when a dog first learns how to sit correctly, communicate to your dog that he has pleased you. It's just as important to condition your dog to know that praise is a good thing and that it means he has done something right as it is to teach him how to do those things in the first place.

From the very beginning, you want to teach your dog what you want him to do. A number of techniques are available for teaching. If correction becomes necessary, use it wisely and fairly.

Note that positive-only trainers don't use correction of any sort. They don't believe in this aspect of training, or even use of the word *no*. Positive-only is one method among many, and in this book I'll present all aspects and choices in training. The differences between "correction" and "punishment" can be vast, at least in my book. This is an issue that is becoming emotionally and politically charged in today's dog-owning environment.

Punishment and correction are not exactly the same thing. Punishment is used to decrease a behavior and must be administered with exact timing to be effective. Correction, on the other hand, properly applied can increase a desired behavior, and in this respect can be acknowledged as negative reinforcement.

Punishment may be necessary where harsh measures are needed, such as in breaking up a life-threatening dogfight or stopping a dog from a bad habit that could also endanger his life, for example, chasing cars.

When you study behaviorism in dogs you'll quickly find many negatives about punishment, and not surprisingly, very few of us really love hard-core punishment. Most of us quickly see that an atmosphere of constant pressure creates a stifling learning environment.

In the case of the car chaser or the dogfighter, harsh punishment is warranted. "The pressure of correction must exceed the pressure of cause" (Rex Carr; personal correspondence with author), and you must communicate quickly and effectively to the dog that worse things will occur if the bad action is not stopped. Such extreme bad behavior must be eliminated.

However, in many ways, saying no to communicate displeasure to your dog when he does something wrong and then guiding him into the proper behavior so that he can learn the response you desire can be very effective training. *Correction doesn't have to be doled out as capital punishment*. Indeed, correction was a part of life while the puppy was still with his mother. Well-timed corrections throughout his life need not be adversely absorbed when applied fairly so that the dog understands and can learn from them.

Certain acts from your puppy will be tough to tolerate, and your puppy should learn his boundaries. Are you going to let your puppy jump on you? Will you let him bite you? Will you let him dig in the yard? Can your dog chew your favorite shoes, robe, and magazines? Is it OK for him to bark whenever he pleases? All of these things will likely come up as the pup grows and will then give you opportunities to establish and maintain your position as the head of the pack. You might choose an all-positive approach and with some dogs this will be effective. However, others may need more levels of correction or communication than others to change behavior. Experiment. Do what works for you, but remember that there is a big difference between a seven-week-old puppy and a one-year-old, seventy-pound terror. The puppy is much easier to teach "No jump," wouldn't you say?

Don't overuse the word *no*. Refrain from repeating it often or you'll negate its importance. When care is used to give this word emphasis and meaning, it's possible that you can get through potentially sticky situations with your puppy by simply saying *no*, causing your puppy to change or alter his behavior. The dog will either choose the correct response or you can then guide him into the proper behavior.

One more thought regarding correction and punishment. Punishment has the potential to produce resentment and fear in the dog, yet this need not happen. Correction, when meted out fairly and with good timing along with communication on how to perform correctly with subsequent success and praise, can develop a successful working attitude. The goal is to phase out the need for correction as proficiency continues to grow. Dogs need to be interested in the whole premise of dog training for the outcome to be successful: a conducive learning environment of stimulation and success is of paramount importance.

Maintenance

As you learn to live with your dog and as you train him your relationship will constantly undergo change. Lessons will need to be honed from the moment they're established, and they'll continue to grow like so many building blocks as they are linked to more advanced behaviors. While you take this journey with your dog, maintain a proper perspective regarding your relationship. Remember that your dog is a dog and you are a person. It's not uncommon to begin to view our dogs as people, but they are most assuredly not people, they are dogs. That notwithstanding, they are often our best friends.

Where will *you* fall on the scale of discipline methods or lack thereof? Quite likely you'll rest somewhere between the positive-only group and those on the opposite end of the spectrum. You may choose one method when you begin training your dog and end up taking different bits and pieces from other methods that you'll learn about as you go along—and that is not a bad thing! If you become aware of something that you feel can enhance your dog's training, go for it. Think outside the box. Many training manuals will tell you to find a program or method and stick with it. Sometimes that is the best advice, especially for novice trainers, but as your training experience increases this is not written in stone. Once you become savvy with dog training, you'll be prone to combine methods as you develop something that works for you and your dog. Remember no two dogs are alike, even within the same litter, and always keep this in mind. The next dog you train may be different and require still another method than the one you used on your present dog.

Beyond the information presented in this chapter, remember there is only so much book material you can absorb, and then it becomes time to gain experience. You might work with an experienced fellow hunter and trainer, or apprentice with a nearby professional or successful amateur, or ask well-conceived questions. You'll also train your own dog with plenty of patience. No matter how many words are written, it's impossible to cover everything that can happen while dog training in the pages of a book. That being said, this book will constantly stress the need to be on your toes, to think like your dog, to walk in his paws, and be observant. As you go along you will learn to listen to the little voice inside, how to read your dog and how to react on the spot to the dynamics of any given moment.

Fundamentals of Training Success

Dog training is not a big mystery. As stated in the Introduction, just about anyone can train a dog. It takes patience, time, and a good measure of common sense. True, not everyone is gifted in the art of really being able to predict what dogs will do and what things are necessary to move them along with the best momentum—that knack of knowing when to simplify, when to push ahead, and when to tread water—but if the desire to do a good job is present, you are well on your way to training your dog as an excellent hunting companion. Your dog needs fairness from you, and in return you require effort from him. With those two things you'll get the job done in an admirable fashion.

Training Basics

Arm yourself with sound principles and training techniques as you set out to train your dog. Many values will immediately put you several steps ahead of the game if you recognize them and incorporate them into your plan from day one.

Listen to Your Inner Voice
You've probably become acquainted with it. Within you is a powerful equator that talks to you and helps you evaluate the things you see.

It often has the best reactions for what is needed at any given moment; it helps you think on your feet. The more you listen to that voice and experience positive results from doing so, the more you will be apt to listen again and again. Since you will be striving to do your best job with your dog, chances are the little voice is urging you toward the right direction.

Learn from Your Mistakes

Keep in mind that since you are training a dog you might not always make the correct decision. When you happen to err in judgment, whether with a correction or the way you progress, don't let it rock your boat. Instead, make book and learn from the mistake and try a different tactic. Keep everything that happens tucked into your bag of growing experience. Take comfort in the fact that no one is right 100 percent of the time. No one.

Think on Your Feet

When you are training your dog, things are bound to come up on the spur of the moment that you just hadn't planned on. Therefore you won't have time to ask someone what to do nor will you have a chance to look it up in a book. While a book can be very helpful in putting main thoughts, ideas, and methods on paper for you to draw from, you must ultimately make your own decisions.

Follow the Golden Rule

Dogs thrive on consistency in their lives. Your dog wants a fair and reasonable set of rules to adhere to that will give him a sense of order as he learns to adapt to you. The dog that is constantly wondering what's right and wrong is always second-guessing his actions and reactions and applies that misguided mind-set to life in general. Conversely, a well-trained dog is one that is content and secure in his purpose and he knows how to achieve and maintain it.

Your Magical Powers

Remember that you have powerful ways to communicate with your dog in body language, voice, and touch. You'll learn to determine when praise is highly effective and when it may erode the situation at hand. Learn about your power of voice and touch for each dog you train and how these things affect dogs in different ways. Use your senses and your instincts to determine your most effective means of communication to talk to your dog and effectively convey your point.

Learn to Read Your Dog—Focus

In order to develop and cultivate a successful training program with progress, you must read your dog. Focus on your dog. Get into his head and walk in his paws. Figure out what drives your dog and you'll know what to do to get him where you want him to be.

You must be able to determine your dog's moods and his temperament. You need to perceive when your dog has slipped backward, whether you pushed too hard, or whether your dog just didn't learn or retain a lesson well enough, and you also need to recognize every step forward. Make an effort to assign a reason to progress in either direction. There is an action or reaction for everything your dog does.

Rules of Engagement

Certain things qualify as solid "rules of engagement" when training dogs. While they are all based on common sense, it is worthwhile to spell them out and to review them constantly. No question about it— these tips will make you a better trainer.

Every Dog Is Different

Flexibility is paramount to successful dog training. No two dogs are created equally. Even brothers and sisters from the same litter will emerge with very different personalities and levels of trainability. This is why experts often advise against one person obtaining two puppies from the same litter. The youngsters will likely be quite different, and it's tough to refrain from constantly comparing the two and possibly making one keep pace with the other.

Train each dog as an individual. Don't make your dog conform to the same schedule as your buddy's dog, and refrain from trying to mold the dog to the successful program you used for your last dog. Instead, develop a program for this dog.

Importance of Timing

Your ability to act and react to every situation when training your dog is vital to your success. When you're teaching your dog, your personal timing will hasten or slow the dog's grasp of each lesson. Know when to give and when to take, when to push and when to back off. Continually sharpening your skills of focusing on your dog and reading your dog will help your sense of timing.

Also, when correcting your dog or reinforcing a behavior, the swift, timely delivery of a correction or a reinforcement will make the lesson very clear to your dog. If you wait longer than a second beyond any given act, you've missed your opportunity to capitalize on the moment. If you choose to administer correction or reinforcement too late after a behavior (instead of waiting for the next chance that comes along) you may set your training program back a little, or a lot.

Be Fair

Any time you train your dog, maintain a level head. If correction is necessary, be certain that it fits the crime—do not go underboard or overboard. Never apply correction just to impress someone else who might be watching. Above all, never correct your dog in anger or to fulfill a need to "get even" with him. If you ever find yourself in this situation, take a deep breath, back up, and punt. It's better to miss a correction when your judgment is flawed than to plunge full steam ahead and perhaps dig a hole so deep that climbing out could be difficult, if not impossible. Also, never correct or punish "after the fact" . . . if you miss your chance, let it go. Keep these things constantly in mind.

An earnest Airedale brings a chukar to hand. (Chris Halvorson/DogAds)

Basset hounds might look small, but they average fifty to seventy pounds. (Francesco Capodagli)

Speed, focus, and strength—such qualities make the black Lab one of the most popular breeds around. (Avery Outdoors)

One of the most versatile hunting dogs around is the German wirehaired pointer, or Drahthaar. (Claudio Cerutti)

A day in the field always calls for good grooming afterward, and the burrs in this English cocker's ear are going to need some careful attention. (Rossella Di Palma)

The English springer spaniel takes to water as vigorously as any retriever. (Kim Kuhlman)

The popularity of the golden retriever as a pet and in the show ring has diluted its working blood, but much good field stock still persists. (Pamela Kadlec)

The only hunting breed native to Scotland, the Gordon setter has excellent scenting abilities. (Jonathan Brandt)

A black and tan hound finds success on a mountainside, baying a cougar against the rockface. (Dennis Ingram)

The Rhodesian ridgeback was bred for big-game hunting, but can turn into a good bird dog, too. (Sharon C. Johnson)

Easy-going and persistent, the spinone works differently than some German pointers. (Vince Robinson)

Yella, a well-known Lab from WaterDog TV. (Shannon Nardi)

Tail up and nose out—this pointer has made game. (Sharon Potter)

A handsome pair of young majestic tree hounds, a breed that descends from
bloodhounds and St. Hubert hounds. (Steve Morrow)

Dogs Learn by Consistency and Repetition

Be firm with your dog and consistent in what you do. Give your dog plenty of repetition to solidify the lessons. Learn to do this in the face of increasing distractions and locations while keeping things interesting for both of you. Use your business tone of voice when you give the dog a command. Do not beg, cajole, or plead to try to get your dog to perform properly.

Train Wisely

Never give a command when you're not in a position to reinforce it if your dog doesn't comply. Likewise, don't give a command if your dog doesn't yet understand it. Don't dish out discipline that's not understood, because such acts will quickly erode your dog's working attitude.

Recognize the Importance of Momentum

If you're a student of organized sports, you're likely aware of momentum and its influence on the overall outcome of any competition. Momentum is an interesting phenomenon that affects virtually every aspect of life. It could pertain to someone's rise or fall on the job and it touches political careers. It's interesting to watch momentum swing from one team to another in football, hockey, basketball, or baseball, or from one individual to another in tennis or golf or skating.

During the dog training process, momentum has a subtle yet powerful effect on smooth or choppy progression, or lack thereof. It can be a study in itself with regard to training and handling performance dogs.

Accent the Positive

Develop ways to positively influence your hunting dog. Eliminate any tendency to nag your dog. Do you learn more quickly when you're encouraged for good effort or when you're constantly criticized and punished? Cultivate a training attitude in your dog that makes him look forward eagerly to his lessons and is not constantly looking over his shoulder expecting trouble. Devise a plan to reach your goals and constantly think of better ways to achieve them.

I liken this situation to a favorite example of mine: the half-full glass. While the same amount of liquid is in the half-full glass as the half-empty one, saying "half-empty" sounds negative while "half-full" accents the positive—there's still some left!

Love and Respect

Which comes first? I was first asked this question over twenty years ago by a mentor of mine in dog training, Rex Carr, and it warrants serious thought. Certainly a dog can love you but have zero respect for you. A dog might also fear you and listen to you but neither love nor respect you. Fear is not the respect I'm talking about.

Solid, special bonds grow within the relationship built on respect and love. Not just one or the other. Show me the dog that has developed a bond with his owner or trainer through sound training and fair treatment. The dog has been given a set of rules and knows he must abide by them; the dog knows his boss is firm yet fair. The dog knows he can count on his owner for all his needs. He has developed a deep respect for his handler, one that gives root to the strongest kind of love a dog can deliver. Respect based on honesty and fairness fosters the strongest kind of love.

Training Journal

Whether you're training one dog or multiple dogs, one of your best allies to a smooth flow of sequence in training is keeping a training journal. You may think this is unnecessary and, after all, you have a razor-sharp memory, right?

Wrong. The best memories fade after days become weeks and weeks become months. It can happen quicker than that. When you've taken the time to jot down specific breakthroughs or setbacks, and little tricks of training that you learned while teaching A or B, you can look back for certain things that may reveal successful tips or steps to enhance future training. It's all worthwhile.

Keeping a training log will reveal when you're dwelling too much on any certain skill while overlooking others. You can track positive and negative tendencies. The act of recording and reviewing highlights in your training may shed light on budding problems, perhaps offsetting them before they get out of hand. When you force yourself to write things down you may record things that could otherwise be forgotten. You'll become more observant. You'll be able to track training momentum and you'll constantly cultivate that all-important focus on your dog.

Teamwork

Realize that this relationship between you and your dog is a team effort in many respects. While in the learning phases, you are the coach and your dog is the player. He gets his lesson plans from you as you outline the strategies. As you progress down the training road and accumulate valuable time in the field, in the swamps, or in the woodlands, this division between the two of you will meld into something intangible and almost beyond words as you become a working team. Your hard work

Ultimate teamwork: a spaniel and handler at UK working test. (Bill Beckett)

will pay in dividends you never could have predicted and, indeed, you cannot begin to fathom, even as the years roll by.

Training Tips

- Reward and praise must be given immediately for effect, but the type and its value will vary from one dog to the next and from one behavior to the next.
- Corrections must be administered immediately for effect; punishments can work against you, so use with care. (See chapter 15.)
- Dogs need to feel the excitement of learning.
- You can teach an old dog a variety of new tricks, but you often need more time and patience to do so.
- Training sessions should be kept short and stimulating.
- End your training session on a good note, even if you have toback up and simplify something in the session to accomplish this.
- Teach lessons in a quiet atmosphere and gradually add distractions, corrections, reinforcements, and advancements to training. Ultimately you will be out in the hunting environment with a well-schooled companion.

CHAPTER
SEVENTEEN

Different Training Methods

O nce you've studied training philosophy and can safely say you understand the fundamentals, you'll need to decide upon the method, defined as "how" you'll train your dog, along with a "curriculum" that will determine what you'll train on to school your dog. There are many different training methods and each of them can be effective, although some work better with certain dogs than others. The success of any method rests in the hands of the trainer and the sound principles of canine learning that are applied with that method. Method and curriculum combined becomes a training program, and there are many programs within different hunting dog pursuits to choose from.

When you talk "dog training" you will quickly find that sentiments run high on which way is best to train a dog. Much of this passion centers on a piece of training equipment called the electric collar, or e-collar for short, and whether it should be used. In training days of old the e-collar was known as a "shock collar" and therein lies the reason for varying emotions regarding its use for dog training. Are these extremes of reaction valid? We'll take a closer look.

In this chapter, we're going to examine the five integral types of dog training. They include conventional training, e-collar training, positive-only training, clicker training, and combination training. Until recently the two primary methods of training have been conventional or e-collar based, and these two remain on top in terms of numbers. However, other methods are gaining increased support. When choosing any one of these methods, you should evaluate your own temperament and that of your dog, as well as your time frame in which you expect a finished product.

Conventional Training

The first method of choice is conventional training, so named because it encompasses all techniques available prior to the advent of the e-collar. Conventional training has also been referred to as "Amish" (nonelectricity based) or "tennis shoe" training because of the additional footwork that's often required to teach or correct a dog that has done something incorrectly. It involves teaching, correction, and reinforcement, incorporating the use of discipline when necessary.

Conventional training can include any number of different training programs that will vary in the sequence of steps and the progression of skills for the dog that usually culminates in the same finished result. For instance—and these things will be covered in detail in part 4—some trainers elect to force train (the trained retrieve) their dogs wherein some may pinch the dog's ear (ear pinch) while others prefer the toe hitch technique. Other trainers choose an "orderly retrieve" sequence instead of force training the retrieve. These would be examples of some of the many differences between training programs within any method.

Conventional training follows sound teaching principles and applies discipline, reinforcement, and repetition during phases of training. While no e-collar is used for correction, other types of correction such as a training stick, leash, or physical shake will be used. Praise is an important part of the training process.

One of the challenges to this type of training is long-distance correction when the dog does something wrong or makes an improper action. The trainer must figure out how to get a timely correction to the dog since, as we've learned, the most effective corrections come immediately upon the act or misdeed. The trainer may need to use help from bird boys or assistants in the field to apply a correction (like a "boogeyman" hidden in tall grass on a point where a retriever might exit the water prematurely) or the trainer may need to hustle out into the field to apply direct physical correction (hence the "tennis shoe" nickname). Because of this drawback, not all corrections will be consistent, potentially adding length to the overall training process as you seek the finished product.

E-Collar Training

In contrast to conventional training, perhaps the biggest asset to e-collar training is the ability of the trainer to apply instantaneous correction or reinforcement to the dog at any given infraction—or to reinforce a good action—depending on the method of e-collar usage. Basically the e-collar offers the addition of an "invisible leash" in training. The trainer can reach out a hundred yards, or four hundred yards, or even a mile if need be to communicate with the dog in a fraction of a second.

With those things in mind the e-collar sounds like an excellent tool to incorporate into a training program—and it can be—but it is not that simple. While the e-collar has been successfully applied by many of today's top trainers and while it has been adapted by many diligent amateur trainers, the e-collar and its power can be abused in the wrong hands. Certain people should never consider using it, but these same people could cause harm with virtually any training tool.

Proper e-collar use involves a series of steps that will ensure its sound application. In other words, each dog should be put through the paces of a conditioning program with the e-collar so that the dog understands it and its application to the rules that have been taught—all of this before it is ever used in the real world. Do you have and will you commit to that time? Let's face it: In today's fast-food society, many of us aren't tailored to applying much planning or forethought in anything we try. If you fall into this category and if you want everything done instantly, you may not be a good candidate to use the e-collar when training your dog.

In addition, if you're hot-tempered you may be the sort to fall on the button any time your dog does something wrong; this could be the worst possible scenario. Why did your dog do something wrong? Was he trying but simply messed up? Or was it from lack of effort? If your dog was giving his best and made a mistake, that wouldn't be an example for e-collar stimulation. Conversely, if the dog was not trying at all that might be a different story. E-collar usage requires the ability to make impromptu decisions on behalf of your dog's welfare and the overall progression of the training program, among other things.

Without a doubt, because of the opportunity to apply instantaneous corrections, and perhaps praise, to your dog, use of the e-collar can be a big asset in the advancement of your dog with a reduction in any confusion on his part when it's wisely used. However, you must be honest with yourself in your assessment of your goals and your temperament as to whether the e-collar is a tool that you can successfully use with your dog. E-collar usage is covered in chapter 24, but please note that the e-collar is just a tool that can be implemented in a training program—it is not a program or method in itself.

Positive-Only Training

This method of training has been gaining popularity in recent years as some people rebel against the generally accepted and conventional means of discipline when training dogs. In short, positive-only training incorporates behavioral concepts in developing methods to teach a dog certain tasks in the absence of any discipline, and instead by shaping behaviors. Based on research, most notably by behaviorist B. F. Skinner and others way back in the 1930s, it applies the principles of operant conditioning versus classical conditioning, otherwise referred to by many as conventional training. (However, Skinner also experimented with things that were not positive-only.) Conventional trainers will disagree on the basis that both classical and operant conditioning principles are applied within their method. (For a review of training philosophy, see chapter 15.)

The objective of positive-only training is to devise ways to teach dogs without aversive or negative forms of pressure in any degree, including the tug of a collar. Instead, behaviors are shaped and rewarded while bad habits are eliminated by time-outs and similar means. Physical discipline is nonexistent in this type of training. Supporters of this training method accept the fact that many lessons will take longer for the dog to absorb and perform correctly. This is a drawback to the training process but is welcomed by people who prefer this approach to dog training.

Clicker Training

Recent years have seen an upsurge of clicker training, which is essentially a method of marking a behavior or conveying praise or "Good dog" instantaneously when a correct behavior occurs by using a gadget that makes a clicking sound. The clicking noise is sharp, quick, and pleasing to the dog. You can condition your dog that the sound is a good thing by initially using a "click and treat" (C/T) procedure.

The way to introduce a dog to the clicker method is this: the dog may be "lured" into the sit position with a food treat and when he assumes the proper position, the trainer "C/Ts." This sequence is important. Once the dog gets the hang of things for any given command, the treat is eventually phased out, as is, ultimately, the click.

Most clicker trainers train a majority of behaviors without initially using commands. The commands are introduced into the process after the dog already understands and knows the behavior. In other words, trainers click on a "Sit" or they work a dog to the ground from a sit to a "Down" with hand signals and treats for compliance without words, and then bring the verbal command into the learning string.

The bottom line is that clicker training identifies good behaviors and then builds upon them with the goal that the clicker will eventually be phased out. Clicker trainers are not necessarily positive-only in approach and most will use sound methods of teaching, praise, and, rarely, discipline to get any training point across. Clicker trainers feel that they can immediately reinforce proper behaviors from a distance with the clicker procedure in a manner and speed that cannot often be duplicated by conventional trainers, although actual distance is limited to what the dog can hear.

Combination Training

As the name implies, combination training takes the best techniques from two or more of these methods and uses them all in a training program to sculpt a well-mannered and skilled hunting dog. In order to be successful, combination training requires a good working knowledge of these different methods and an understanding of what makes them work, as well as an understanding of the principles dogs use to learn.

As political correctness becomes more important to an increasing number of individuals, the ranks of those who use combination methods will continue to increase in size. The most popular combination method is a pairing of conventional training with moderate e-collar reinforcement. Some trainers have had good results with these methods teamed with clicker reinforcement and a better understanding of the principles of operant conditioning.

There is no doubt that the continued refinement of combination training, as well as other methods, can result in an approach toward dog training that is also applied by many child psychologists who believe the optimal child-rearing method pertains to applying one or a few well-timed spanks in the hopes of eliminating them altogether. While physical discipline and certainly spanking is frowned upon by most mainstream child behaviorists, a few experts have deemed spanking as beneficial when applied properly and in the right situations. Physical or other corrections with dog training are looked upon by many in the same way, as trainers strive to improve methods and reduce the need for discipline while methods are perfected for training with less pressure.

Which Method Is Best?

There is no one "best" way to train a dog. All of the described methods have their merits as well as drawbacks. Evaluate the positive and negative aspects of each method and the programs that are available for your choice of hunting dog, and determine which one works best for you. You may want to train with experienced professionals or amateurs who employ these methods before deciding on any one approach. You might even decide that you'd rather secure the services of a professional trainer. For more information on this, see chapter 28.

Once you decide on an approach that you feel will best suit you and your dog, do not be afraid to change in the middle of the process if you realize that other methods may suit you better than the one you are using. Remember—adaptation is one of the biggest keys to successful dog training.

CHAPTER
EIGHTEEN

The Tools of the Trade

O nce upon a time a hunting dog could be trained with an al-
lotment of time and just a few essentials such as a leash and
collar coupled with a bumper, drag, bird, or fur hide. Indeed,
sometimes when I take an inventory of all the gadgets and gear I possess for retriever training and bird dog training and hound training, I'm
often taken aback at how times have changed. But have they? Are things
that much different from what they were twenty or thirty years ago?

When I was a youngster, I managed to train renegade local dogs in
the neighborhood armed with nothing more than a piece of rope and a
plain old flat collar. And for that matter, when a collar was absent I made
do with a makeshift "slip-rope" collar—and to think if I had patented that
idea, I might be sipping margaritas on a tropical beach—but no, that's
not exactly true, either. Not to detract from the wonders of such a place
. . . but, well, more than likely I'd be found hiking distant hills in search
of elusive birds or freezing in some remote duck blind in a magical place
or trekking through a swamp at midnight in a secret honey hole—every
waking chance at least.

But, I digress. Those early students—the various volunteers that I remember so fondly—willingly (for the most part) learned to sit and shake
and roll over and heel and come and stay. Quite an impressive repertoire
of tricks, I thought. And above all we had a good time reaching that level
of accomplishment.

Fast-forward a few years and you'd find me in some ducky,
marshy-looking place with my dad's dog and eventually my own dog,
and they'd find birds and make "blind" retrieves, with help from tossed
shotgun shells or rocks, that is. Their telltale splashes offered clues to
the downed birds' whereabouts.

Dad saw I was pretty hooked on the dog thing and bought me a gift,
now well worn and dog-eared from years of constant reading and refer-

ence: a book on dog training. In those days it was known as the retriever trainer's bible: *Training Your Retriever*, by James Lamb Free (New York: Coward-McCann, 1949). In its pages I was able to pursue my quest for dog training knowledge in earnest.

When it came time to find gadgets to train my dogs with, I came up pretty empty-handed. A priceless find was a metal coach's whistle. For bumpers I used those plastic, oversized, white floaters you'd find in a marina, and I made others out of stuffed fire-hose material. Wings from game birds were used for bird work, and a hide took the place of a whole raccoon. I never knew the trick of stashing whole dead birds in the freezer so I didn't even attempt to try that when I was growing up; my mother would've probably skinned me alive if I'd have done so, anyway.

Little did I know that even in those days there were mail-order catalogs that specialized in all types of dog training supplies and gear for the aspiring dog trainer. Nowadays, there are catalogs with all types of training equipment and also hunting supply superstores with dog training choices galore. Indeed, at some stores and in some catalogs the selection is so great that you are left wondering what you really need to train your dog.

Let's take a look at how things have changed. This section not only covers the brass tacks of dog training essentials, but also the other gear necessary to get the job done, such as transportation and high-tech accessories. Some of these things are very expensive, while others can be made yourself for little to nothing invested.

Dog Gear

The basic essentials include a flat collar for your dog, catch rope, and a short leash.

Flat collar—Made from leather or nylon, collars come in many widths, from one-half inch to one inch to two inch. These collars usually have either a D ring (near the buckle) or a C (center) ring built in to the collar to attach a lead or training rope. This collar should fit snugly but not too tight; you should install a brass engraved nameplate by riveting it to the collar. The nameplate should include pertinent information including your name, your phone number, and maybe your address. Name and phone number are most important. If you add "Call Collect," "Reward," or "Needs Medication" on the nameplate you will increase your chances of getting your dog back should he become lost. Don't include your dog's name.

Regarding the nameplate, also invest in a slip-on brass plate for use when you travel and your contact information subsequently changes, or put your cell number on the plate. The bottom line is to make sure your dog is wearing a collar with a *current* phone number. Collars can be reflective, fluorescent, leather, or camouflage.

A note on collar safety: It has recently become fashionable to hunt and travel with dogs sans a flat collar. Some say the collar could get hung up on a snag in the water and the dog could drown, or that it could get hung up on brush in the woods. Make your own choice on the matter, but the odds of something like this happening are slim compared to the security of providing information on a nameplate for a helpful individual to contact you in the event someone finds your dog. I've hunted dogs in every kind of environment you could possibly imagine and all types of dogs at that, often with more than one collar (tracking collars, flat collars), and fortunately I have never had such a tragedy occur. In the face of the odds, I'd rather give someone the means to call me so that I can get my dog back. Ultimately the decision and the weight of risk is yours to make.

Catch rope—A short rope that attaches to the flat collar and hangs down about three feet, usually made out of lawn mower starter cord (doesn't snag or tangle easily). This is invaluable when working with young dogs that don't know what "Come" means. It also provides the means to round up the dog without getting into a game of catch me if you can.

Six-foot leash—Handy for teaching obedience commands. The Delmar Smith Command Lead deserves mention here and can be effectively used to teach beginning obedience such as "Sit" or "Whoa," "Here," and "Come."

Training Gear

Checkcord—These can be any of several lengths, from ten feet to fifty yards or more. Uses abound for checkcords in different training

A typical checkcord. (Author photo)

regimes. Checkcords come in handy whether you are working retrievers, bird dogs, versatile breeds, hounds, or beagles.

Checkcords can be homemade in various lengths by using nylon ski rope with a brass snap. Cut the hollow ski rope to the desired length and burn both ends until they melt, then take your moistened fingers and quickly flatten the melted ends (use caution) into a point. This prevents fraying. Thread one end of the rope through the ring of your brass snap, then take the splicer, or a pen, and thread it through the hollow inner portion of the rope where you want to run the rope through to secure the snap. Remove the splicer and insert the rope end, carefully weaving it up into the remaining body of rope until there is a snug fit between the rope and snap. It's best to weave the rope into the main portion at least eighteen inches. Short leads and long training ropes can be made for pennies on the dollar. Cords can be purchased in a variety of cotton blends specifically made for training dogs.

Training collars—These would include slip-chain or choke-chain collars, prong collars, and J.A.S.A. leather pinch collars. Some words about these collars are in order.

The slip-chain or choke-chain collar, as with any training tool, is only as effective or humane as the person using it. When a too-large chain collar is used, or when it's put on the dog incorrectly, injury to the neck area can result. With correct use and proper fit, this collar can be helpful in training a dog as it delivers mild discomfort when the dog isn't complying. Wild, uncontrollable dogs should not be fitted with a slip-chain collar; instead, the prong or pinch collar should be substituted for the purpose of teaching commands such as "Here" and "Come."

Note: The choke chain received bad press in an alleged study from Germany about slip-chain collars versus prong collars that was repeatedly quoted as fact (supposedly forty-eight out of fifty dogs trained with choke chains had physical injuries or spinal injuries while only a few of the pinch-collar dogs had problems). This study is an urban legend and never took place as stated. Its widespread and fallacious use, however, deserves strong words of caution: don't jump on a bandwagon just because dramatic facts and figures are used to highlight what could otherwise be hearsay.

Metal prong collars and leather pinch collars look like archaic and brutal instruments of torture when in reality they can be blessings in disguise for trainers who must work with unruly, wild, uncontrollable dogs. They should be used wisely and fitted properly, but can help humanely deliver lessons to the rogue dog.

Whistle — Used in most forms of hunting dog training for one thing or another, even if just for recall at a distance. There are a number of popu-

A small Munsterlander with prong collar. (Ken Przybyla)

THE ULTIMATE HUNTING DOG REFERENCE BOOK

lar brands and models available, including the plastic Acme Thunderers, Tornadoes, Fox 40s, Gonia Specials, and Mega Whistles.

Lanyard—The contraption that hangs around your neck to hang your whistle, dog-box key, and hunting calls on, depending on your lanyard options. Available in a variety of styles and materials from inexpensive nylon to different grades of leather and even braided horsehair.

Heeling stick—This resembles a riding crop and has many uses in some training programs. Usually about three feet in length, this tool can be used for guidance or for discipline.

Training bumpers or dummies—Generally made from rubber, plastic, foam, or canvas in several shapes, sizes, and colors, used for teaching and training retrieving on land and water. Today's rubber bumpers are usually "knobby" and come in a variety of colors including the most popular white, white with black, orange, gray, black, blue, green, and glow in the dark. White or white with black bumpers are most extensively used to train on marking drills, while the other colors are used for marking, drill work, and blind retrieves. Dogs are somewhat color-blind and cannot readily distinguish certain colors. Plastic bumpers have a tendency to crack and break in cold weather, while rubber holds up better in all weather conditions and will not rot with extensive water use, as canvas sometimes does. Foam may absorb water and might develop an odor over time.

Canvas cork-filled bumpers come in white, olive green, and orange, but have a tendency to mildew and they also harbor dirt. They are many dogs' favorites, however, generally preferred over knobby bumpers. A new canvas model includes white or white with black and incorporates a streamer for better visibility for the dog.

Fire-hose cork-filled bumpers are commercially available in today's market and come in standard fire-hose material.

Training dowel or buck—This object has two "ends" to keep it elevated off the ground and therefore easy for a dog to pick up. Its shape also helps teach hold as the dog grasps the center portion.

Dokken's Dead-Fowl Trainers—Developed to teach puppies and older dogs the proper hold and grip on game birds, the Dokken's trainers have a soft urethane body, come in all sizes and shapes, and look and act like real harvested birds. Available in small-bird sizes such as wood duck and teal, to larger sizes such as mallard and even geese.

Foam bumpers and simulated birds—New retrieving objects that float well; their texture is pleasing to the dog.

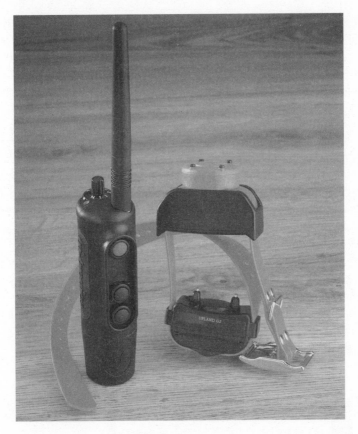

E-collars are much improved from their earlier versions, but still call for judicious and fair use. (Author photo)

Training pistol—Used to simulate gunfire. Cap pistols and .22- or .32-caliber blank pistols are available.

Shotgun popper—A modified shotgun, usually a single shot, used for shooting blank popper loads.

Drags—Usually made out of canvas and shaped similar to a retriever training bumper, the drag is used with scent to lay a trail for the dog.

Rolling cage—This is a round wire cage that will roll and is used with live game inside to excite young dogs in training. Primarily a device used for training coonhounds, the rolling case isn't legal in all states.

E-collar—Previously known as the "shock collar" or "electric collar," the e-collar has in recent years undergone a politically correct change and *not* in name only. Today's available models offer much more humane options than their predecessors of thirty years ago. This training tool offers instantaneous correction at any distance within its range. The e-collar can be misused or wisely used by the person in control.

Shovel—To assist in digging an earth dog from a deadly underground tunnel.

Training scents—Some scents are far more realistic and therefore more successful than others. Scents are usually applied to a training drag or dummy.

Telemetry equipment—Tracking equipment consisting of a locator collar (transmitter) and a receiver that can help the user find a lost dog. This is a valuable piece of equipment for bird dog, hound, and beagle trainers.

Clicker—Various models of clicking devices used to "mark" a behavior when it is done right.

Target stick—Used in clicker training.

Calls—Appropriate calls for use in training such as duck call, goose call, or raccoon squaller.

Silhouette backing dog—Automatic, electronically controlled, or standard silhouette staked into the ground used for bird dog training to work on honoring and backing another dog.

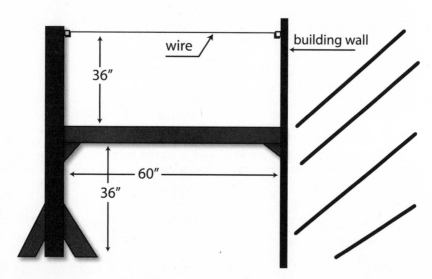

A styling beam configuration for those who want to build their own. (Jim Wurtz)

Styling beam—Used with bird dogs to teach proper stance and style when on point. A barrel can also be used.

Bird harnesses, hobbles, tethers—Various pieces of equipment to restrain birds from flight; enables reuse in bird dog training and forms of upland retriever training.

Bird crates and bags—For transporting birds from the pen to the field for training.

Bird pen—Used to house ducks, pigeons, or pheasant. Options will vary.

Lighted collar—Shows up at night, is available in different colors, and is used in hound hunting and for hunting dogs to help with visibility when airing at night.

Harness—Used for roading exercise and pulling exercise.

Dog bell—The bell comes in many sizes and tones and is used on some bird dogs to determine when they are moving and on point, for beagles in thick cover, and even on some hounds to determine if they are out hunting.

Beeper collar—Various sounds reveal if bird dogs are on point or out ranging.

Dog boots—Made to protect the pads of dogs' feet in the presence of rocky or thorny ground cover.

A vizsla under leather harness. (Jeff Malone)

Blind stakes are easy to make at home. (Author photo)

Dog vests—Of the two models, one protects the dog's abdomen in thick brush and the other is insulated for use in cold-water weather.

Tie-out chains—The single tie-out is for one dog. The "chain gang" model allows a number of dogs to be spaced out at regular intervals along one system.

Blind stake/marker, flag—Used to mark the spot of a planted bird for live-bird work or a dummy or bird for a dead-bird retrieve. Homemade blind stakes can be made by using poly posts from a farm supply store or garden stakes, and fitting a "swimming noodle" of fluorescent pink or orange Styrofoam to the stake by cutting one vertical slit the entire length of the noodle and slipping the noodle around the post. Clorox jugs, white buckets, and traffic cones can also be used effectively, depending on how visible you want the markers to be.

Rattrap or floater—A floating contraption to attach a dead bird to for a blind retrieve, it is placed out in the water and is connected to an anchor. There are a few ways to make these floating gadgets that will secure a bird for blind placement. These are used for "out-to-sea" and open-water blinds in retriever training. They are also helpful whenever you want to run a blind but don't have a handy place for the bird.

The most popular one is simply called a rattrap. This commercially available rattrap is secured to a piece of thick Styrofoam with waterproof glue and is usually spray painted fluorescent orange. An anchor rope is attached to the bottom board of the rattrap through a hole in the Styrofoam. Take into consideration the type of water where you'll use the rattrap when choosing your anchor weight and rope length: Is there a current? How deep is the water? Place the beak of the bird under the metal spring clasp. When the dog grabs the bird, it will come free.

A homemade rattrap for a water blind retrieve. (Author photo)

A rudimentary version can be fashioned from a spent shotgun shell and a log section. Tap the used primer from the shell and run a string through the resulting hole; tie a washer to the other end so that it catches inside the brass cap of the shell and the string is secured. Wrap the shell to the log with the length of string coming out the primer hole. Add an anchor of appropriate length and weight for the local conditions. Push the bill of the duck into the empty plastic of the shell where it will remain in place until the dog reaches the bird and grabs it. Note: Either of these gadgets should be introduced to your dog in a short retrieve situation where you can manage the variables. In this way, your dog can become accustomed to this new twist in retrieve work.

Transportation Options

Crates—A variety of crates are available that can be used in the home as well as any suitable vehicle such as a truck or SUV. Collapsible wire models are available as well as plastic, fiberglass, aluminum, wooden, and stainless steel varieties, in all sizes.

Dog boxes come in all styles. This one has carpet tacked to the top to give a rigging for dog traction. (Author photo)

Dog boxes—The most popular dog boxes come in models with partitions to separate two dogs, although custom slide-in boxes designed for pickup truck beds can be made in any size and with a number of different options. Dog boxes should be well ventilated but also provide adequate insulation. The doors and any storage units should be lockable. Wood, aluminum, and stainless are the most common materials used.

Chassis box—Professional trainers and some amateurs often choose a large chassis-style box that replaces the bed of their truck with a "kennel on wheels" that sports all the comforts of home. These are usually built of stainless or aluminum, and can hold as few as a couple of dogs up to twenty in one rig. They are well insulated with the ultimate in security and convenience built in.

Bed-rail box—A cousin of the chassis, the bed-rail model fits on and is bolted to the bed rails of the truck. It can be made from stainless, aluminum, wood, or fiberglass. A drawback is the height that dogs have to jump to enter the compartments. Manufacturers also make an optional jump-ladder to assist with this.

Dog trailer—Dog trailers come in all shapes and sizes and a number of different materials. Safety features should include full-size tires including the spare, a strong axle, insulation and ventilation, a stout tongue and harness setup, and visible lighting including double brake lights, back-up lights, and amber accent lighting. All working parts should be regularly inspected for wear and tear.

Other Considerations

ATV—Many of today's trainers have incorporated one or more ATVs (four-wheelers) into their daily training regimes. Gear and people can be replaced in the field more quickly with these. ATVs are also used to exercise dogs.

Bird launcher—Another relatively new training device, bird launchers come in quite an array of makes, models, and options and can either simply toss a bird well enough to interest a flushing or pointing dog or it can

Dog boxes can often be used with an ATV. (Author photo)

fling one out at a distance suitable for testing marking with a retriever. Wingers are included.

Dummy launcher—These devices, such as Retrieve-R-Trainer, shoots a loud blank while propelling a foam bumper at a distance for the dog.

Remote stations—Human-shaped mannequins or makeshift human-simulating devices placed in the field to mimic people are used extensively in retriever training. These can be handmade. Twenty years ago I had some "station markers" made by a local steel company that had made similar gadgets for other area trainers. The markers resemble roadside speed-limit signs in shape with a main rebar "spine" and a height of five to six feet. Near the bottom of the spine—which has a sharp, pointed end to pierce the ground—is a crossbar to step on. When this contraption is placed in the field with a T-shirt, pillowcase, lab coat, or Tyvek disposable painter suit hung on the speed-limit part, it works well to simulate gun stations. My markers are still used today and they've held up exceptionally well.

More modern versions of this marker system, called "stickmen" by many trainers, can be made with convenient lightweight materials. Step-in poly posts or plastic-coated garden stakes can be obtained from feed or farm supply stores for under five dollars and come in six-foot lengths. These materials are less likely to scratch your vehicle, although a rebar is still a popular spine and is very sturdy. When you fasten a simple coat hanger with a coat or painter coveralls attached, you have an instant low-cost marker station.

Live traps—Used to catch raccoon, rabbits, foxes, and opossums for training purposes, these traps are not legal in all areas.

Pigeon traps—Used to catch feral barn pigeons for use in dog training.

Recall pens—Generally built for use with quail in bird dog training.

Water jugs—Should be mandatory in anyone's dog training rig for carrying a suitable supply of water from home.

Cooler—A cooler stocked with ice should be a mandatory piece of training equipment during warm weather to provide an extra means to cool down a dog in an emergency situation.

Stopwatch—Comes in handy when timing training tests to determine how much can be done in a day with multiple dogs and people in a training group. A stopwatch is a necessity in coonhound night hunts and therefore a helpful addition to training at night.

A winger behind holding blinds. (Author photo)

Mules or horses—Often used when coon hunting and sometimes used during bird hunting. Also used extensively during some forms of bird dog field trials.

Boat—Johnboats or canoes are often used in retriever training.

Holding blinds or hides—Used to accustom dogs to waiting prior to taking their turn in a competition or hunt test event, or to hide gunners out in the field from the dog's view. If you know someone handy with a commercial sewing machine, you can buy any waterproof hunting material and make two- or three-sided holding blinds with rebar or poly push-in posts at each "seam" of the blind. A handy pinch-hitter for the holding blind that provides a "retired" gun effect is a camouflaged umbrella; the oversized versions work best.

Anchors—Boat anchors and rattrap anchors can easily be made by filling pails with concrete. A rope of adequate length is inserted into the container, with the end touching the bottom and the rope held in the center and controlled so that just the proper amount of length will be set in the concrete. Wet concrete is poured into the container; when set and dried, remove from the container and you have a great, solid working anchor.

Bird dryers—Particularly useful in large training groups when you are using birds to help keep them off the ground and to aid the drying process when they are wet. A bird dryer can significantly increase the usage life of a dead bird. These gadgets are now commercially available and can also be handmade.

Game enclosures or fenced pens—Used for training and running game.

There you have it! However, it seems new training accessories and tools are developed every day. This list doesn't include necessary clothing and hunting gear and supplies to complete a day or night afield. Those items are covered in chapter 37. Take heart as you peruse this equipment list, however, because it is still a belief of mine that you can train an excellent hunting dog with bare essentials. You'll need a whistle and at least one training rope, a few bumpers or drags, and some birds for retrievers and bird dogs, or hides for hounds or beagles. Of course you'll need some means to transport your dog, but with those items you can get your project rolling. Whether you choose to incorporate some of the more high-dollar and high-tech gadgets into your training program is entirely up to you. The primary ingredients for your success include quality time spent in teaching and training your dog what you expect from him and then putting your dog in the woods or out in the field to gain real-world experience.

CHAPTER
NINETEEN

Finding Training Grounds

As time goes by and civilization continues to encroach on rural America, the availability of training grounds for working our dogs will continue to shrink. This continued exodus out to the "country" simply has to interfere no matter how we try to ignore it. It helps to know where to look for places to work your dog and how to garner permission from the landowner for many of those priceless finds you come across along the way.

Requirements

Exactly what types of grounds do you need to train your dog? For your dog's yard work sessions, any quiet secluded place will do and your backyard is likely just the place. If for some reason your own yard won't suffice, try to find another convenient spot nearby—perhaps even a vacant lot or field—since you'll ideally work twice daily for fifteen to thirty minutes per session during this phase of training.

You'll also need wild areas to introduce your puppy to the outdoors where he can experience freedom in an unrestricted setting. Walks with your puppy help build a bond between the two of you and will also expose him to short and tall grass, streams, ponds, muddy areas and swamps, underbrush, new sights and smells, and game and scent trails. Without an area like this close by, do some exploring; you might be surprised with what you find just around the corner. Sometimes park areas suffice for recess-type walks, but beware when taking a puppy without a complete set of vaccinations to any place frequented by many dogs.

If you have a bird dog, you'll need various pieces of land with cover as his training progresses. You may want to do some water work as well. Once you determine your goals, you'll know what you need to get the job done. Retrievers need both land and water as their training advances, along with more complicated terrain. Hounds and beagles need appropriate hunting territory to explore and to run a track.

Public Land

Often gems of public land beg to be discovered. Most of these lands aren't adorned with signs that say "Use me!" Small lakes with public access areas often work perfectly to introduce your dog to water and sometimes have room for marking tests and blind retrieves. These areas may be suitable for introducing other hunting breeds to water as well, especially when the water entry location is uncomplicated and without growth. Public land is often well suited to dog training with its terrain changes and various types of cover in different heights.

Universities often have terrific land for public use, but you must work to find these spots. If you live near a college that owns land, check out possibilities that might be right under your nose. Observe all regulations and usage rules.

Parks usually have leash laws so be prepared to work your dog on a long rope if required. Flexi-leads work wonders with young puppies in such places. One good thing about these park areas is they often have streams and small ponds with groomed land suited to teaching young puppies concepts such as crossing water to get a bumper on land.

Be up to date on requirements on all public lands. In the United States, most state game and hunting management areas require possession of a valid hunting license to train dogs during the year. There may be firearms limitations and restrictions on bird usage. Some months are off-limits to dog training in certain states, while other states have no restrictions. Permits and sign-in boards may be required.

Private Land

If you locate property near you that looks fabulous for hunting or training, find the owner's identity and pay the person a visit. Introduce yourself and explain what you do with your dog. Respectfully request permission to train or hunt on the owner's land. In the process, make it clear to the landowner that you'll not only leave the land as you found it, but even better if possible. You'll not leave trash behind and you'll pick up anything you find. You'll close all gates behind you and keep a watchful eye on fences. Finally, you won't hold the owner liable for any accidents that may occur. If permission is granted you may also need written permission to access the land. You can carry preprinted business card forms, which on one side releases the landowner from liability with room for your signature, and on the other side provides for the landowner's signature along with permission to train and hunt on the property.

Some private landowners are willing to allow use of their land for a fee. If this comes up, ask if you can work off the price by helping on the farm throughout the year. If not, see if you can round up a few other hunters and dog trainers to contribute to the fee. If this arrangement gives you exclusive use of the land, ask if there are times when you're not welcome. If other parties use the property, find out if there is room for everyone or how use will be governed between individuals. Still other private properties levy a day-use fee per visit.

In any event, remember your gracious private landowners with a Christmas card each year and possibly a token gift such as baked goods, nuts, or fruit. At the end of each year, renew your intentions with all of the property owners by visiting them in person. Politely issue thanks and ask whether you can be of any help in the coming year for proposed projects. If you're hunting on the property in addition to training, offer some of your harvest.

Building Your Personal Training Property

If you own land you may consider grooming it for hunting and dog training. This could include planting food and cover crops, perhaps thinning some timber or planting trees. It may mean redesigning or replacing aged fence rows. Perhaps you'd like to use a feeder program on your property at certain times of the year. You may want to build ponds and berms to use in training. In addition to the training opportunities presented by pond construction, your efforts may support waterfowl populations and overall wetland restoration.

Check local laws before beginning any topographical land construction. Contact the state extension office and state and federal agencies. Grants are sometimes available for wetlands projects and other supportive game conservation projects. Pond structure and design can be obtained from some of these agencies as well as from retriever trainers. Aerial photos of properties with manmade training ponds can be quite helpful during construction.

A Model Training Organization

The state of California has an innovative organization that has been formed by interested retriever trialers to secure, develop, and provide lands for both amateur and professional trainers on a pay-membership basis, renewed annually. The California Retriever Trainers Association (CRTA) has grown from a humble beginning in 1999 because of the efforts of Stephen Bechtel Jr., Gary Bechtel, Bill Daley, Glenda Brown, Charles Tyson, Gary Ahlgren, and others, and today it enjoys a healthy membership.

If this idea works for retriever people, why can't similar projects work for other types of hunting dogs? A core history of CRTA is included here to help other prospective projects get off the ground.

Originally, CRTA sought to secure permanent grounds for training and trialing in both Northern and Southern California. Members began with the thought of pursuing wastelands that could be funded by private contributions. It quickly became evident that land was not only tough to find but prohibitively expensive, while private contributions were difficult to secure and inadequate.

The goals of CRTA became more expansive as members decided to work with charitable organizations and associations with successful track records in projects involving wildlife and waterfowl restoration and protection. This premise was expanded to include the potential for upland game and land development. Help loomed from Ducks Unlimited, California Waterfowl Association, California Audubon Society, Nature Conservancy, and the recently formed California Conservation Fund. It seemed feasible that if retriever enthusiasts worked hand in hand to support the causes and projects of these organizations while working toward a combined effort for new grounds that would benefit everyone, the project might become a reality.

Today beautiful grounds in Northern and Southern California— grounds used regularly by members for training and used by host clubs for holding events—remain a testament that different organizations can work together toward a common goal. The CRTA Goose Lake Grounds in Kern County encompass four different properties totaling over 6,000 acres with 3,500 currently available acres, while northern properties are under advisement and construction at this writing. Both areas will be groomed, improved, and maintained with construction of lakes, channels, and wetlands that enhance retriever training while providing habitat for waterfowl, shorebird species, and upland game.

What is necessary to get a project of this magnitude off the ground? The timing was good in California since nearly 95 percent of the state's wetlands had been lost to cotton and rice farming, and recent movements to reclaim some of these valuable wetlands had begun.

In 2005 California Fish and Game removed certain training restrictions and instead instilled a requirement that state hunting licenses be obtained for training or trialing on private property. CRTA members can now use properties for training throughout the year, while California's Fish and Game demonstrated the recognition that recovery of game birds is essential to conservation efforts.

Annual dues are tailored to individual, family, professional, and club memberships. No daily usage fees are required of members. However, members sponsoring participating guests (those running dogs) are assessed a $20 per day fee. Nonparticipating guests must accompany a sponsoring member but are charged no fees.

A look at CRTA's charter reveals important factors that can be used in other states to model similar projects. CRTA is a nonprofit group committed to preserving and restoring native habitat for California's wildlife and providing access for retriever training to retriever clubs, individuals, and professionals that support it. In addition, CRTA is an advocate of providing quality grounds for AKC-sanctioned field trials, hunt tests, and picnic trials, as well as for in-state and out-of-state professional retriever trainers. There are no daily fees for use of the grounds, but annual membership or guest status is required. Membership fees are used for land usage, restoration, water, maintenance, and management of the properties.

CHAPTER
TWENTY

Training Partners

Depending on your breed of hunting dog and your type of hunting, you may want to seek help and advice from experienced trainers, or you may want to join a training group to get your dog additional exposure to different hunting situations. How do you go about finding this kind of help? Where do you turn?

Keep in mind that not everyone you find with your interests and dog choices will have the same training goals and schedules that you have or harbor the same scruples and ethics toward hunting that you hold dear. However, this isn't always a bad thing. Something very useful I learned long ago that still holds true today is that there are times when the most valuable lessons you'll learn involve how *not* to do something.

Training partners come in all sizes, but as long as they're committed to the dog and his work, age doesn't really matter. (Author photo)

Clubs

In the United States most states have at least one retriever club and one bird dog club that are either hunt test or field trial oriented, or both, while some states have numerous clubs. The same applies to hound organizations. An Internet search might provide clues for locating names of clubs in your area or in your state. If this doesn't help, try adding the names of your breed and state in the search. The universal willingness of dog people to help each other can usually be taken to the bank—you just have to find those people in the first place. Many countries throughout the world have breed organizations and related training groups.

If you come up empty and cannot find specific dog training clubs, locate the national breed club for your dog and either e-mail or write expressing your desire to find local field clubs that cater to your interests. The secretary of this club should be able to give you some leads toward real contacts. Another suggestion is to contact one of the field organizations directly. These include AKC, UKC, CKC, and American Field. Ask for help and suggestions to find other interested hunters and dog people in your home area.

Once you locate a regional or state club within driving distance, find out when membership meetings take place, how to join, and how to become involved. Brief the secretary about your particular situation, the type of trainers you are seeking to partner with, and whether there are any training days. Participation on your part will be your best bet to secure the help you need in the quickest fashion.

Individuals

Low-profile individuals might be nearby, perhaps in your town, and you just aren't aware of them. Perhaps they are avid hunters but don't belong to any trial/hunt test clubs. Where are they hiding, however? You may find them and secure their help through a local shooting club, such as a sporting clays range or skeet and trap range. Maybe the county has a local sportsman's club. Beyond that, find the most popular sporting goods store and go hang out and listen. Ask questions. Perhaps the store manager will allow you to post an announcement or leave a card on file requesting help or information.

Another source for finding dog people who have your same interests is the veterinary clinic. If your local animal hospital cannot produce any good contacts, branch out and check clinics of surrounding counties. Ask for breeders or owners of pointing dogs or retrievers or hounds, depending on your wants and needs.

The local feed store or farm supply business also may be able to put you in touch with like-minded dog folks. Again, use the bulletin boards that many of these establishments provide; you can usually find them near the entrances.

Media and Publications

Most dog people enjoy receiving publications pertaining to their chosen sport, and chances are you're not immune to that propensity. There are many available dog-oriented and hunting dog magazines and event publications that are full of informative articles and helpful tips and contacts. In addition, these periodicals are usually an excellent place to begin a search for professional trainers, should you ever need help, and breeder and stud dog listings when the time comes to look for either a new puppy or a suitable mate for your exceptional female.

Internet forums have become almost mainstream in popularity for attracting specialists of all kinds to talk and share problems, questions, and answers, and there is no shortage of them when it comes to hunting dogs. There are talk forums for every type of hunting dog expertise and they're based all over the world. These forums, although addictive— you've been warned!—are often very helpful for securing sound advice for training problems. It doesn't take long to discern which posters are knowledgeable and helpful and which ones have little to offer.

The good news is this: This book does much of your homework for you. Located in the Resources of this book is a comprehensive list of national breed clubs, registries, Web sites with forums, and a list of magazines and periodicals, all of which should help you on your way. Also a list of books under References covers a variety of subjects pertaining to dogs in general and hunting dogs specifically.

CHAPTER
TWENTY-ONE

Things You Should Know

What are two of the most significant elements that affect not only dog training but also hunting success and indeed any field trial or hunt test work as well? Scenting conditions and weather factors should be consciously monitored at the same time we are evaluating our dog's work because they directly and indirectly influence his overall performance. When your dog is doing well, or when the dog seems subpar to his trained and natural abilities, what can you determine about the scenting conditions? Good or bad? What about the weather and the barometric pressure? Before you throw the book at your dog, consider these things and how they might have an effect on dog work on any given day or night.

The Knowing Nose

First of all, it helps to recognize the difference and the power of the canine nose compared to other animals and to the human nose. The dog's nose is superior to ours, to the cat, and to most wild animals, including red foxes, coyotes, and raccoon. Indeed, the Army Research and Development Center concluded this in a 1985 report and that in addition, no mechanical or electronic devices were more effective in detecting mines, booby traps, and explosives than the dog.

Generally speaking, humans have approximately 65 square inches, or half a meter, of olfactory (nasal) membranes, while dogs fall in the 900-square-inch, or seven-square-meter, range, an impressive difference to be sure. Consider that also generally accepted is the fact that we humans have about 5 million scent receptors in our noses, while large breeds of dogs have a whopping average of 220 million olfactory receptors. Although the 220 million receptor number is widely used, research has proven that many smaller breeds of dogs have less millions of receptors than their larger counterparts, although they remain superior to us. For instance, a dachshund has around 125 million, still a staggering amount compared to our paltry 5 million olfactory receptors.

My original fascination with the way scenting works with our dogs really expanded when someone gave me two books, one called *Hunting by Scent*, written by H. M. Budgett (London: Eyre and Spottiswoode, 1933), and a small paperback book called *Scent and the Scenting Dog* by William G. Syrotuck (Rome, NY: Arner Publications, 1972). Indeed, the latter work is somewhat of a classic in the search and rescue field. Since then, advanced scientific finds have discovered even more about how scent discrimination works.

We are only recently beginning to understand the complex way that a dog manages his scenting, and we do not know how he perceives certain things, such as the ability to detect pending earthquakes and tidal waves or seizures in a loved one, although one of many theories is that a dog smells electrical signals from either the atmosphere or the person well before the event. The subject is intriguing and plenty of ink is devoted to it.

Have you ever seen a male stud dog "chatter" when smelling a ripe female in estrus? This is yet another aspect of the dog's olfactory system. Dogs can scent pheromones (body scents) and smells through an organ in the mouth, which is separate yet still part and parcel of the olfactory system. This process perhaps helps them "taste" the smell. Known as the vomeronasal organ or Jacobson's organ, this is an elongated structure consisting of two fluid-filled sacs that opens at one end into the mouth or nose just above the upper incisors. When a dog uses this vomeronasal organ to process scent from a female, he will chatter with his teeth and also often work his lips in an effort to bring the scent into this tubular structure. You probably have seen a stud dog doing this when checking out a bitch in heat. We just mentioned earlier the inexplicable ability many dogs have to sense earthquakes, tidal waves, and epileptic seizures. Some experts speculate that this organ—of which much is not known—may have something to do with the ability of dogs to process and identify these events and more, such as cancer and even heart attacks. That being said, the actual ability to sense these things may have to do with this particular scenting process or another process or a combination thereof or a mixture of elements we cannot yet begin to understand.

How Scent Works

We do know that a dog has mobile nostrils, and this feature can help a dog determine the actual direction of scent. A dog also "sniffs," which is different from what we would consider a normal intake of air. When the dog sniffs, the air passes over a bony structure called the subethmoidal shelf. This is important to our purposes—that of knowing what happens with our hunting dogs when they work—in that as the scent brought in via a sniff passes over this "shelf," some of it remains behind and accumulates while other air from regular breathing travels through the nasal passages and goes to the lungs. Without getting too complicated, the dog's nose is structured to screen odors as determination is made in what to do with odors and where those molecules will go and which receptor cells the molecules will adhere to as the chemical smells convert to electrical signals en route to the brain. Our dogs are pretty amazing in that they are often doing all this and processing such information while focusing on their objective at hand.

Let's talk a bit about scent and, better yet, how the dog processes scent. Take a coonhound, for example. As long as I can remember the old-timers have described distinct kinds of track dogs, those that "drift" a track and those that "straddle" a track. The dogs with the ability to drift a track run with their heads up and are generally much faster than the hounds that straddle a track. These track drifters "cut and slash" along a scent trail, often running from one side to the other of the actual scent as they continue to work it. This type of dog would be similar to a bird dog that runs with his head up searching for bird scent. In contrast, the straddler takes the track one paw print at a time.

Two types of scent are left by a moving animal. One is the scent made by disturbed vegetation (the technical name is diaminobutane)

Summer vegetation can interfere with scenting of game. ("Major" NAI, SDX-Judy Balog Photo)

from each foot or paw print as well as from brush disturbed by the body as it passes through woodlands or grasses in fields, and there is also raft scent (called diaminopentane) actually coming from the body, more or less in a scent cone. With the first type of scent the track will actually be riper after time has lapsed and bacteria have had a chance to form among the disturbed vegetation and soil. Many hounds use both types of scent when running a track. The dog's objective becomes more complicated when game such as deer or even other dogs and humans cross the path.

Now add other variables to this scent picture, such as wind. When wind blows off a living being, the scent particles are carried downwind and are further affected by obstacles in the way. All things being equal, this wind factor accounts for the drifting track dog that runs twenty feet to the side of the actual track, for example, because that is where the strongest concentration of raft scent is at that time. If obstacles interfere with the wind and funnel scent in a certain direction, the dog may seem off course as he responds to this scent, when in reality the dog is not.

What do we know about scent and how it pertains to the effectiveness of our hunting dogs? Scent is water soluble. Dogs with cool, wet noses will do a better job of working with scent than those with dry noses. A hound needs to replenish his magical nose with moisture, not to mention his whole system, and so should our retrievers and our bird dogs when they've been hunting for a while.

Other factors besides a dry nose might interfere with your dog's ability to smell. Certain medications will impede olfactory ability, as will diseases of the respiratory system. Although the dog will eventually rebound, recovery from a damaged respiratory tract could take weeks. If your dog suffers from an illness such as tonsillitis or infection from tooth decay, his olfactory ability could be profoundly altered or rendered almost useless.

Scent conditions will be much worse when the air is hot and dry than when it is hot and humid—high temperatures disperse scent rapidly—yet scent conditions might be best in moist, warm situations and adequate when it is damp and cool.

Also in the summer vegetation is much more abundant and will impede the disbursement of scent. Scent is more apt to remain concentrated in smaller areas because it is trapped by vegetation. Also, some vegetation is very pungent and many young dogs will overlook such areas for bird or game, while their older counterparts know from experience how to find birds or game in such places. During fall and winter much of this plant growth dies and shrivels up, making room for better scent distribution in the area.

Did you know that scent has a constant weight and that if unaffected by other things it will travel downhill? It will do so at a rate of fourteen feet per each degree of slope in the terrain. Add wind, which disperses scent ten feet per each mile per hour of measured wind. Thus, it follows that if you hunt on a day with no wind, you should start at the bottom of a slope and work your way up instead of going down the slope, unless your dog is compensating for this condition by using his own hunting pattern. If you add a wind blowing up the slope and a stand of trees where the wind will bank scent, things can get really complicated in a big hurry.

Optimal scenting conditions are met when the ground temperature is slightly warmer than the air, such as is regularly the case at early evening. Are there other times of day when this can occur? The answer is yes, depending on what the weather is doing and how it changes throughout the day or week or as a weather system moves into any area. Also, the dew point can affect scent. Dew falls in the evening; fog often develops in early morning hours.

Training and Hunting Variables

Keeping in mind that since arid, hot weather is just about the harshest environment for scent, you should be conscious of this when working a young dog in the event you bring down a runner. There may be no scent for a young dog to follow on a hot, dry day. Pick and choose your opportunities to work on these situations because the experience could prove frustrating for the developing young dog. In other words, don't send a *young* dog on such a bird when conditions are so bad that the experience could be less than fruitful.

On the same note, if you bring down a dead bird, in the first few minutes there may be very little scent surrounding the bird, especially if it falls stone-cold dead with wings folded. Birds that tumble from the sky will leave more scent than the one that plunges hard and fast, but in either case, on a windy day scent will be quickly transported from the area of the fall. In such an instance it would be wise to send in a dog from the downwind side.

A dog ordered to retrieve a bird freshly fallen may well not come up with the bird, yet the same dog when sent ten or thirty minutes later might be quickly successful. In a situation like this a certain amount of bacteria has built up while the bird has been on the ground. When a second dog is brought into an area where the first dog was unproductive in finding the bird immediately after it fell, the second dog has the often not recognized advantage of the strong scent that built up over the elapsed time. The second dog finds the bird and has "wiped the eye" of the first dog, but perhaps not fairly so.

This same phenomenon can be observed many times when working young coonhounds. You are riding along and suddenly a raccoon crosses the road. As luck would have it, you have permission to hunt right there, so without further ado you slam on the brakes and quickly get your young hound out and turn him loose on that "hot" trail. Sometimes, sure enough, you have a pretty fast, productive race. Yet other times, your promising young hound disappears into the night without so much as an extra sniff at where you know a track is located. This may be attributed to the fact that you acted too quickly, before bacteria could react with the disturbed ground left by the fleeing raccoon. Had you waited a few minutes the whole scenario could have turned out differently, provided that it was not too hot and dry to boot.

Another aspect of scent fools with the talents of young bird dogs. Until they learn to discern real body scent, many a youngster will false point strong scent in an area where a bird has recently been but vacated for greener pastures. What about the innate ability some dogs possess to determine the flight status of a creature, whether furred or feathered? For example, I've seen some bird dogs—and I'm certain you have, too—that point their quarry as close as ten feet in some instances and then in others they'll be back forty yards from the covey, and all of this appears to be governed by when these birds were apt to flush. How do dogs know or sense situations like this? The leading theory has to do with the amount of adrenalin a bird or animal is giving off depending on its level of fear or flight tendency. Perhaps the birds are restless and moving or about to burst up into the heavens.

Keep an eye on terrain when attempting to recover game. If your bird has fallen in a ditch or low place, it is likely that your dog may not get in position to wind any scent coming from the body lying in such a depression. Similarly, if you and your dog are both on high planes with a fallen bird below and between you, especially if there is no wind, you will need to work to put your dog in position to get that bird.

Also, and this is often the subject of heated debate, not all dogs smell alike. Just as some people are born with a more sensitive smell ability, or taste ability, or better sight, so it is with dogs. Many a hunter will argue that all dogs are born with the exact same scent ability, and it is a matter of their drive, or lack thereof, that stimulates the scenting to work for or against their overall performance. Chalk me up on the side that believes dogs and their noses are not created equally.

Weather or Not

Consider the matter of weather and how it affects scenting conditions. Probably most of us as hunters can attest that we've been told as far back as we can remember that when the barometer drops, the game starts moving. Yet, in contrast, scenting will deteriorate as it pertains to dogs. When a front approaches, game usually stirs. Far enough in advance of the front, yet within a time frame that affects wild creatures, the scenting conditions will probably be at least adequate, but as the barometer spirals downward so does the ability to scent game. It pays to keep in mind that when a front is moving in on you, quite often some of your best hunting opportunities will be presented. Then there are the high-pressure bluebird days where scent holds tight . . . and sometimes, so does the game.

What about rainy weather? Game often moves during rain and then demonstrates a tendency to hold tight immediately afterward. If you can stand the conditions you may do well when hunting in this weather, and certainly training is a good idea in the rain—unless dangerous lightning is present, of course—because there will be times when rain will otherwise ruin your best-laid hunting trip plans or times when rain will interfere with an important field trial or hunt test. If your dog is not prepared to perform in these conditions, you could be mightily disappointed. Your dog will be as good as the exposure given to him. Hard rain will interfere with and pound out scent, while a misty rain may help it.

Weather extremes will affect scenting ability. Also, wet, really muddy swampland will be less conducive to tracking than wet, firm ground. New snow conditions and heavy frost offer little scent as does the swampland's deep mud.

What Is the Bottom Line?

On the whole, not a great deal is clearly known about how dogs are able to smell so proficiently. By the same token, it is readily evident to all experienced dog trainers and hunters that there are times when scenting conditions are deplorable and other times when scenting is exceptional, and these things can change categorically within even a day's time, and they are reflected in our dogs' performance.

When training a dog, keep this in mind and constantly assess what might be happening with scent as you evaluate your dog's performance. What about the direction of the wind? Use the wind to your advantage when training your dog. Teach your dog how to use the wind by wisely using it yourself and by putting your companion in situations that set the dog up for success so that when conditions become more challenging he can figure out productive solutions based on previous experience.

Although we don't know everything about our dogs and their sense of smell, all the experts seem to agree that training and experience will expand a dog's olfactory abilities even more. This translates into getting out there with your dog and working him in all types of conditions and weather and terrain and cover so that he can develop a catalog of experience to draw from. In the meantime, have realistic expectations based on weather and scenting conditions.

Note that factors affecting scenting ability and weather conditions all blend and can reflect upon your dog's performance, as can feeding times for game. This is excellent material for your training journal, as well as your hunting journal. Truth be told, I've been faithfully keeping training logs and hunting records for several decades now, and although I can draw comparisons about certain conditions, fronts, temperatures, and the like, it is a mystery to me when all the variables affecting scenting conditions turn out to be wrong, no matter how right they should seem.

PART FOUR

Let's Go Training!

CHAPTER
TWENTY-TWO

Head Start Training

In the old days, rare was the dog that received any formal training before a year of age. We could draw an analogy with the way children used to be schooled versus modern methods. Nowadays children are in head start programs that lead to preschool that lead to kindergarten and beyond. Why wouldn't our alert, inquisitive puppies benefit from the same type of head start, preschool, and kindergarten training? What could possibly be wrong with such an idea?

More fodder for heated discussion. Should you start your puppy's schooling at seven or eight weeks of age or should you wait until he is nearing a year? Keep in mind there are pluses and minuses to both sides of the coin, but why not take the best of both worlds and create and nurture an intelligent puppy budding with talent so that you can take him to the top of his game? Of course there are right ways of doing this and wrong ways, and from that standpoint, some would say it might be better to err on the side of caution and do nothing at all. Instead, get out there and learn the things that will help your puppy become the best he can be, and then do it!

During your puppy's early months you have a chance to positively influence everything from his personality to his temperament and trainability to his confidence. Doesn't seem that anything bad or harmful can be found in such an approach.

No matter what type of hunting dog we are talking about, puppy training has always fascinated me. For instance, retriever people in the United States are pretty definite about starting the training process at seven weeks of age. Puppy bumpers are thrown, with or without wings attached, birds are introduced, and soon all sorts of little training sequences are under way. Depending on your type of bird dog training method, many similarly aged pups are started on quail, grouse, chukar, or pheasant wings. Hound puppies are started on a piece of hide or raccoon tail. Of course these are generalizations and do not intentionally omit HPRs, which are essentially included in the categories above, or beagles, or earth dogs such as dachshunds and Jack Russells. The same principles apply across the board.

However, in all fairness, there are a number of very good, if not exceptional, dogs that did not receive obedience training or bird work as puppies. Many retriever trainers from the United Kingdom refrain from using any birds until their dogs are quite obedient and steady in training with bumpers. Note: They train—just not with birds. Some successful upland bird training methods refrain from structured lessons in bird use and obedience at an early age and turn out well-schooled hunting dogs. That being said, in my humble opinion, the key to success for these types of training is not so much the method but the means, and that could be applied across the board. The young dogs are being worked—that is the means—and therefore learning is being accomplished, often in spades. This is key to success. Develop those minds and get the learning and thinking processes under way instead of letting them stalemate, never to be fully resurrected in later life.

We touched the surface of the critical stages that puppies go through when we peeked in on the issue in chapter 13. As you may have guessed, this chapter will take a closer look at those phases. Older dogs will of course have long since said good-bye to such things, but some of the straightforward training herein can be beneficial to older dogs devoid of much exposure to training.

Look at the options. How many puppies, young dogs, and for that matter older dogs can you think of that are just sitting in backyard kennels? There is no way to learn how to learn anything within the walls of a kennel, other than neurotic habits such as pacing and barking. Make a difference with your dog's socialization and training progress, if not every day, then at least several times a week.

While indeed this is a "head start" chapter, its contents can be applied to dogs of all ages that need a place to begin. The bottom line? Training should begin with positive experiences and basic, simple approaches to learning. Name recognition is key as is basic vocabulary retention. Formal structure should not be an issue with many breeds of dogs or in several types of training yet, but exposure to life—to facilitate that all-important ability to learn how to learn—is paramount.

Those Critical Stages

We left the critical stages in chapter 13 with the puppies emerging from stage three, recognized from day twenty-nine to the seventh week, or the forty-ninth day. Stage four continues from that point—some experts blend stages three and four into one continuous stage beginning with the fourth week and concluding at the end of the twelfth week—and we will examine the important aspects of this stage, as well as stage five from the thirteenth through sixteenth weeks.

Ideally, you've purchased your puppy at about seven weeks of age. Hopefully he has had a fulfilling life up to that point at his first home. From this point on your puppy enters one of the most critical (there's that word again) periods of his life and certainly one of the most significant.

Stage Four

At this point, brain waves can be consistently recorded in puppies. Various studies have determined that prior to this phase, interaction between littermates is vital to proper social skills development between dogs, but by the seventh week human interaction can begin in earnest. (No, this does not mean that a puppy obtained a few days earlier will necessarily be stunted socially, nor does it mean that puppies secured days or weeks later will be social wall flowers, but more on this in a moment.)

At the time a puppy leaves his littermates he experiences a void for the first time in his young life. The puppy will crave love and security and will need human socialization to provide those things. The dog will look to you to remove his vulnerability. This is something you should be immediately aware of as you bring the new puppy home.

You are catapulted into the role of human caregiver. Almost as quickly, while you are providing a nurturing environment, you may have to "growl" at your new little charge occasionally, as he will have to learn boundaries within your household. If you should have to issue any discipline, do so gently and fairly. This will be the first act of dominance that you will impress upon your puppy.

Permanent bonding takes place during this stage more so than at any other stage in your puppy's life. Puppies will learn about respect for their owners during this stage and it is a new and exciting thing to them. It should also be handled wisely by us.

Housebreaking should be introduced at this time, also. All new changes in surroundings and environment should be gradually and positively introduced. During this stage puppies learn about and develop confidence; as owners we can make or break this important quality at this time.

It is now that puppies learn how to learn. Every little thing you do will have an impact on your puppy and the development of his mind. Take your puppy for short rides in your truck and for walks out into the world. Introduce him to creeks, cover, and the strangeness of his new home and environment. Anything and everything you do and expose your puppy to during this phase—mini obedience lessons to bring a bit of order to life, a leash or a tie-out, horses, ATVs, strangers—will contribute to teaching him to learn how to learn.

Be on the lookout for some manifestation of fear in your puppy in the eight- to ten-week range, although this is just an average. Some puppies demonstrate a certain amount of trepidation to things in their world during this time and just need some extra encouragement to overcome their fears. Watch for this and help him through it if necessary.

Stage Five

This developmental stage begins at day 85 and culminates at day 112. All of the things that have become important to the mental and physical development of your puppy are still desperately needed, such as love, security, and essentials such as food. Also important is a sense of structure in your puppy's life, and of course more socialization.

During this time there is a likelihood your puppy will exhibit some rebellion toward something you want him to do, toward a learning phase, and ultimately toward you (occasionally, some alpha-type puppies will actually show this tendency in stage four). One of the most common times this happens is when your puppy is told to "Come" and he decides he would rather entertain himself than you. What you choose to do in reaction to this disobedience or willfulness will strongly shape your puppy's attitude toward training and correction in either a positive or negative way. Proceed with caution. This is not the time—nor is there ever a time—to lose your temper with your wayward puppy. Be particular, for you are laying a foundation that will mold and shape your puppy for years to come.

Without a doubt, early experience to gentle handling and touch, neurostimulation, and proper exposure to stress, noise, other dogs, people, places, and things will shape the personality and trainability of your puppy as well as solidify the bond he has with you. At this important stage, your puppy's potential will be unleashed with proper handling and socialization by your puppy's caregivers and ultimately by you. Because of the significance of this time frame toward your puppy's mental well-being, if you should consider buying a puppy over fourteen to sixteen weeks of age, do all you can to determine the quality of time that has been invested in the puppy up to that point. In some cases, you'll be getting a happy, healthy, well-adjusted puppy; in others, you'll be inheriting social problems and learning disabilities that will haunt you and your puppy for a long time to come, if not for his entire lifetime. Think hard before making this decision.

When you go to visit a litter in the hopes of picking out your puppy, be wary of shy, timid puppies. These puppies haven't been properly socialized on a regular basis or they are genetically challenged in this department; the extra baggage will be difficult, if not impossible, to overcome. Concentrate on locating reputable breeders that devote the necessary time to these valuable factors in the development of puppies. Raising a litter of puppies is a tremendous amount of work, and the labor and effort is more seriously regarded by some than others. Most good breeders take pride in raising bold, personable, clean-natured puppies that have obviously had much handling. Once you pick out your puppy, what happens from that point forward is entirely up to you. Make these critical stages of your puppy's life count in spades!

If the puppy you acquire is older than seven weeks, you now have a working knowledge about the things necessary to healthy mental development. You are aware of how his growing mind and body respond to life. By the same token, if you purchase a started or trained dog, you know that how he was handled as a youngster has shaped his learning capacity and trainability.

Always remember that everything you do with your puppy will affect his development. Often actions speak louder than words—be conscious of them. Also, remember to speak calmly around your puppy so that your voice will have emphasis and impact during the times you need it. Your techniques of communication are vital.

Puppy Acceleration Programs

The little minds of puppies are active and very receptive to stimuli and all sorts of training-related lessons in their budding lives. Doesn't it make sense to take advantage of this? Just like we mentioned at the beginning of this chapter, using this time to its fullest is not unlike the head start and preschool programs that are now accepted as standard procedure with children so that they are better prepared for kindergarten. Indeed, the advantage to us in seizing the opportunity to make good use of this early time with our puppies is to stimulate their minds and expose them to as many elements as we can while laying the groundwork for learning and future hunting.

Puppies gain many positive attributes from being exposed to the timber, fields, ponds, and places that birds or game frequent. They should have plenty of opportunity to roam and explore these wonderful places to absorb all the sights, smells, and sounds they find out there, as this will make up their real working world in the future. They will gain confidence in themselves as they range farther and farther from you in their forays and will no longer be compelled to remain underfoot.

During these times, allow your puppy his freedom. Don't turn him loose only to immediately start henpecking and frequently calling the puppy back to you. Let your puppy explore his world! Choose your locations wisely so that you haven't turned your dog loose close to a busy road. Find a safe place and let him romp at will. When it is time to collect him, put yourself in a position to round him up without a lot of calling, hollering, screaming, or begging.

With some breeds of dogs, such as hounds, it can be advantageous to let a young puppy run loose for the first few months of his life. As long as the puppy doesn't show any learning problems or difficulty in being caught and handled, by running loose he will learn many valuable lessons on his own, like how to roam and then return home, and how to run scent trails from rabbits and other creatures, and often how to tree squirrels and cats. Puppies raised in this fashion should still receive human contact several times a day through handling and regular feed and maintenance schedules. The puppy-owner bonding process should not be replaced by the mere fact that the pup is loose in the yard. At any rate, however, most folks do not have the proper facilities and land available to make this a viable possibility.

More often than not a new puppy will conform to variations of this schedule: confinement through part of the day combined with frequent short lessons and walks. This provides needed structure in a puppy's life, and he looks forward to each new lesson and exposure with you, the center of his world.

Simple Manners

Your puppy may show typical signs of wanting to jump up on you and other folks and he may want to engage in puppy biting. Is it a good idea to let your puppy do these things for attention? Although deep down we know the answer to that question, actually doing something about it is often another story indeed. However, these problems usually begin during puppyhood and this is where they can quickly escalate out of control. When puppies are six, seven, ten weeks of age they are cuddly and cute and it is easy to say, "Aw, just let it go for now" and fall into that mind-set and consequently allow your new small pup to jump on you or bite you.

Of course right now you are big and puppy is little—but that is going to change! Let's take the jumping issue first. If you let your new puppy jump up on you and then all of a sudden one morning—when you realize that your new little puppy is a six-month-old monster—after you are dressed for work are you going to have a fit and take it out on your puppy? Are you—out of the blue—going to come down like a ton of bricks on your puppy when he jumps on your clean clothes, when all this time you have let him do just that and he naturally thinks jumping up is OK? Do you think your puppy will understand why you are so incredibly unhappy with him on just a moment's notice?

As the handler, you must be the one to decide if jumping is acceptable behavior or not, but bear in mind that others may not approve of it. (Rossella Di Palma)

There are other things to consider as well. If you have small children in the family or in the neighborhood, or elderly people in the household or close by, you are inviting trouble by allowing your puppy to jump. Although you may think it's cute when your pup or dog jumps up to greet you, it may be dangerous for him to do the same thing to a young child or an elderly, fragile person. Your dog may not know the difference.

What can you do? First and foremost, it helps to recognize what "jumping up" is to your dog. This is a form of greeting and normally occurs during times of excitement. However, as I just mentioned, it can be downright dangerous to both young children and elderly people once any dog reaches a significant size and weight. If you are going to let your dog run loose, or if he will be in the house at least part of the time, teach him proper "greeting" manners. This should be done with puppies that are kenneled as well. Ideally, I want my dog to greet me in a front sit position and I will teach "Sit" or "Stand" to a very young puppy.

OK—teaching sit or stand to a puppy of any age can be easily done with treat rewards. Although I'm not really a big advocate of using food or treats to train a dog—because food can fade in significance, and because I might not always have it handy—there are places where its use is helpful to teach lessons and this is particularly true with puppies. I will then insist that my puppy always assume a front sit or stand position before he receives any greeting or positive reinforcement from me.

Words such as "No" and "Off" can be used when the puppy or dog jumps up; simultaneously, you can turn your body into the puppy or dog to make the action less inviting. I like to advise people not to respond in any other way to your dog's greeting/jumping behavior, or you might run the risk of actually reinforcing the jump-up action. In the manner described you are effectively counteracting it.

As with all training, it is up to you to use good timing and almost simultaneously command "Sit," "Stand"—or "Down" if your puppy, or an older dog with this problem, knows this command—then upon compliance by your dog you can return his greeting once all four feet are on the ground. This is another good reason to teach "Sit" at a young age, by the way. You can also possibly reward with a treat. It is much easier to teach a young pup proper response than an adult dog, particularly one that has reached his adult size and has been allowed to indulge in this bad habit unchecked for any length of time. Therefore, teach your puppy an acceptable greeting position right from the start and accept nothing less. Do not encourage your cute little puppy to jump all over you when he is seven weeks old and then become upset when he is jumping up at seven months old. Teach good habits from the start.

With the older dog that already has this very annoying habit, you still have options. My first choice is to use the body block with a dog that jumps up. Simply put, I will turn into the dog, then firmly command "Sit" or "Down" to counteract the jumping up. As soon as the dog complies I will use praise—probably just verbal—and maybe a treat. Why just verbal praise? If you come right back with some physical petting for praise you are going to get the dog excited all over again and by doing so you may encourage more jumping up—not what you want. Another favorite move of mine is to grab the front paws and hold them tightly high up in the air, in effect making the dog maintain an upright position—which is uncomfortable to the dog—for an extended period of time. Then I will lower the dog to the ground and at this moment command "Sit" with praise upon the proper response. And again, particularly during teaching, I might give him a food reward.

What treats can be used? My favorites are dried liver, hot dog pieces, or little chunks of cheese. Of course the treat is gradually phased out and/or seldom used, with the greeting from you becoming the reinforcement for good behavior, and no treat needed.

For some, clicker training is an option. If you are a clicker trainer, this action is a good place for it. You can click as soon as the dog sits and give him a treat. Again, click/treat can be used when the dog assumes the sit position, or praise/treat, or just praise.

But again, let's say you have an older dog that is really bad about jumping up and absolutely insists on this bad habit. You must realize that it is critical to be very consistent when working on this problem. Certainly an ingrained bad habit will be more difficult to break. Once you begin to tackle the problem you must insist on the correct behavior every time. Again, I've found that the procedure of firmly grabbing the front paws and holding them up, thus forcing the dog to maintain an uncomfortable upright position until you let him down, works quickest and most effectively. However, this older dog must know either the sit or down command for best results. If your dog does not know this command you will have to teach it. When you hold your dog in this position, you will find that almost immediately your dog will attempt to lick at your hands and/ or struggle to get away. Once you are certain he gets the picture, lower the dog to the ground with an immediate sit or down command, followed by praise and possibly a treat for correct behavior. If an older dog has a severe problem, you may have to restrict the amount of praise—don't overdo it—until he learns to respond calmly and correctly. Also, refrain from any type of greeting—positive or negative—to this dog until he is sitting or lying down.

Another thing that might work: attach a short (foot-long) piece of rope to the dog's flat collar, and whenever the dog attempts to jump, grab the piece of rope. Give a few short tugs toward the ground while commanding "No" and "Sit" and guide the dog into place to begin with, and then insist on the correct behavior once the dog comprehends the lesson. Use praise and/or a treat, followed by a greeting when he behaves properly.

Keep in mind that, particularly with an older dog, you may need to set up this lesson several times a day and possibly enlist the help of visitors to your home, yard, or kennel—people that have been previously instructed on how to react with your dog—and each time insist on consistency from your dog.

This brings up another important point: what are the rules for other people that will come around, and what about the kids? What about when you are not around?

The absolute golden rule of training through *any bad habit* is that anyone around a dog must be firm and consistent. Jumping up is not cute to most people and should not be rewarded by attention from others. Adults and children should be instructed to at least ignore your dog if he becomes excited and wants to jump. You can suggest to them to turn away from your dog and give him the cold shoulder if this happens, at least for starters. Better yet, ask them to command a "Sit" or at least a "No" if they are comfortable in doing so, with a mild greeting to your dog allowed upon compliance. If you cannot expect other adults or children to react properly to your dog, consider confining him when you are not around and/or lock the door to your kennel or dog run.

Sometimes dogs learn over time that it is OK—or rather that they can get away with jumping—in certain places or areas. This is because dogs are basically place specific. Here again, consistency is the key. Quite simply, if you allow any dog to jump up occasionally he will have a difficult time figuring out when or where is OK and when it is not acceptable. Therefore, always insist on good behavior and do not allow anyone to ever encourage jumping up with your dog. Teach your dog your greeting position of choice and insist that he always respond properly no matter where you are and regardless of distractions. This will pay off in the long run with an obedient, mannerly dog that reacts well to other dogs and people whether you are at home, traveling, hunting, or at a dog event.

Let's approach the biting problem. Now, there are very few of us that can resist the adorable smell—strange as that seems—of puppy breath. It is intoxicating to dog lovers—a sweet, musky smell that emanates from the mouths of young pups—and when the silky smooth tongue of the little puppy is added to that, and as he washes your hands and face in adoration, well, you get the idea. This is a pretty contented picture between puppy and new owner that we're painting. However, now let's add a set of sharp teeth to the equation and suddenly this picture of bliss is abruptly interrupted.

Many times puppy biting seems cute, even a sign of affection toward the recipient on the part of the puppy. It could be a quest for attention. And, no one likes to adversely affect the "infant" period of a young canine, so it is tempting to overlook those nips. After all, the puppy is little and is going through important mental developmental stages, we reason, and we tend to refrain from rocking the boat. This tendency is compared to how we "grown humans" might not want to correct or influence our babies or young children for some misdeeds that in actuality could grow into serious problems if left unchecked.

Puppy biting ranges in various forms from light play biting to very aggressive mouthing and applying teeth with pressure. The occasional light puppy bite might be innocently applied and this sort of tendency may gradually go away with time, particularly if it is ignored and not encouraged in any way. However, when left unchecked, puppy biting can escalate into additional problems as the youngster becomes an adolescent and then an adult. Since biting can lead to aggression and even possessive dominance, this behavior can create a number of negative behaviors or bad habits that can be exceedingly hard to break, which is why the problem should be addressed when it first crops up.

What can you do to positively influence your growing companion's world without fussing at him? Make sure that your puppy gets lots of activity so that he doesn't have an opportunity to become bored. Often, the act of biting human hands can transcend into biting other objects as a matter of course. Give the puppy plenty of exercise, and play games with him.

You can encourage a number of different games, from simple, fun obedience lessons and such timeless classics as hide-and-seek and keep-away. Be consistent with these games, the rules involved, and your expectations. Don't let your puppy rule each play session. You must be in charge and you must establish that fact so that your puppy begins to look at you as the boss from early on in his relationship with you.

When talking about games we should discuss a popular puppy/owner game: tug-of-war. Should you play this game with your new puppy? Can bad habits emerge as a result of engaging in this activity? This could be a concern particularly with retrievers that might be used for hunting and organized retriever games. Will tug-of-war create problems for your dog?

That depends. Literally. There are three schools of thought regarding tug-of-war for retrievers. As you might surmise, one school vehemently believes that tug-of-war games will nearly always lay the foundation for hard mouth while another school believes that the game has absolutely nothing to do with subsequent hard-mouth problems. And the third school is undecided. Yet, tug-of-war is fun to play. There is no question that it is a game that involves the mouth and therefore the teeth and all that go along with it. Will this game encourage biting? Will it create tendencies to grab at objects, or worse, develop an overly possessive attitude toward retrieve or tug items?

It seems logical that playing tug-of-war with a puppy that is destined to become a hunting dog, hunt test, or field trial competitor may be playing with fire. However, there are some die-hard and successful trainers who think tug-of-war games help develop retrieve instinct. If you choose to experiment with this game, be sure to employ a few rules.

First of all, make sure that you—as the boss in charge—are the one who starts and ends the game. Most dogs like to tug instinctively so this game is usually easy to teach. While the puppy learns to "Tug" he should also learn to "Drop" . . . these are rules of the game.

"Drop" is a valuable command in the delivery portion of the retrieve process, whether your dog is retrieving birds, fur, or tennis balls. For a retrieve to be successfully executed the object must be delivered to hand or at least near you, such as at your feet. A dog that retrieves something and then won't "Give" it to you or drop on command is not properly performing his retrieve for your benefit. Surprisingly, tug-of-war can encourage a good drop response, as long as the rules are properly and consistently observed every time you play the game.

In addition, because your dog learns to drop, he is also learning tenderness of the mouth which carries over to subduing biting tendencies and helps to further eliminate those tendencies. However, trainers opposed to tug-of-war feel that the risks of encouraging hard mouth are too great, and they simply prefer to teach "Drop" as part of the retrieve process, or game, in the case of young puppies.

Besides playing games and making sure that your new puppy is adequately entertained, what can you do to discourage puppy biting without being too harsh on your youngster? Watching the interactions of littermate puppies and even puppies with their mother gives us important clues on the best way to deal with sharp, unpleasant puppy biting. What do you see happen when one puppy in a litter suddenly gets too rough with his siblings? Often they will retaliate and let the offending puppy know that he should cool it and lay off the teeth thing, or they will yelp and in effect say, "That hurts." Mom does the same thing. When a puppy gets too rowdy with his teeth, she will quickly put him in his place with a warning growl or nip. Bottom line—your puppy needs to learn that biting is not acceptable interaction with you. Perhaps you may be able to teach him to use his jaws without applying the power of his teeth. However, discouraging puppy biting is best.

An effective way of accomplishing this with young puppies might not surprise you at all, once you spend a few moments to think about it. When your puppy attempts to bite you say, "Ow!" or "Ouch!" with a hurt voice, then turn away and ignore the dog for a minute or two. Your puppy wants to play with you, and when you disengage yourself from him you are sending a loud message that usually won't go unnoticed. Pay close attention to your puppy when you do this; a certain number of puppies could become more excited when they hear you exclaim in pain. With these puppies it might be better to counteract that excitement with a growl in pain as opposed to a yelp or protest. But always turn away and end the play.

Another method is to lightly put pressure on the gums of the mouth against offensive teeth while saying "No" or "No biting" until the puppy squirms in discomfort and then immediately release the source of pressure. Care must be taken if this method of correction or behavior modification is applied as it is easy to squeeze too hard.

Overall, encourage your puppy that abstinence from biting is his best bet. From day one, do your part to teach your puppy that you will not tolerate biting. Don't let even a day go by where you might think the biting is cute and let your pup get away with any portion of the activity. Biting just won't cut it, and the sooner your new puppy realizes it the happier you both will be. Indeed, think about the overall benefits of discouraging biting from the start of your relationship with your dog. You are using this opportunity to help establish yourself as the boss and that is a good thing. In addition, you are molding a good citizen that can be trusted with children and even infants because he has learned, through your efforts, that his teeth can hurt and he must refrain from using them around people of any size. The benefits of this good behavior are substantial and long lasting. Keep all this in mind when you evaluate and build your puppy's good manners.

To Be or Not to Be—Obedience Training

It is a natural tendency to want to spend lots of time with your new puppy, and it therefore follows that many of you will want to go straight to obedience class with your new companion. Indeed, you will probably receive lots of unsolicited friendly advice urging you to do just that. The argument is that these classes will expose your puppy to other dogs and will give him needed manners, too.

However, be cautious about doing this. First of all, the obedience class may have an instructor who insists you do things a certain way—his or her way—and you may have already decided upon a different method of training. Out of respect for your instructor's knowledge and time, you should either conform or resign. Avoid confrontation—it's not worth it in this case.

But far more important, what are your overall hunting goals? You may have a breed that could be set back by too much formal obedience at too early an age. What about the commands issued in obedience class? A retriever might get along fine with early strict obedience. If you have a bird dog you may not want him to learn to sit until much later in his training regime; instead, you want him to stand. Strict early heeling lessons often impede upcoming training lessons for hunting and quartering because those early strict lessons often produce a dog that is dependent on heeling at your side. The dog becomes hesitant to range out or hunt on his own initiative, making many disciplines such as quartering, for a bird dog, or hunting, for a hound, very difficult to teach. This is not written in stone, as each dog is different, but is something to consider at this vital point in the learning process.

In addition, many bird dogs and hounds need exposure to freedom, birds, and game during their early learning stages, with a minimum of structured obedience. Certainly a measure of obedience is necessary to keep a manageable handle on "field" or "woods" lessons, but moderation is often the key to success. Obedience training should be done more as an extension of fun and games during this time than as a strict schedule of events. However, all of these "freedom" lessons and moderate obedience are vital parts of head start and the learning process.

Early Training

Crate training and housebreaking procedures should be started as soon as you bring your puppy home. The crate should quickly come to signify a place for good things and a safe sanctuary for your puppy. It should be his den, his place for sleeping and naps, and even a place for meals where your puppy can eat undisturbed. You should never use the crate for discipline as a time-out location or for anything similar. Associate all good things with the crate for your puppy or your dog.

There are all sorts of crate models and sizes to choose from. You will find wire collapsible crates, wooden crates, plastic and fiberglass crates, even aluminum and stainless steel crates. You can line the bottom with layers of newspaper for ease in cleaning and as a layer of insulation against the cold crate floor. Eventually, a properly sized mat can be added for comfort once your puppy is past the chewing stage.

The crate will be a handy transition to a dog box as your puppy learns to ride in vehicles for pleasure, when going to the veterinarian, on training excursions, and on hunting trips. It is also handy for use in a motel or hotel room when you need to confine your dog but want to bring him inside. Many hotels will allow this with a deposit, provided your dog is crated while in the room. A previously developed comfort zone with the crate experience will make this seamless and enjoyable for both of you.

In addition, crate usage makes house-training more black and white for your new puppy or dog. By nature a dog does not want to soil the area where he sleeps. He will try to keep the crate clean and will succeed with the proper help from you. House-training is actually pretty simple but takes commitment and effort from you, particularly when your puppy is just seven or eight weeks old, because he is not capable of the waste retention of a grown dog just by virtue of his size and his inexperience in learning to "hold it." And that is where you come in.

How do you get the correct message across to your puppy? Every time your dog wakes up from a nap, or after sleeping through the night, take him immediately outside to the spot in the yard you've deemed appropriate for potty business. Praise him when he complies. Every time after an extended play session, or after a meal, or after drinking water, take your dog outside to that spot. If your puppy wakes up in the middle of the night and seems restless, take him outside to that spot. Your puppy will soon begin sleeping through the night, but the first week or two he may need a late-night potty trip. You can help regulate the dog by removing his water source after a certain time each evening and doing the same with his feeding schedule—for example, last meal at 6 p.m. All of these things will contribute to a consistent schedule that your puppy will soon adapt to with success.

In the event that your puppy has a mistake, do not rub his nose in the excrement. This is one of the most common "old" remedies of dog training you will hear or encounter and also one of the least grounded and nastiest. Not only are the chances slim that your puppy will make a connection with the deed, but this could also encourage unpleasant habits. Instead, if you catch your puppy in the act, scoop him up and take him outside to his spot to hopefully finish the job there. If you discover a mistake and don't know when it was made, just clean it up and go forward. Discipline after the fact is never a good thing, and although it may help you feel some closure over the incident, it won't help your puppy at all and could promote distrust, something you don't want to cultivate at any cost. Develop a routine with your puppy and stick to it; the rewards will be evident before you know it.

Make walks with your puppy count, no matter what breed of hunting dog you own. Give your dog exposure to his new world—at this time it is a huge playground full of interesting sights and smells and all sorts of stimulating things—and allow him to adapt and familiarize himself to all of it.

Take your puppy for short rides in your vehicle. Condition your dog to the motion of the truck. This will be necessary for most hunting trips and training excursions. It is surprising the number of puppies and young dogs that have a tendency to be carsick. They truly become upset over the motion and stress of the car ride when not properly introduced. Worst-case scenarios are young dogs that vomit, defecate, and drool all over the inside of the dog box during transport—not pleasant for either you or your dog.

This can be nipped in the bud with frequent exposure and pleasant memories associated with the vehicle. When you begin this process keep those first rides short and stress-free. Don't schedule a ride just after your puppy has eaten a meal. Many puppies get claustrophobic in the confines of a crate or dog box so you might consider letting your puppy ride around the block on the floorboard or in the seat until he gets his "legs" under him and then put the dog in a box. The addition of a mat or some wood shavings will add to your puppy's comfort while in the box and he won't be as apt to slide around either. Once your puppy is used to motion, make the trips longer, and also expose him to rides on your ATV if you have one and plan to use it when hunting. Most important, realize that the earlier you start this business of riding in the truck, the easier it will be for your puppy to acclimate himself to the process. Car or truck rides should signify good things to your puppy and not be viewed with dread.

Accustom your puppy to a flat buckle collar. Doing so at this age will be relatively painless. Your puppy will quickly adjust to the feel and weight of it on his neck.

Introduction of the Tie-Out, Leading, Dragging a Rope

These are all combined because they are related, so to speak. First of all, it is often handy to be able to tie your dog out when you go to a hunt and you want to get your dog out of the truck but you have no opportunity to let him run loose. A dog that is comfortable with being staked out will make life much easier in many instances.

Some puppies will immediately adapt to the tie-out stake while others will buck, cut flips, and carry on at the prospect of being confined to a certain space. Make sure that when this happens, the collar is snug, but not too tight, so that it won't slip off your puppy's head during his antics. Also be watchful during this process so that there is no way the dog can hurt himself. In short order, your puppy will discover that once he quits acting up he can roam at will within the confines of the lead or chain. Puppies that have been introduced to the tie-out procedure are very easy to teach to lead or to heel.

If you do not want your puppy to heel at this stage of his life, attach a checkcord or long line to his collar, and allow him to drag it as he explores so that he becomes accustomed to its weight and feel as the cord goes everywhere the puppy goes. Soon your dog will disregard the rope. You, however, will have an added means of control over your puppy, should you need it, anytime that checkcord is attached.

Introduction to "Here" or "Come"

This command should be taught through careful observation on your part—choose your times wisely in calling your puppy to you, in other words when you are about 100 percent sure the dog will come anyway—and then reward him for a deed well done. Now is a good time to introduce the whistle for "Here" as well. (Or "Come," as you prefer—these commands mean the same thing.)

Clap your hands and move in the opposite direction—your young puppy is likely to find you irresistible. This illustrates a valuable lesson: for every action there is a reaction. Make this always work for you and not against you.

Depending on your goals, you may want to take the here command a bit further by working your puppy on a check cord. Command "Here" and if your puppy comes arunning, good job! Tell him so. If not, say "No" and "Here" while giving a gentle tug at that very moment. Hopefully one tug will guide your puppy to you but if not, use a few more. Give plenty of praise when the dog complies.

Introduction to "Sit" or "Stand"

There are a number of ways to do this. Positive-only trainers will guide the puppy into position with a food bowl over his head, for example, and then click and treat. Another method for "Sit" is to gently push on the dog's rump, command "Sit," and praise and treat with compliance. Same for "Stand"—use a supportive hand(s) under the abdomen and/or chest while giving the command, with praise and possibly a treat upon compliance. In either case, accept the position for just a flash of a second. Duration can be increased once the command is understood.

Regarding puppy obedience, it is often best to keep the sessions from becoming too serious. Refrain from becoming bossy or overbearing unless you have an exceptionally unruly puppy that might benefit from some firm measures. At this point you are just teaching these few commands in short sessions. Avoid the temptation to overdo it; don't test your puppy's attention span. Keep things simple and fun and create a positive learning atmosphere. Your puppy should regard his training as fun and interesting. At the same time, you want to cultivate good training habits within yourself. Remember this golden rule: never give a command that you are not in position to enforce.

Exposure to Scent and Instinct

Most puppies are very receptive to learning about scent. Help your dog become acquainted with the wonders of his nose. This may or may not include use of a coon tail or a grouse wing initially—you may want to start with tempting pieces of hot dog. You can get a young hound to start looking up, or a retriever or bird dog to start searching for things of interest.

With a hound, beagle, cur, or earth dog, take the training a step further by using a coon tail, rabbit hide, bear, squirrel, rat, or cat hide. Remember that your puppy is pretty little at this stage, and a full-sized coon (for example) could intimidate him. You want your puppy to think that life is grand, that you are wonderful, that learning is grand, and that raccoon smell is awesome—or rabbit smell, or bear smell, or cat smell. Without using actual game hides you can scent a canvas drag and use it to entice your hound puppy to trail scent and perhaps tree. (Use caution with any treeing by sight. This should be kept to a minimum to prevent this crutch from developing.)

With retrievers and bird dogs you can use a wing, a dove, or perhaps a pigeon, depending on how outgoing the puppy is. For those who elect to keep birds out of the training process at this early stage, use a bumper or tennis ball, some object to jump-start the retrieving instinct.

Any time you have a puppy that shows interest but seems a bit intimidated, try introducing another puppy of about the same age to the equation. Young puppies are always braver when they have teammates as they encourage each other to get with it.

The big key at this stage is to lay a successful foundation for the team effort between you and your new hunting companion. Remember, at this time you are the coach and your puppy is the developing athlete. When you ask any sports coach what are the most important variables to successful team development, the coach will invariably tell you the most important elements for young team members are the basics and a foundation.

CHAPTER
TWENTY-THREE

Basic Training and Foundation

At this point your puppy is between three and six months of age, unless you've purchased an older dog. You have developed a strong bond with your dog and his learning environment has been influenced in a positive manner. The breed of dog you have and the type of hunting you are training for will even more strongly influence your decisions from this point forward than they have thus far. In addition, you should explore within yourself whether you might have some abiding interest in dog sports, such as field trials or hunt tests, as this decision may affect the order of the steps you take to train your puppy from now on.

A number of additional steps will help prepare your dog for involved training procedures, including loading, fencing, and increased exposure to noise and gunfire, as well as a proper introduction to an inactive e-collar if you plan to use one. The proper approach can be invaluable to the overall training picture. Horses and other applicable hunting equipment such as ATVs can be continually used around your dog.

Loading in the truck is a relatively easy project by now because you've already attended to a number of fundamental details in your puppy's training. Of course your dog is already well accustomed to a crate and the dog box and is convinced that rides in the box signify good things. Indeed, some puppies are so eager to tend to the business of life and rides in the truck that they've begun loading on their own by this time. They want to get on with things—life is grand!

However, if your puppy hasn't taken it upon himself to start loading for you, your dog is in the majority rather than the minority. Do your part to make the loading experience a positive one and help your pup learn quickly.

One way to begin the process is to place the dog box on the ground with the door open. With a lead rope on your dog's collar, command "Load" or "Kennel" and guide him inside. The dog should start going in

Eventually, the well-trained dog doesn't need commands to do things he anticipates, like loading up. (Avery Outdoors)

on his own after just a few efforts. Next, use a low truck, such as a two-wheel-drive Toyota instead of a 4x4 full-size Ford diesel, and pull the dog box near the tailgate edge and command "Load" or "Kennel" while deftly guiding your dog up and into the box. The only added effort here is that your dog has to expend a bit more energy to jump or hop into the box.

Another option is to push the dog box, with the door open, way into the back of the bed to give you some room to stand up on the bed and guide your dog up gently from the ground to the proximity of the bed with the load command and then into the confines of the box. Remember, you are not way up in the air when you do this but in a truck bed that is low to the ground. Encourage your puppy while gently tugging on the rope. Nine times out of ten your puppy will at least attempt to jump in the bed. More encouragement will usually do the trick. This is a situation where you can employ food as a reward if you'd like.

Then, put the dog back on the ground and repeat the procedure. Don't stay at this too long in one session, but in just a few tries most puppies will load into a low truck. Once they find out that they can load they will make a larger effort to jump or load into a higher, bigger truck.

However, once you've accomplished this, the job is not necessarily complete. You are still up in the bed of the truck and calling your puppy or dog up there with you. Next, put yourself on ground level with your dog and command "Load." The first few times you should include some wrist action with the lead or another similar movement to encourage the dog to load.

Some trainers prefer to teach this command from the ground through the entire procedure. However, when difficulty is encountered, putting yourself in the bed of the truck to call and tug your dog up inside the truck will often help to simplify the lesson. From ground level, stand next to the tailgate and put some pressure on your dog's collar in an upward, lifting manner with the lead as you give him the load command. You can grab your dog's collar and the hair near his rump and physically start the motion of lifting him off the ground. Another thing to try would be to push the dog box back into the bed again with the door open but with you standing on the ground so that once you get the dog up in the bed there is room to guide him into the box with ease.

As soon as your dog makes an attempt to jump, use praise. Timing is important, just as it is with most training procedures. Another trick is to get a running start at the truck—you and your dog—and jump into the bed together. First of all, you definitely need a low truck so that you can smoothly make the jump, and also be prepared to shift gears in midair if you make the jump but your dog does not.

Some dogs haven't had the benefit of early conditioning to a crate or dog box. You can easily rectify this, however, by acclimating your dog to the truck box before teaching him to load into it. Make it a pleasant and safe place rather than an intimidating scary mountain. This can be initially accomplished by feeding and watering your dog in a box placed on the ground.

The main thing to remember when you teach the load command is patience on your part. It can be very upsetting when a dog won't load because this seems like such a simple task—don't let it get to you! Blowing a gasket and taking it out on your dog will only create more problems. Take your time and your dog will soon grasp what you want.

Fencing is a necessary talent for many hunting dogs. Most all hounds will need to negotiate fences throughout their lifetime. Many bird dogs and retrievers can also benefit from this exercise. Indeed, retrievers are often required to negotiate fences during hunts and also in events in countries such as England, Ireland, and even Australia. What is fencing then? It is simply the act of learning to negotiate various fences encountered out in the real world while hunting. There may be barbed-wire fences, tight mesh fences, hog panel fences, stone and wooden fences, and even electric fences.

Often the best means to teach fencing is by hunting your young dog with an older, more experienced dog. This works particularly well with hounds. Monkey see, monkey do. With regard to formidable fences, sometimes the only way to deal with it is to find a way to cross through or under it instead of over it. Smart, savvy dogs soon learn to look for places along the fence where the ground dips in an area the fence cannot accommodate, or they look for breaks in the fence.

In contrast, most traditional fences are much easier to negotiate. When given the opportunity, most dogs quickly learn to jump them. However, there are things you can do to assist your puppy with solutions regarding fences. First of all, you can arrange walks where you know you will encounter small or low fences and walk over them yourself. Encourage your puppy to join you on the other side. You can also erect some fencing or a similar barrier in your puppy's kennel and put his food and water on the other side. You may have to show your pup how to cross it, but this simple teaching lesson will help your dog understand fences.

Another option is to construct a realistic obstacle course in your yard if the art of fencing still seems out of reach for your dog. Always look for sensible solutions and ways to simplify training problems.

What if you should run up on an electric fence while out hunting? In the event a dog hits an electric fence, he could be adversely affected for the remainder of the day or night, or longer. It helps to do your homework in advance. If you know of electric fences on property you will be hunting, chances are the owner will allow you to turn off the charger while you are using the property, as long as you remember to turn it back on when you are through. Forget just once and that could be the end of your good relationship with that landowner.

Increased exposure to noise and gunfire can be effective during this stage of your puppy's training. During times of high excitement or pleasure, including feeding time, make some noise. You can accomplish this by banging stainless steel feeding pans together, or shoot a cap pistol at a distance, all the while carefully watching for any reaction from your puppy. Do this intermittently to begin with and bring the source of

Noise introduction created with feed pans. (Author photo)

the noise within closer proximity of your puppy as his reaction, or lack thereof, warrants. Soon you can change the cap pistol to a .22 blank pistol. Shotguns should not be used at this time; their introduction will come a bit later in training. However, horses, horse trailers, ATVs, and any accessories that are large or make noise can be introduced at this time.

Pointing, Retrieving, Tracking and Trailing, Treeing

Most retriever trainers want their young puppies solidly retrieving with gusto as early as possible. The majority of hound trainers want their young dogs to show intense trail and tree tendencies early on as well, although some do not. Many flushing trainers want their young dogs keen on birds to facilitate training.

The biggest division of early ability in hunting dogs and whether to foster it or not perhaps exists with pointing breeds. Some trainers believe in teaching or bringing out pointing instincts before any other lessons are learned, while other trainers refrain from any pointing lessons until hunting for birds becomes instinctive.

Once again, these things are all critical to the progression of any training method. Depending on the breed of dog you've selected, you must do your homework and decide how you wish to proceed along these lines with your own puppy or dog.

Teething can be quite uncomfortable for some puppies and can alter their personalities and prompt a refusal to retrieve. It is complete by six months of age; then, much more can be expected of youngsters because this painful phase is behind them. Read your own puppy, as some enterprising youngsters are ready for additional work well before teething commences or is concluded.

Advanced obedience can be brought into daily life now for those breeds that need it and within training methods that require it. Obedience should include "Sit" or "Stand," "Come" or "Here," "Heel" or the ability to range with a checkcord, and "Down." It might also incorporate work on "Whoa" from a barrel, or place-board (place specific) work for any number of commands that can enhance the ability of all types of dogs.

Keep in mind that ultimately a strong platform in obedience training is the foundation for almost all successful hunting dog work. There are a few exceptions that we will continually refer to as we go along. It bears mention here, however, and repeatedly throughout these pages because obedience is often viewed with disdain by trainers. This is in part because the act of teaching and reinforcing obedience can be boring and dull. That, however, depends on you. Change your attitude and bring some animation to the obedience lessons and drills you do with your dog. It will pay big dividends in the years to come.

Yard work should incorporate teaching drills for all actions that will be required of your dog in the field. Teach, add distractions, and reinforce those lessons. We'll see much more of this in upcoming pages and in problem solving.

CHAPTER TWENTY-FOUR

E-Collar Conditioning and Application

Theere is a popular saying well worth its weight in gold that goes like this: if you can't train a dog without an e-collar, you shouldn't train a dog with one.

I'll go out on a limb and guess that the e-collar needs no introduction. Some of you will be die-hard e-collar users and some of you will be adamantly opposed to its use. A certain percentage of you are undecided but think you might want to use this tool one day. Regardless of where you fall in the mix, this chapter is devoted to a proper explanation and the pros and cons of this training tool. Because it is difficult to find good information about the e-collar we will go into some detail for those of you who want to learn more about its judicious use.

Development of the E-Collar

Often called the shock collar, this training tool was, once upon a time, just that. Back when these instruments were first contrived, nearly fifty years ago at this writing, those rudimentary tools delivered a wicked jolt when used. Then, in 1969, Tri-Tronics Inc. of Tucson began manufacturing the first really reliable commercial models that had just one high level of stimulation. No question that dogs had to be mentally tough to take the pressure in this punishment form of training.

Times have changed drastically but the stigma that developed back in the early collar days still remains with a significant percentage of the population. Indeed, the very mention of this tool evokes all sorts of unpleasant mental images for lots of folks. Today many people still regard it as a cruel and crude implement for dog training. However, there are virtually no similarities between today's e-collars and yesteryear's dinosaurs. Also, the training methods that have evolved along with the modern e-collar features have catapulted into the twenty-first century as well. Today's successful e-collar trainers emphasize fundamentals of how dogs learn and employ this knowledge within a working system of teaching, reinforcement, performance, and praise—not the harsh punishment-only training of days gone by.

In the early to mid-eighties, variable intensity features became available on the transmitter, which proved invaluable toward training dogs of all temperaments. Since then, modern trainers have developed methods that produce highly motivated and stylish dogs. Today's trainers have the ability to use the e-collar to mold and shape learned behaviors into reliable, consistent performances. Variable intensity has allowed trainers to use the e-collar like an invisible long lead to gently remind their dogs that they can always reach them, thus eliminating the ten-foot dogs that only obey when they are within the distance of a conventional leash. Eventually, the e-collar can be phased out of training as the dog becomes reliable off-lead.

However, make no mistake. The e-collar is only as useful and effective as the person operating the transmitter. This tool can be misused and abused, and just one instance is too many. If you are hot tempered, find another method. If you have intentions of trying to shortcut your training with this tool, choose another way. Shortcutting with any method only invites problems that are generally compounded when the e-collar is brought into the picture.

Fundamentals

Basically, the e-collar consists of two parts: a collar (receiver) that is placed on the dog's neck, and a transmitter that is held by the trainer and is used to send a signal of "stimulation" to the dog when necessary. The primary advantages of e-collar use include the "invisible leash" premise as well as the ability to deliver instantaneous correction or motivation for any behavior, independent of the distance between dog and handler. (Actual distance is governed by the limitations of any specific e-collar model.)

A multitude of features are available on today's e-collars to accentuate preferences of different trainers. For example, some units come with a nick, or momentary (extremely brief), factory-set stimulation and continuous (up to eight seconds, depending on the model) stimulation modes. Models are available for single and multidog use.

Most units have a wide variation of levels of intensity to choose from. Many models have this option available on the transmitter while some have intensity modes that must be changed on the collar itself. The lowest levels, when touched by a human, resemble a tingling effect, perhaps compared to something less than static electricity when one crosses a carpet, or discomfort less than a mosquito bite. It is amazing how many dogs respond to these low levels, therefore never needing a more uncomfortable higher level except in cases of extreme behaviors such as car chasing.

Also, some models have a tone, buzz, or vibration feature that can be used to deliver praise, warning, or to signal a desired response without ever using electrical stimulation. Response to audio mode must be conditioned with each dog. Many possibilities are available with this option, but only one can be used effectively. For instance, when the tone is used for praise, a trainer can communicate "Good dog" by applying this audio mode up to whatever distance the unit will reach. Dogs could be praised from a few hundred yards up to a mile away. Conversely, the tone used as a warning would clue dogs that without immediate compliance, stimulation will follow; this is a means of obtaining a behavior or action without using actual stimulation and is avoidance training.

An example of using the audio feature for a desired response is for recall. This is used in many law enforcement departments that have canine units since it enables officers to recall their dogs with a tone heard only by the dog. In this manner the officers don't have to reveal their position when in dangerous situations. Recall is helpful to many companion dog owners who want to be able to communicate with their dogs at a distance without hollering or blowing a whistle.

Applications

There are a number of ways to use the e-collar in training. The oldest method is to apply stimulation strictly as punishment. However, contrary to popular consensus, the majority of successful trainers have long recognized the pitfalls of strict punishment training. Innovative trainer Rex Carr said of punishment back in the 1960s, "Punishment does not represent the most constructive form of control and guidance. Individuals are more apt to learn by positive encouragement and direction based on love and understanding" (Personal correspondence with author).

However, it should be noted that still today certain situations exist where old-fashioned punishment training is applicable. Chasing cars and running deer/fast game are two examples of bad habits that can jeopardize your dog's life. In instances like these, dogs often require higher levels of intensity to counteract the obvious enjoyment they experience in their indiscretions. With proper use, the e-collar has the capability to help shape new responses.

Another method is by compulsion in using the e-collar to teach desired behaviors. Some trainers have applied this method with success. However, many trainers feel that the presence of this compulsion can impede learning and mental development, and that many dogs emerge from training with reduced self-esteem, a quality never desired by the conscientious trainer. This method may be used successfully by some professionals but should probably be discarded as an option by the novice.

By far the most common and arguably most popular method used today is teaching each dog a set of rules that he must live by and then reinforcing those rules with minimum stimulation applied with the e-collar to solidify results. In other words, teach any command or action by conventional means and then reinforce with the e-collar. This approach applies throughout the learning chains, beginning with citizenship and obedience, continuing into gun dog and hunt test behaviors, all the way through advanced field trial work for those who desire this challenge.

With this method, dogs are "conditioned" to the e-collar so that they are familiar with it during training. Taught commands are reinforced with low-level intensity. When infractions occur during actual work, the trainer has the option of using a conventional correction—although this will result in a delay of delivery of the correction—or using an e-collar stimulation using either direct or indirect pressure that produces immediate correction and a greater likelihood of comprehension of the lesson.

An example of using direct pressure with an e-collar correction in the real world would be the dog that ignores his owner and keeps chasing a rabbit toward the highway where a car could injure or kill him. The owner gives a "No" immediately after the disobeyed command with an e-collar stimulation, which would be direct pressure, and a repeat of the here or come command. Likewise, direct pressure to correct a dog for jumping up on people would be to apply a stimulation while the dog is in the act of jumping, while in contrast indirect pressure would result when the dog jumps up and the trainer commands "Sit" with a nick. Thus, the correction comes with the sit command, but this is employed to stop the dog from the act of jumping. Consistent use of this method will quickly bring the jumping-up problem under control. (Note: The term "indirect pressure" is not recognized by the scientific dog behavioral community but is recognized by active dog trainers because of the effectiveness in its application.)

Even within this method there are variations to usage. Some trainers prefer to use low-level continuous stimulation until a command is carried through, while others nick to start compliance and let up as soon as the dog begins to perform the command or action. Still others will use a tap-tap of the nick feature or a manual tap for a nick in the continuous feature, tapping for as long as necessary.

Because of the importance of the timing of corrections when undesirable behaviors occur, overall training results can usually be relatively quickly achieved. In today's fast-paced world this is an important factor because many people don't have time to do anything in slower, old-fashioned methods—or they don't make the time. Also, people want instant drive-through quality results. Indeed, the option of using an e-collar to train a dog or correct unwanted behaviors may mean the difference between sculpting a well-mannered dog in a reasonable amount of time instead of giving away the family pet that has grown into a wild, unruly hooligan.

Again, it is important to remember that the e-collar is just a tool. It is inanimate. It is only as effective—or as detrimental—as the person using it. Like any training tool, the e-collar can be used successfully but can also be abused.

Allow me to repeat that golden rule we started this chapter with: if you can't train a dog without an e-collar, you shouldn't train a dog with one. The ramifications of this statement go far beyond the words themselves. What this means is that for anyone to achieve success when training a dog with an e-collar, the individual must first understand training fundamentals and the basics of how dogs learn, and then must know how to use that information and methodology to actually train a dog without the aid of an e-collar.

Without question, use of the e-collar should be judiciously applied in a fair, consistent manner. The e-collar can be of great help to trainers aspiring to take their dogs from basic citizenship levels on to well-trained hunting dogs and even up through advanced field trial work. This tool can assist folks who need to be able to control their dogs from a distance, and today's models give a variety of options and features to complement virtually any training method. Sound e-collar methods are largely used in the competitive, advanced world of field trial sport with much success.

Using the e-collar strictly as a punishment tool is largely a thing of the past. Today's modern e-collar trainers advocate sound use of this tool to help accentuate each dog's abilities. From high working levels to basic obedience, emphasis is put on placing the responsibilities of each dog's actions on his own shoulders while ultimately phasing out the use of the e-collar, thus producing long-term, consistent results and a happy working companion.

Thoughts on Application

Allow me the opportunity to explain why you should take the time to properly introduce your dog to the e-collar if you are bound and determined to use one in training, even if you are only going to use it for something like trash breaking your dog from off game. There is a fundamental flaw with the idea of strapping an e-collar on the dog and pressing the button with no preparation for your dog. You are placing your dog in a position to deal with something he's never experienced before, and chances are you are compounding the issue by using a relatively high level of intensity.

If the very first stimulation your dog receives occurs when he is out hunting—in other words your dog's out there cruising along, doing something he is beginning to love—when all of a sudden, *wham*! The dog gets jolted out of the blue in a way never before experienced. The dog likely will not even begin to understand what is happening. Walk in your dog's paws and try to imagine what he is thinking and feeling.

Your dog is likely to respond in one of several ways. Either the dog will try to shrug it off and continue what he was doing, or he will freeze in place, afraid to move, or the dog will quit what he is doing and come in, or he will bolt and run away from this awful thing he doesn't understand, or the dog will quit the behavior he was stimulated for and continue on.

Obviously, most of these reactions are not at all acceptable. In the first instance the dog will eventually learn to run through the e-collar stimulation, rendering it useless for further training. In the next the dog will withdraw and you'll have difficulty training him, while in addition you may have to go and get the dog when he freezes. In the third example, should your dog quit, he may refuse to go back out and hunt. In the fourth, your dog could become lost or could run into danger such as the front of an eighteen-wheeler on a road somewhere.

Because of the possibility of any of these negative repercussions, you should commit the time to properly introduce your dog to all that the e-collar means and stands for in his life if you are going to use one. This is called conditioning a dog to the e-collar, and yes it is time consuming. As far as I am concerned there is no other way. Conditioning is the process of establishing a set of guidelines between you and your dog, using the dog's foundation of simple obedience commands to not only introduce the e-collar but also to teach proper responses to the e-collar and how to ultimately avoid its use.

Every dog should be accustomed to the feel of the inactive e-collar for some time before the real thing is introduced. You can accomplish this by placing the e-collar on your dog before training sessions, before walks, before feeding. Always use the same mannerisms during this phase that you plan to use once you start using an activated e-collar. Be sure to place it properly on your dog—high on his neck behind the ears and snug but not too tight—as an improperly fitted e-collar will not function correctly, if at all.

Once you have introduced the dummy (inactive) e-collar, and you've done your homework with obedience, your dog is at a point where he handles well for you regarding obedience, he understands you, and he knows that you will be fair with him. One more thing you must do before you begin any introduction of the e-collar with your dog is that you must become familiar with its use before you try the real thing. Just as a medical resident will practice suturing an orange before suturing a real, live, breathing human being on the operating table, so should you practice handling the transmitter and pressing the buttons so that you know which ones are which and how to make them work before you try them on your dog.

A few parting comments. Never, but never, strap an e-collar on a dog in anger and then start pressing the button to get even with him for something the dog did that embarrassed you in the field, or worse. If you are prone to do this you might be better off without a dog, but in any event you certainly don't need an e-collar. And strive to phase the e-collar out of your dog's training as he becomes reliable in his work.

CHAPTER
TWENTY-FIVE

Adding Skills

A t this point you should have your puppy well started. He will most likely have been introduced to the type of game that will be a prominent factor in the rest of his working life. If your dog is a pointer, a hound, or beagle you may have used a fishing pole with a bird wing or a coon tail or piece of hide attached to pique his interest and wake up his senses. You may even have your bird dog pup pointing already or your hound puppy treeing already or your beagle puppy running tracks (as we've seen, some folks prefer to start these things early and others wait until later in the training process). Retriever puppies should be retrieving like gangbusters already, and chances are you've introduced your own puppy to birds, unless you are using the method that keeps feathers out of the equation until other skills are honed. If you have a versatile breed, you may already have your dog doing all of these things, or your dachshund or terrier may be retrieving or treeing or running through little makeshift training tunnels in the backyard.

Now it is time to begin introducing skills that will accentuate the performance of your soon to be hunting companion. Of utmost importance to the bird dog or coonhound is the buildup of confidence to range out and hunt boldly. This quality—confidence—is also a significant part of the retriever's work but is enhanced and encouraged in somewhat different ways in his training, as he learns to believe in his eyesight for birds he's seen fall, and to believe in you when sent on blind retrieves. However, first and foremost, unless you have a hound or an earth dog, there is a training issue that you must honestly confront at this time and make an educated, informed opinion on how you want to proceed. Please read on.

The Trained Retrieve—Yes or No?

If your dog will be required to retrieve in his working life, you must decide whether you want to "force fetch" the dog. Force fetch is also known by other names such as "force training" and the "trained retrieve." It is a process or program of orderly steps and drills that is supposed to take away any "option" your dog may think he has to perform with regard to the retrieve.

In simple terms, force fetch is a procedure that teaches your dog he must retrieve on command. Because during the procedure the owner inflicts at least a small amount of pain in getting the point across to the dog that he must fetch when told to do so, no ifs, ands, or buts about it, many folks develop an immediate aversion to the process. Therefore, it is helpful to understand your options and what those options mean.

Force fetch first received attention way back in the 1800s so it has been around for a long time. Over generations of dog training, trainers in favor of force fetch have become adamant about their position and the reasons why they do what they do, and those opposed have become equally solidified in their own beliefs.

Force training has become an accepted practice to teach a retrieving dog (this can be any breed of dog—not just retrievers) that when told to retrieve he must do so. It is not acceptable for the dog to retrieve when he feels like it and to shirk the duty when he does not. This training procedure sometimes becomes a battle of wills, but the trainer must ultimately win. Whether it actually gets to this point is largely a matter of genetics regarding the degree of stubbornness in the dog and the manner of application by the trainer. Force fetch is viewed by some as just a cog in the wheel, however, in the much larger picture of training; it is used to solidify the trainer's dominance over the pupil and to show the student that when pressure is applied, there is always a way out—by compliance.

What about dogs that are not force fetched? Is it possible for them to be reliable retrievers in the field? This is the basis for the argument that is constantly waged between those that force fetch and those that don't. Some say yes. Others say no. But it is not nearly as simple as all that.

Any number of retrieving dogs have been trained over the years to go out and retrieve objects—or birds or rabbits—and then return to their handler and deliver that object to hand, without the addition of the force fetch procedure to their training program. Contrary to what you may read, many of them have been quite good at their jobs and have earned performance titles and qualified All-Age status, not to mention accolades in the duck blind or in the field. How can this be? These dogs have been taught "order" in the retrieve process.

Before you begin with either process, be prepared to praise your dog for correct behavior each time he makes an improvement. Don't plan on drudgery or your dog's performance will reflect the same. Be sharp and use exceptionally good timing with each step, each command, and each communication of "good dog" as your dog grasps more pieces of the procedure.

The orderly retrieve process—as I call it—involves a sequence of steps:

1. The dog is taught obedience. This is mandatory because proper response to obedience commands and subsequent respect for the trainer is necessary to the success of these next steps.
2. The retriever is taught to hold an object in his mouth while sitting. Usually this begins with a dowel or other object easy to manage. The dog should not mouth or roll the dowel in any way.
3. Once the dog will hold the dowel properly, he is taught to "Drop" or "Give" and release it to your hand.
4. When the dog will sit and hold for several minutes, he is taught to walk at heel and hold the object. This usually takes some doing. Many a dog will be a champ at sitting and holding an object, but when the time comes to take that first step and actually get in motion, the dog spits out the dowel. Plenty of patience is necessary in putting the dowel back in the dog's mouth and commanding "Hold."
5. When the dog has learned to walk and hold an object, the dog is placed on an extended sit not far from the handler—say five or ten feet—and then given the here command. This works on the delivery process because now the dog is coming to you.
6. The dog is taught to sit in a front finish (in front of and facing you) and to deliver the object.
7. The dog is taught a complete finish: to deliver to you and then to assume a heel position by your side.

8. These steps are repeated with a few different objects, such as a canvas bumper, a rubber knobby bumper, and finally a fresh, dead bird that is in good shape with no blood.
9. The extended sit is done at longer distances to simulate the delivery of a retrieve. Hunting retrieves usually cover a distance and this step simulates that.
10. Be animated. Let your dog know that you're pleased with his advancement and success.

The force fetch procedure actually involves many of the same steps just described, but adds several additional measures.

1. Once the dog learns to hold an object he is taught to open his mouth for that object and "reach" for it. An ear pinch causes enough discomfort or pain that the dog will open his mouth in protest to the ear pinch itself. "Fetch" is said immediately and the object is put in the dog's mouth. The most popular methods for this step are the ear pinch or the toe hitch, but the ear is easier to fall back on as a reminder in the field. It usually doesn't take many applications before the dog learns that when presented with the object and told to "Fetch" he can avoid the ear pinch by reaching for the object.
2. Be certain to convey "good dog" the exact instant the dog reaches for the bumper or dowel. You want him to know exactly what you want, and how pleased you are when he complies.
3. The object is gradually lowered to the ground where the dog has to make more of an effort to reach down to get it.
4. The object is placed on the ground—but this usually presents quite a mental obstacle for most dogs as they won't reach for and then pick up something off the ground even though they've been grabbing it from your hand. So, it helps to keep your hand on one end of the dowel the first several times it is placed on or near the ground.
5. The object can be picked up off the ground without the presence of your hand on one end.
6. The object is placed several feet in front of the dog, and in order to fetch the dog must take several steps to the object and then pick it up. This is often another mental obstacle for the dog.
7. The object is placed as much as fifteen to twenty feet out and the dog will go to it, pick it up, and return to deliver it to you.
8. This process is done with other objects.

9. Several additional fetch-type drills are employed to solidify response to the fetch command, such as "Fetch—No fetch" where several bumpers are placed on the ground and the dog is walked at heel and commanded to fetch some of the bumpers while leaving others alone. He learns not to grab everything in sight, but to retrieve when told to do so.
10. The dog is "forced to a pile" of bumpers about twenty feet out. At this point some trainers will use additional means of stimulation, such as the heeling stick or the e-collar, or both, but must have used these things through all the steps.

All steps in your chosen approach to the retrieve must be thoroughly completed to end up with a happy, confident dog that is stylish in his work. If you elect to begin the force fetch procedure you must commit to finishing it completely. If you stop partway through the process you could end up with a dog that might retrieve every time you tell him to do so but the dog won't be happy about it; his retrieve will not be pleasing to the eye.

Whether you are using the orderly retriever process or the force fetch procedure, these steps should not be taken in a humdrum fashion that will quickly become boring to most all dogs. Begin with sessions that are just a few minutes long at a time. Be sure to use praise for good performance. Break up sessions with a little lighthearted fun such as a play retrieve or happy bumper, but when doing so keep it just that. Don't counter your action by fussing at your dog for doing something wrong during the play retrieve. He doesn't know all the accepted steps to the retrieve yet. And in either case, do not subscribe to the "hell week" theory that you may have heard about elsewhere—that of completing the force fetch in just one week—as very little good can come of rushing your dog through this process. Yes, advance in an orderly fashion, but don't rush your dog too fast on these steps and do not skip any steps, as this could cause confusion and you will likely experience the fallout most definitely later on at some point in your dog's training.

Nowadays you hear that without force fetch, no dog will reach his full potential. You hear that if your dog is not force trained there will be days when he will refuse to do his job, either because he just doesn't feel like it right then, or because it's too cold out, or he's tired, or there is ice on the water. Don't get me wrong, these things can happen, and do happen with some dogs. But, what you often don't hear and are not told during these arguments for and against force fetch is that these things are going to crop up with certain dogs even if they have been force fetched, but with the force fetch procedure you have a means to fall back on to communicate and remind your dog that he must retrieve for you. By using whatever measure you employed during force fetch you tell your dog he must go and get that bird—but then the weight is on his shoulders to do so or not.

In a perfect world, there are hunting instances where some dogs, no matter how thoroughly they've been trained, may refuse, no matter what you do. The best example of this that I can come up with is when a dog is faced with big, intimidating water for a long retrieve. Some of them may attempt to go in, but not all of them are going to carry through. Of course that in a way is a training issue regarding big water that can sometimes be resolved with work, sometimes not. Heart and bravery and courage also come into play, and not all dogs have what it takes in that department to execute the really tough work.

Here are the brass tacks of the matter. Force fetch need not be an exercise in brutality. How quickly it is done, how thoroughly it is done, and how much pressure is used to get it done are all a matter of personal preference aside from the dog's responses and ability. But, as a general rule, in the early stages of using this procedure, some measure of discomfort is necessary to get the dog to open his mouth as the first step of actually reaching

for an object. In addition, discomfort will be necessary as the procedure progresses to "force" the dog to comply.

In contrast, with the orderly retrieve process, you must already have a dog with a high desire to retrieve. Your dog must demonstrate the desire to work for you and do as you wish. If your dog does not have either of these qualities, you are behind the eight ball from the very beginning and these steps in the retrieve process may or may not resolve the issue for you.

Proper attention to the commands "Hold" and "Drop" in the early stages of either of these procedures will be great strides in eliminating the possibility of mouth problems for many dogs. However,

Using a force fetch table for teaching soft mouth. (Author photo)

once a dog has demonstrated the desire to roll or play with birds or, worse yet, to munch on them, your chances of fixing the problem become quite complicated. You can try attacking the problem with strict "Hold" and "Drop" drills, and perhaps the "remote drop" where you teach your dog to spit out the bird while the dog is in a remote location. In this manner you can make the dog release the bird at the point of "munch" if he is destroying the bird on his way in to you. Working on a mouth problem with birds may make your dog quit retrieving, at least temporarily, if you have a non-force-fetched dog. Sometimes, the procedure of force fetch is the only chance you have to cure or contain the mouth problem.

It becomes obvious that any dog that is a candidate for the orderly retrieve process should possess a keen love for retrieving. The dog that halfheartedly retrieves one or two tennis balls or puppy bumpers and then quits is usually not a good candidate for this process and will likely need force fetch to resolve his issues.

This means that it is pretty important to cultivate the retrieve instinct from the time your puppy is a very little guy, but some pointer folks prefer not to do any retrieving at all until much later in the training process. To each his own, but when those dogs do not develop natural retrieve desire later on (they may or may not—the proverbial remains to be seen), the only option to train the retrieve at that point is to use force fetch.

All this being said, it is not my intention to imply that each dog trained through the force fetch procedure lacks the proper amount of retrieving desire to do his job well. That is often far from the truth. It is a matter of personal preference and choice of training program whether you decide to force fetch your dog for any of the reasons or combination of reasons outlined in this section.

Steadying, Advanced Obedience, Whoa Work

In training for any advanced obedience procedure, such as steadying on the retrieve, work on "Whoa," or for things such as "Go to your place," the inclusion of a pretty simple gadget can do wonders to make your communication perfectly clear to your dog on what you are teaching and expecting him to do. The place board is a valuable and inexpensive training tool that can be used in your backyard as well as out in the field.

When you are hunting, your dog may often be required to work from a platform or a designated spot. If you choose to participate later in events such as field trials or hunt tests, your retrieving dog will be expected to work from a certain line where a mat or piece of Astroturf will be used to mark the area the dogs start from. Quite simply, the use of a place board in training helps get the point across to your dog that he must stay in a certain spot, that he must work from a certain spot, or that he must go to a particular area. It also helps to introduce whoa work.

What is the purpose of a place board? This item can be used to teach basic and advanced forms of obedience in virtually any stage of training, whether simple good citizen work around the house or work on steadying in the face of short, shot fliers (shot live birds). Basically, it is using

a "place" from which the dog must learn to work. To simplify training, a place board can be set just about anywhere a session warrants. It can even be used to convey "Go to your place" when your dog is in the house.

Several different items can be used for a place board, or you can easily construct one. Raised versions work well to start with because the board is more defined to the dog. In other words, if he moves or takes a step it will usually be down from the board instead of just off the board. You can make one by using a rectangular piece of plywood that sits on a base constructed of 2 x 4 wooden pieces or PVC pipe, either of which will elevate the board from two to four inches off the ground.

Use of an elevated place board helps give a dog clearly defined boundaries for work within a training session. (Author photo)

Usually, these plywood place boards are then covered with outdoor carpeting to provide more traction for the dog. Place boards can even be
made by covering small pallets with carpeted plywood.

Generally, trainers who use place boards begin with relatively large
boards—such as 20 x 30 inch platforms—so that the dog can easily grasp
the concept of staying on the board or going to the board. A basic rule of
thumb: whatever training is required with the board will be easier for the
dog to understand with a larger platform—he'll have more room to work
with until his performance reaches a higher level. Also, an elevated place
board helps simplify beginning training even further.

Once your dog understands the principle of the place board, you
could actually remove the element of elevation and go to a lighter and
more mobile mat or carpet, or a carpeted piece of plywood with no base.
As training progresses, board size can decrease whenever this modification can help sharpen any particular training lesson, such as using a
small, square board for a sharply defined "Sit."

To begin using this gadget in training, it should be introduced with
either the sit, stand, down, or whoa command and then transferred to the
extended sit or down—otherwise known as "Stay put until told otherwise"—which then can easily be transferred to steadying drills for retrieving work. It is a relatively easy concept for the dog to grasp that in any
scenario, his world is fine until one or more of his feet leave the board in
an attempt to step down from the platform. This is precisely why an elevated board is best for initial lessons on this concept, and the board—as
mentioned—should be of sufficient size so that the dog feels comfortable
once positioned on the board's confines. Be sure to have your dog on a
training rope when you first introduce the board. You can use the same
steps for the sit command in conditioning your dog to the place board that
you have already applied in regular leash training, such as standing at the
end of a six-foot length of rope and progressing in a circle around your—
hopefully—stationary dog. This way, if he tries to get up or reposition himself, you have a means of control to put him back in place with little ado.

In training, approach the board and guide your dog into position on
its platform. Take a moment to use appropriate touch and voice reassurance so that your dog doesn't become intimidated or spooked by the
board. Chances are that you will use the board a good bit in upcoming
training and hunting situations, so you want to start off on the right
foot. Remember how your dog sometimes balks during weigh-in at the

veterinary office when he is required to step on the scale platform? This is a similar situation until the dog becomes comfortable with the routine.

Whenever a dog tries to leave his commanded sit, stand, or down and begins to dismount from the elevated board, you can apply conventional correction with the leash or a tap with your training stick to put the dog back in place, you can use low-level e-collar stimulation until he retreats to the confines of the board, you can use a combination of these methods, or you can simply reposition the dog on the board. As soon as sessions are going smoothly from this six-foot (leash length) circumference, you can gradually increase the distance between you and your dog until you are out of sight. When a dog has mastered this level of difficulty, distractions can be added, such as a child playing with a ball nearby, another working dog retrieving various objects, or a walking wing-clipped pigeon nearby.

From this point you can begin working on steadying and the line from which he should run (sometimes called "mat work"). The place board becomes a point of focus for your dog, and can actually make steadying work more trouble free. Again, at this point, an elevated board helps remove any gray areas in communication between you and your dog, regarding what is acceptable behavior and what is not allowed. A step down off the board is easily recognized by your dog, particularly with good timing of correction. This is important. By the same token, a step off or down from the board breaks the stand or whoa command.

Once steadying is learned with the place board, it can be used as a "line" during training. This lesson often will effectively remove tendencies of creeping (inching forward toward a bird when not told to retrieve) by certain dogs as they learn they must not leave the board until instructed to do so. Certain genetic lines of retrievers are more prone to creeping than others, and sometimes using the board can help to curb these tendencies from developing, or can help to instill training cures when this bad habit is already a problem. Gradually, the elevated board can be lowered from four inches to two inches to ground level. When flush with the terrain, a carpeted 20 x 30 inch piece of plywood or simply a piece of outdoor carpet or other type of mat can prove sufficient for your purposes.

Next, after steadying drills and using the board as a running line for training, the board principle can be applied to places the dog will find itself in many hunting situations. For example, these would include the transom of a boat, a dog platform in green tree-flooded timber, or a perch in a pit blind. The possibilities are endless.

The place board can also be used to solidify obedience in the house and to teach arm signals. You can teach your dog to go to his place with an elevated place board out in the open where the dog can see it. Begin work with you and the dog a short distance from the board. When you introduce this command, you have already worked on "Sit" or "Down" on the board, and possibly steadying from the board as well, and your dog is quite comfortable with it. Therefore, initially command "Go to your place" while your dog is on his familiar six-foot lead, and guide him to the board. Keep working with whatever measures necessary until your dog will readily mount the elevated board on command, then add more distance between you and your dog and the board. You can add an arm signal as you give your voice command, then remove the voice command and only use your silent signal, if desired. Eventually, you want to be able to put the dog on an extended sit at a distance from the board, with you another length of distance from the dog, and to be able to command your dog to his place from your remote location.

In this manner you will be able to tell your dog to go to his place when you are in your home once you designate what that place is. The dog's place might be a dog bed in the corner of your den, your bedroom, or the kitchen. You may need to use the board in the house to make things clear, but it will quickly be replaced with an open crate or a dog bed. You will also be able to tell your dog to go to his place whenever you are in a strange location, such as a motel room or a hunting lodge, by using that familiar board or bed.

Once a dog understands going to his place, the board can be used to even teach casting (directional signals) on a beginning baseball field configuration, chosen for its shortened baseline distances. A board is placed at each "base" and one on the pitcher's mound. Some trainers actually teach these directional commands without using bumpers at each location, but simply by using the place board as a destination for each cast until the dog becomes familiar with moving on direction. While most trainers prefer the traditional baseball casting drills (see chapter 26) with bumpers and retrieving work, this procedure may well do the trick for you to teach your dog cast and arm signals if your dog is not force fetched (that makes teaching casts relatively easy). Dogs introduced to whoa on the place board can then progress to barrel or styling beam work with smooth transition.

Place Board Construction Suggestions

You will need a 20 x 30 inch (or custom sizes for different training goals) plywood platform in a thickness of 3/4, 5/8, 1/2, or 19/32 inches. Cover the platform with outdoor carpeting for traction and use enough carpet to extend it a few inches on the underside all around. Secure with heavy-duty staples or carpet adhesive. Bases can be constructed of PVC pipe (lighter and stays white longer without paint) in 1/12-inch, or smaller, pipe, with pipe cement to secure your piping. Then use U-clamps—one to a side—to secure the PVC-pipe base to the platform. Or you could construct a base from 2 x 4s secured to the plywood with wood screws and with 3-inch wood screws in the ends of the 2 x 4 base for added stability. You could also use paling materials (as for deck construction) secured with drywall screws with 6-inch gaps on the opposite ends for places to grab and pick up the board. Wood bases are usually painted and sealed with something like oil-based deck enamel to protect and keep out moisture. Small pallets can also be used; secure a carpeted section of plywood to the top, seal, and paint.

Flat place boards include carpeted and sized plywood, carpet runners with rubber backs, rubber mats, or Astroturf.

Gunfire

Hopefully your puppy has been properly introduced to gunfire with no repercussions and he now thinks loud noises are part of life and that gunfire means good things—and these things are only going to become more significant as the dog's training and hunting career commence in earnest.

That being said, arguably one of the most serious problems a hunting dog can face is sensitivity to gunfire. Much has been written on how to prevent this potential disaster from occurring, but what—if anything—can be done to cure gun shyness, to fix the dog that's already got it? There are many manifestations of this problem, ranging from a mild to a severe affliction.

Another question would be—what are some of the ways dogs can become gun shy? One of the most common is when an overanxious owner of a young dog takes him hunting before the owner has done much if any preparatory work with the dog, and then sticks the pup in the corner of a cramped blind with three gunners surrounding him and firing repeatedly over his head—this is the dog's introduction to gunfire. Or, a young hound is happily treeing away, not tied or anything, never having been fired around prior to this, and someone starts shooting .22 longs at a coon and missing repeatedly, all the while scaring the fire out of the dog. And since the dog hasn't been tied, he takes off to boot.

While there are varying schools of thought on whether this problem is genetically rooted in a given dog or whether it is man-made, it could be one or both theories working together that produce the problem. From the genetic standpoint, a timid streak and sensitivity to all noise is often prevalent, yet one could argue that this still would be affected by outside influences and stimuli by man—by you or someone else careless about loud noise around a young dog.

The mildly gun-shy dog will noticeably flinch and may cower every time a gun discharges anywhere nearby. This dog may also show some sensitivity to loud noises. However, in contrast, the serious case shows so much fear that he attempts flight—bolting, running away, trying to hide, or even digging a hole—essentially, any action that says, "Get me outta here!"

You may even need to visit a professional trainer for this one. Basically, when a trainer assesses a dog with this problem, there are a few serious factors to consider. What is the overall potential for the dog in question? Does the dog possess intelligence and willingness to learn? If he will be a retrieving dog, what is his retrieve drive, or the level of his intensity to retrieve? Otherwise, what is the dog's overall prey drive toward his game, such as rabbits, raccoon, bear, or cougar? This is a vital factor. Finally—and this one is possibly most important—how birdy or gamey is the dog?

Of course part of the cure is also part of the procedure for prevention. Professional trainers and their dogs have a different situation because, in the case of bird dogs and retrievers at least, the dogs quite simply get used to riding on the truck and hearing gunfire from a distance all day long.

Even so, shooting should be first introduced with a cap pistol and then a .22 blank pistol fired from a distance, gradually worked in closer and closer until it is being fired in the immediate proximity of the dog. This pistol should be replaced with a shotgun or a rifle, depending on your type of hunting, using the same steps. An advantage of retrieving dogs in overcoming this problem is that dead birds, fliers, or live wing-

Gun-shy work with a .22 pistol. (Author photo)

clipped pigeons can be used for each retrieve while conditioning the dog to the gun. With a hound, the excitement of treeing, which can be compounded even further when other dogs are present, and being able to get his mouth on the game he is so crazy about helps a great deal, but .22 shorts or CBs (less noise) should be used and the dog should be restrained during shooting until the game comes down.

Many times simply a good and thorough socialization and constant exposure to distant noise can help break through the initial fear that the gun-shy dog exhibits. Then, the gradual introduction of gunfire to the retrieve process or hunting scene from a distance and with a pistol, and graduating to the same steps with a shotgun—and use of birds or game—is perhaps all that is required.

Sometimes severe cases need additional methods. One of the harsh old-timer cures was to withhold food until a dog would eat with gunfire in close proximity. If you work on this problem you will note that most dogs that fear gunfire will refuse to eat if a gun is discharged just prior to feeding. Thus, this old method was to fire a gun, place the food down, give the dog just a few minutes to start eating, and if he didn't eat, then remove the food source until the following day, repeating this procedure for as many successive days as necessary. Again, this is a harsh method.

A variation of this method, however, that works well is to use the feeding time for training and conditioning of this problem, but to do it in a more humane way. However, it takes more time. Just prior to feeding your dog, make lots of noise, such as the loud banging of heavy metal feed pans. Once the dog is accustomed to this activity and will eat his dinner, you can take a cap pistol and fire it from a distance prior to each meal. The pistol is worked closer until it is being fired nearby while the dog eats without reservation. Then the shotgun replaces the pistol in the same progression of steps. An addition to this procedure is to use a sound system in the vicinity of the kennel with noise conditioning tapes that contain claps of thunder and gunshots blended with other soothing sounds.

Once your gun-shy dog can tolerate extreme levels of noise and subsequent gunfire during feeding, you can begin the gun introduction process in the field or woods. With patience and time, many dogs can be cured in this manner.

More extreme cases can be much more difficult to overcome. Most trainers agree that without relatively high levels of retrieve intensity and birdiness or gaminess, the situation can be pretty bleak. Dogs with an extreme desire and love of feathers or fur will eventually work to overcome their fear of interfering noise in order to complete their job.

Quartering and Upland Hunting

The art of quartering, whether we are talking about a pointing breed or a flushing breed or an HPR or a retriever, is beautiful to watch as the dogs learn to successfully work birds. It also leaves many trainers scratching their head over how to go about working on this skill with their dog.

The act of working and quartering in front of the hunter has far more to do with all the skills and experience necessary to work those birds—birds that may be inclined to sneak away or otherwise disappear—than it does the actual movement back and forth within gun range for the hunter. This has been put quite succinctly by Julie Knutson of Gunclub Labradors in a letter to the author, as follows:

> Upland hunting requires that a dog understand the nature of birds. The schooled upland dog must have learned to use its nose, eyes, hearing and the other dog "senses" that make the good hunters aware of bird activity and presence. Acquisition of these skills is not acquired by directing a dog's movement through a field. These skills are acquired by exposing the upland dog to the places in which birds live, while the birds are actually

present. A dog will learn how to use the wind to locate the most likely places birds may reside. A dog will learn how to interpret the smells and the sounds it is taking in and through experience, will act upon increasingly seasoned interpretations; learning to avoid being mislead or to "guess wrong," and to actually locate the birds.

To be able to properly develop the bold hunting skills of quartering in the dog so that he acquires confidence about where to look for birds and how to work the wind—so that he learns what birds do out in the field or woods and how to use those activities to produce those birds—requires a certain amount of uncontrolled freedom. This is why, many chapters ago, I stressed not teaching controlled heeling to any young hunting prospects that would be required to quarter later on or for hounds that would be expected to bust into the woods and big country to strike, track, and trail their game. Just like you need to put the hound in the woods so that he can gain the real-time experience necessary to become a top hound, so must you put the young bird dog in the field so that he can learn about birds—and their habits—from the birds.

Spending formative time out in the field after you first get your puppy and giving your young dog freedom to range, hunt, and explore without constantly putting the moves of control on him, can be one of your most valuable investments of time with your dog. By taking your dog for walks out to the field and allowing him to explore these areas several times a week, the two of you are developing and solidifying a bond and the dog is learning valuable things out there about scent and bird activity that you cannot see. Leave him alone to learn those lessons. However, your puppy or young dog must know to come when you call, whether you are around the house or in the field, and when it is truly necessary to call the dog, such as if he takes after an ill-chased bird—one he cannot recover, one that you cannot shoot, or one that places him in danger such as along a road—or to keep him away from places he's not allowed to go, you can give the subtle control necessary to mold him into an excellent hunter and quartering dog without using pressure, force, and complicated training techniques. You'll give him his freedom to learn to work in front of you, but subtly work "Here" into the session to control his range.

Tracking for Versatile Dogs

Simple tracking lessons can jump-start the tracking instinct of virtually any dog, but they are particularly useful for versatile breeds that will be required to track at times when hunting, or for hounds or beagles. These same steps can be used to teach Labs and other dog to take blood trails to find wounded game, such as deer.

Working in the cool hours of morning or evening, exercise your dog for several minutes and then put him in the house, dog box, or somewhere out of sight. You should begin in a relatively flat field with short cover. Take a pole, such as a cane fishing pole (you may have used one with your puppy when he was seven or eight weeks old to spark his interest in a bird or game), and attach wings from a bird such as a pheasant, or a coon tail, or a partial hide from a bear or cougar, or even a strong commercial scent, and "lay a short track" by dragging it in the grass in a straight line for about forty to sixty yards. Leave a few feathers or bit of fur at the beginning of the track and perhaps in a few places along the way, and put a bird (a quail or chukar won't show up as readily by sight at the track's beginning if the dog is visually searching for something in the field) or reward, such as fur, at the end of the track. Bring your dog out and put a checkcord on his collar (which the dog is accustomed to, of course), bring him to the start of the track where the feathers or fur is, and get him excited. Give the dog a command that you will use when hunting, such as "Hunt dead" or "Find it" or "Get your track," and then walk slowly with the dog to make sure he gets the idea he is following the scent. Use a low, normal voice when talking to your dog once he

Checkcord work. (Author photo)

gets the scent, not a continued excitable voice. Praise your dog when he gets to the end of the track and finds the bird or the fur.

Most dogs quickly catch on to this game. After just a few short tracks like this you can complicate things by lengthening the track to one hundred yards or more and add terrain and higher cover and perhaps changes of cover and terrain. However, as soon as your dog is tracking well, quit these contrived lessons, for you can overtrain just as you can overtrain any aspect of your dog's learning process.

Skills for Hounds, Beagles, Terriers, and Dachshunds

Besides nurturing the instincts in trailing and treeing with your young dog or running tracks of your chosen appropriate game, you should instill a sense of manners that you can count on once you get to the woods or the field in earnest. Having a dog that will come when called by either voice or whistle (or hunting horn) will be not only a pleasure, but can help remedy many training problems and may save your dog's life. Do you want to hunt a dog that gets out there on a bad night when no game is moving but won't come back in for any reason until he gets good and ready—and you've got to get to work at 7 a.m.? What about the dog headed for posted land where he might be shot or toward a busy highway where he could get killed?

For some reason it is often said that these breeds of dogs must not be "tampered with" or they will lose their drive to an extent. If you do your job properly, nothing could be farther from the truth, but you will have a dog that you can manage and control when necessary.

Your young dog should come when called in simple situations by now if you've done your homework while he was a little puppy. Here is how to build on those lessons: Put your dog on a rope so that you can control him. Wear gloves to protect your hands from rope burn. Give the command for an extended sit (yes, you will need to teach this to your dog if you haven't already) in your backyard or other convenient training area and call him by voice or whistle or both. If your dog does not come immediately, give a brief tug on the rope and use the "No" "Here" sequence we visited in chapter 22. Your dog need not be e-collar trained, but if he is you can eventually slip in a well-timed nick with the e-collar in the same sequence. Your dog must have a working knowledge of "Here" before beginning this procedure. Patience and repetition are key components of success.

Once you can place your dog on an extended sit at different lengths and he will reliably come when called, add distractions that will tempt the dog to disobey and then insist that he obeys. The next step is to move to other locations to add the distraction of strange environments and surroundings with different sights and smells. By increasing the distance of recall, along with variation of surroundings and the addition of distractions—including other dogs, animals, people, and things—you will build the reliability of your dog's response so that when he is recalled under extreme distraction he is more likely to comply. If not, then you have to continue this work in the field or in the woods until your dog understands that this command is something that must be adhered to no matter what he is otherwise doing. Use common sense, of course, and you will succeed without interfering with any hunt or prey drive.

These steps are important because dogs do not readily understand the concept of "generalization" and therefore must be trained to do the same thing in several different locations and with increased levels of distractions until they learn what is accepted behavior or response to any given command. This principle of instilling different places and distractions applies to all commands throughout dog training so that the dog becomes consistent and reliable without the aid of training tools.

CHAPTER
TWENTY-SIX

Advanced Training

Retrievers

Retrievers require more advanced training work than just about any other breed of gundog from the standpoint of handler/dog teamwork as opposed to putting the bird dog in the field or the hound in the woods for advancement. Many hunters are well satisfied with a retriever that is steady to shot until commanded to go and get birds he sees fall and bring them back and deliver to hand. However, other hunters need retrievers that can mark and remember several birds at once. They also need dogs that will "handle" and take a line, or direction, out after a bird they have not seen fall, then stop on a whistle and take hand signals to the area of the bird. This training is time consuming and can be a bit technical, but is not overly difficult to do. The following is an outline of the principle components of handling. Many bird dog and HPR breeds can also learn how to do advanced retrieving work.

Multiple Retrieves

When your puppy was young, you may have started throwing two bumpers at the same time to help develop your puppy's memory. You can throw two bumpers by tossing the second one after the first one hits the ground and your puppy has had a chance to see it fall, or you can introduce the concept of "bird in the face" by tossing out another bumper while the dog is in the process of returning with a retrieve. This is an excellent method of introducing another retrieve to the equation. When you first begin the lesson of "memory" bird retrieves (any birds besides the last bird down), you may need to send your dog quickly for it and then work on his line manners (remaining staunch or still) once he is going for the memory bird(s) with confidence. When you use helpers in the field they can holler "Hey, hey" to get your dog's attention again just before you send him out, or they can holler when he is en route if it looks like the dog is losing momentum. The help tactics should be phased out as soon as possible.

Casting Levels

Many young dogs are receptive to the introduction of *fun casting* into their daily games. Once your puppy knows the extended sit, you can hand toss a bumper to the left or the right and let him go and get it. Keep these games unstructured, with no pressure. If your puppy shows adeptness for this exercise, start working the verbal terms "Over" (arm to the side) or "Back" (arm upraised for direction to a bumper behind the dog) into the scheme of things. Many puppies can learn about casting in this manner, and when more formal casting is begun an understanding of the maneuvers required is already somewhat in place.

Three-handed casting is rather easily introduced on the heels of the force fetch procedure, because the act to fetch is so ingrained at this time. If you have elected not to use the force fetch procedure, you can use the place board method outlined in chapter 25, or you can work on the basis of your dog's natural retrieving ability. Also, any puppies who have had the benefit of fun casting in months prior to this time will respond quite well to the new game of learning and combining casts in one drill, called "three-handed" casting. Envision a baseball diamond. You will put your dog on the pitcher's mound and you will stand at home plate and cast your dog "over" to the right (first base) or "back" (second base—directly behind the dog) or over to the left (third base). (See diagram, page 307.)

For the handling gun dog, casting will be an important part of training and hunting once this skill is taught. Therefore, it is important to instill a positive attitude toward casting and handling, right now, at this time of introduction. Be patient and refrain from any excessive use of pressure or negative reinforcement. Make the three-handed casting procedure as positive as you possibly can.

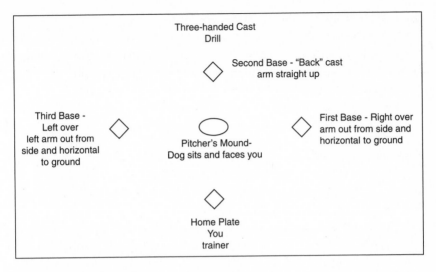

Three-handed Cast
Drill

Second Base - "Back" cast
arm straight up

Third Base -
Left over
left arm out from
side and horizontal
to ground

Pitcher's Mound-
Dog sits and faces you

First Base - Right over
arm out from side and
horizontal to ground

Home Plate
You
trainer

Diagram for simple casting.

Remember the indirect pressure we discussed in chapter 24? It can be of infinite use in training, with or without the e-collar, and casting is as good an example as any for the use of indirect pressure—use "No" and "Sit" or sit whistle (one short whistle blast) when the dog heads for an incorrect bumper, put him back in place, and then resume work on the cast you just requested. The pressure of correction (verbal "No" or slight e-collar bump in conjunction with "No") occurs in conjunction with the sit command or sit whistle—which should be a strongly ingrained command by now—instead of occurring when the dog is well into the wrong cast.

Patience is the key at this point. Use a minimum of pressure and use it as a last resort for most dogs. Concentrate on teaching and on repetition. Three-handed casting is a vital place in training to build a good attitude toward the important components of handling.

Mini-T is an extension of three-handed casting that requires that while you again stand at home plate, your dog is now either at your side or at a front finish instead of being out at the pitcher's mound. With the two of you on home plate you will send the dog from your side to the "back" pile located at second base, and the "stopping" point for the whistle will be the pitcher's mound where the dog was just casting from when he performed the three-handed casting drill. Distance and length should not be an issue for this exercise; keep things short. You should strive to teach your dog the components of putting the previous lessons together with some action and momentum. Go-stop-cast. Those are the elements of the Mini-T. With patience and proper teaching, insist that your dog learn this T properly and thoroughly, and work on a good attitude from your dog as well. This is important, and a good attitude comes from within each of us as trainers. (See diagram.)

Finally you reach the *Double T* with your dog, yet another extension of what you've done thus far. In the Double T you will be putting together everything that your dog has learned while adding distance and difficulty. You will probably start it with your dog on a long rope so you will need a pair of gloves to protect your hands. Work on your "back" pile, by starting fairly close, 20 yards, and then back up to 50 or 60 yards and finally your full distance. Wear gloves so that when you stop your dog at either of his initial two stopping points you can reinforce

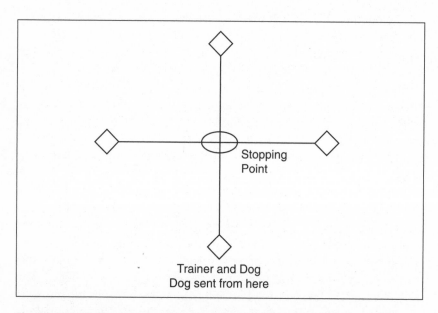

The Mini-T Drill: The same configuration as three-handed casting, except that both the dog and handler are on home plate and the dog is sent from home plate. The pitcher's mound is used as a stopping point by whistle.

the "Sit" with your rope and make sure that the dog stops and sits, if necessary.

Note that when you work on the "Sit" at these stopping points, a flare could develop from your dog, where he deviates from a straight line

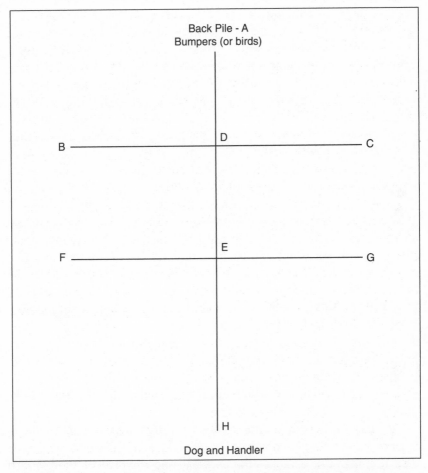

The Double T Drill: The longer cast is often taught first, where the dog and handler begin at E and the dog is sent to the back pile, A, and then right over to C, and then left over to B, while stopping at D. Next, the handler and dog back up to H and use E as the stopping point for cast overs to G and F, with a back cast to A. Sometimes a handler will send the dog from H to A with no stopping to prevent the tendency in the dog to anticipate a whistle stop by "popping"—stopping when the handler doesn't whistle.

to the second base "back" pile, or a pop (dog stops, turns, and looks at you without being given a sit whistle) could crop up at this time. This will need to be addressed in the manner you've decided to train your dog. First of all, if your dog pops, cast "back" immediately. Do not blow a whistle, as this act would just further encourage the pop. You may need to move up to simplify the situation and remove stress or pressure from the situation. Work it through and get it right and then back up again.

Certainly the Double T will instill many important things in your dog's work. This is why you must insist on a good straight line to the back pile, A, as well as crisp, prompt sits on the whistle and clean casts. If you accept flares on the back pile, sloppy sits, or slow turns and shoddy casts, that is what you will likely get from your dog in the field. Set some standards and stick to them. If you need to back up (in training) or move up (physically toward the back pile) to simplify something in order for your dog to grasp what you want, do so, but don't accept substandard work from your dog when he's been taught correctly.

However, certain things can be overlooked while you are insisting on good performance out on the Double T. For example, you might want to let your dog deliver without a perfect heel and sit in exchange for some praise on a job well done in the field. This might seem contradictory, but it is up to you to read your dog and determine where to give and where to take. What is most important through all of this work? Your answer is a good work attitude, and it is up to you to make sure you not only keep a positive attitude instilled in your dog, but that you continue to build upon it. Therefore, throughout the introduction and subsequent work on this drill, keep your dog's attitude up by beginning and ending with happy bumpers, short hand-thrown bumpers with no pressure, if necessary. You can also use wing-clipped pigeons as well to keep an upbeat atmosphere during this important part of training.

Usually it is best to put the Double T together in increments, and the most popular method of doing so is to introduce the back part of the drill first. That is to say, establish the back pile and what will be the farthest stopping point and the farthest set of "over" casts. If all goes well, add the additional stopping point, which will be the one closer to your predetermined, actual starting spot for the Double T drill, along with that set of over casts. If you have any difficulty with putting this together—if your dog exhibits any major problems—it might be helpful to revisit your Mini-T for more work before continuing with the Double T.

Once you have the Double T drill going smoothly, you can incorporate additional bumper piles for more casting possibilities and advanced handling, or you can deviate from standard casts. An example of the former would be putting "angle-back" and "angle-in" piles in conjunction with your four standard over piles. For the latter, you can stop at the first point

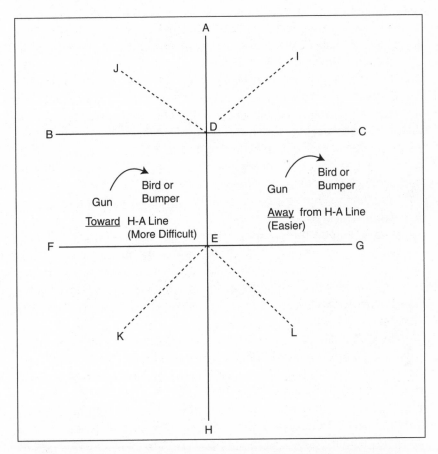

Advanced Work on a Double T: For additional training, add gunner or throwing stations and use dry fire (shotgun only) as distractions for running blinds and handling, or do marks in conjunction with a Double T pattern. Angled casts can be done by stopping at E and giving an angle-back command (arm halfway between horitzontal and straight up) to either C or B, or by stopping the dog at D and casting to I or J. Angle "in" casts from E can be executed to K and L. Lines can also be run from H to any location (H to F, or H to G).

and give an angle-back to the more distant corresponding "over" pile. Advanced handling is an advantage of the extended Double T.

Trainers who use the e-collar should take care to solidify performances with this tool while on the Double T so that the dog has been conditioned to all responses before work out in the field. Of particular importance is the straight line and elimination of any negative habits. Many trainers used to feel that once these things were addressed on the Double T drill it was time to head to the field for transitional patterns, drills, diversion, and cold blind work. However, there is much that can still be done in relation to the Double T.

Because of your dog's familiarity with your drill location and the bumper piles—particularly the back A pile—you can capitalize on the introduction to advanced diversions and concepts with a minimum of confusion for your dog. Examples would include running your pattern past a gunner in the field, then picking up a mark and running behind the gunner on the Double T. The easiest version of this is to simply place a stationary gunner out in the pattern field somewhat off the line to pile A. Take the time to choose a good location for your dog's first introduction to a gunner out on the pattern field.

If you position the gunner strategically, that location will also be a good place from which to throw the first mark on your pattern field in conjunction with your Double T. You don't want too much suction at the beginning so keep the gunner's position a distance away from the line to pile A. The key: strive for success as you introduce these new variables.

Next, you can introduce the art of running past a gunner who has fired a dry pop (a nonproductive shot—no bird is thrown). Your first gun station—identified above—works well for the introduction to the dry pop. Of course you can also do dry pops so that your dog eventually learns to run both behind the gunner and off the front of the gunner, and this is where your creativity and the current readiness and prowess of your dog will come into play. Finally, you can add a thrown poison bird (a bird the dog should not pick up) that should be thrown "out of the picture" or away from the line to pile A. Your gunners can be moved about your drill pattern to best suit your purposes on any given day.

Any combination of difficult principles that you may encounter in the field can first be introduced in this manner. Once you reach this level, by all means exercise creativity, but remember your dog's fundamentals. Work and build upon them.

Whenever your inner voice tells you that you might be pushing the envelope and progressing with your dog just a bit too fast, remember the first key word in training: simplify. Don't hesitate to move forward or break up a principle into simpler steps, no matter how much time you have spent on the Double T in general. Every new variation will produce difficulties for your dog.

A Water T can be set up in a clear pond on a windless day. Again you should use your training rope to teach your dog to stop nicely in the water; you can make sure he turns all the way around to look at you. Let the dog tread water for just a second before giving him a cast, and as he becomes more proficient at stopping in water you can teach your dog to tread water for a bit longer, and then cast.

Blinds

At this point you will be ready to start running blinds with your dog. By now you realize that your dog must have a sound, basic foundation of retrieving, delivering to hand, and work on casts. Initial work on blinds can be done with any number of different training methods. To do blinds successfully you need to recognize the elements of teaching a dog to take a line. These include (1) alignment of the spine and head, (2) fixing attention of the dog, (3) normal position of the handler, and (4) push and pull. Every time you have gone through a drill of any kind thus far in training, you have been working on these things. As you and your dog advance you can put more conscious effort into the dynamics of these elements toward good lining on both marks and blinds.

A dog's initial momentum will carry him through at least his first several strides in the direction his spine and head are pointed. This is not an absolute fact, as I have known and some of you may have also known dogs that have had an uncanny way of coming up with birds no matter where their handlers had them pointed. But, overall this is the first step that you as a handler can do to influence your dog's direction. With time you will become experienced at knowing how you've got your dog lined up. But, it often helps to ask someone to stand behind you to advise you on how you are doing in this category until you do gain some experience.

I remember often being quite surprised that where I thought I had my dog pointed was in fact far from the actual position my dog was in. At any stage of your handling career it pays to stay sharp on this detail.

It is also up to you to fix your dog's attention on his job out in the field. You have been working on this through your body language and the steps you've instilled in your dog throughout yard drills. The steps you used and the care you've taken contribute greatly to this focus and attention.

When your dog is green, generally speaking, you should cut him loose for his retrieve as soon as you have the dog looking in the proper direction. If you spend too much time in trying to fixate your dog "out yonder" or put him in a sweat in an effort to get him to take a perfect line or direction from you, in actuality you could be inviting a problem such as a no-go situation when you least want it to happen. Don't invite trouble at the wrong time. This is a perfect example of how there is no stringent bookwork on the nitty-gritty how-tos of dog training. Know when to push your dog toward advancement and when to back off in the name of progress.

Whether you realize it, your normal body position with relation to your dog has also been established by this time. This is different for varying dog and handler teams because of standards that have been set through a multitude of drill work exercises and marked retrieves. What this means is that between you and your dog there has been a "place" your dog accepts as the "normal" spot you should be in, in relation to sending him to retrieve anything.

This leads us to the all-important concept of push and pull. To demonstrate this, take your dog and sit him next to you out in the yard. Take a step up, or forward, on him from your normal body position—which we just identified and defined. Most of the time when you do this it will affect your dog somewhat and he will shift a bit, from nearly imperceptibly to quite noticeably. When you step up on your dog, this "push," as it is called, will influence the dog's position, usually moving him sideways.

Therefore it follows that when you take a step "back" from your dog in relation to your normal body position, you will again influence his position, whether a little or a lot. This is called "pull."

Basically, through the phenomenon of push and pull you are taking advantage of your dog's natural tendencies to accentuate the direction you need when training and handling on line or when hunting. To further illustrate this, while still out in the yard experimenting with push and pull, throw out a few bumpers in different directions and use—as your main influence for lining (blind retrieve)—the push and pull factors to send your dog to retrieve the bumpers.

Because of the importance of these elements in lining, you should develop an awareness of them and recognize and cultivate them as you continue to advance your dog's training and ability. The better you become at using them, the better you will be at training and handling and the more teamwork you will develop with your dog. It is rewarding, exciting, and fulfilling; it's one of the best parts of training and working with your dog.

Several methods can encourage your dog to run blinds. One is identifying the blind with a helper who yells excitedly while waving a bumper to entice the dog to look out and build the dog's desire to run or swim out without actually seeing something being thrown. As soon as the dog keys in to the bird boy (the helper) he is sent on his name by his handler—you—and when he is moving well out into the field the yelling and waving ceases. However, should the dog slow down in the presence of any cover change or water, the commotion resumes to again attract the dog to the destination and to build the dog's momentum. When the dog is nearly at the pile location the helper throws the "waving" bumper to the pile. This should all be done at the discretion of the helper as that person watches the dog en route, and the helper may further guide the dog by moving either left or right while the dog proceeds toward the bumper pile location should the dog veer off course—the counteraction of the helper will serve to straighten out the dog's line. This is called "marking blinds" and it should be noted that the use of a helper should be discontinued as soon as possible. As soon as the dog indicates that he has caught on to the procedure, remove the helper and send the dog to the pile using the back command. Sometimes when changing over to "Back" as a release, confusion may set in so be prepared to reinstate the helper a time or two if necessary.

Short sight blinds can be run on land or water with no cover present where the dog can readily see the bumpers. For success, the dog must have either been force fetched so that he will go when sent or he must possess a keen desire to retrieve and to respect your commands. As soon as the dog is consistently running these short sight blinds, the distance can be extended.

Long sight blinds can be put out at anywhere from one hundred to three hundred or more yards. Various objects can be used to mark the blinds, such as a Clorox jug on a fence post or elevated stake, or an overturned white five-gallon bucket. Using this method, your dog will learn to look out into the distance for a final destination point.

Many trainers prefer to introduce cold blinds (unknown blinds) as soon as possible once a dog is through the handling (casting) drills so that the dog learns to constantly seek new blind destinations with confidence. There is much merit to this line of thinking, but many professional trainers feel that one of the most common mistakes made by inexperienced amateurs is proceeding to cold blinds too quickly or advancing to difficult cold blind concepts too soon. Doing so can cause any number of problems, one of the most common of which is lack of confidence. The key in training is always balance, and there are few instances in the overall training progression where balance is more important than easing into the running of cold blinds. However, each dog is different and some thrive from instant challenges while others wither on the vine. Read your dog and proceed with his training accordingly.

Multiple (several in one session) cold blinds are quite effective in introducing a young or inexperienced dog to going when sent to unknown locations. In other words, rather than placing one or even two blinds out in a field, put five blinds (not too long) out there. As long as your dog is in good physical condition and will go, stop, and cast, you can work on these five-blind drills that will quickly advance the ability of your dog as well as his belief in you that you are directing him to something "out there." Common sense should of course be used, and the five-blind drills should neither be too lengthy in distance nor too close in proximity to each other—at least initially—and you should make sure to do this during the cool part of the day.

When doing this drill you can proceed by constantly handling your dog whenever he drifts off line—and some dogs will actually eventually learn to line better if they are consistently handled each time they veer off line—or by allowing him to run, even if off line, to build momentum and perhaps eventually even recover a bumper different from the one you had originally intended, all in the name of momentum. The factors of momentum and handling/casting should always be weighed, and you should adjust the types of blinds you set up accordingly so that your dog does not become deficient in one or the other.

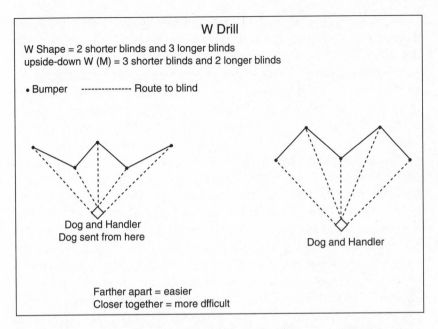

W Drill

W Shape = 2 shorter blinds and 3 longer blinds
upside-down W (M) = 3 shorter blinds and 2 longer blinds

• Bumper   -------------- Route to blind

Dog and Handler
Dog sent from here

Dog and Handler

Farther apart = easier
Closer together = more dfficult

The W Drill: In the W shape, the drill is two shorter blind casts and three longer blinds. Upside down, in the M shape, this becomes three short blinds and two longer blinds.

With regard to the five-blind drill, or W drill (two short and three long in a W-shape formation), your placement of bumpers or birds can enhance your dog's performance. It often accentuates good progression to have three shorter blinds and two longer ones in any one drill. Look at it this way: You have to go out and plant blinds anyway, so take advantage of the opportunity to run your dog for a few extra minutes on several blinds instead of one or two. The extra sending, stopping, and casting will help your dog get into the swing of things. Start with simple expectations in a field with few variables, and add terrain and changes of cover as your dog becomes more proficient at the whole blind-running game.

Whenever you run a drill like this or run any blinds with your dog, pay attention to good habits from your dog and you. Each time you set your dog up, your body language should be the same. Build good posture on line and create good lining movements that will be with you and your dog forever.

Also, once your dog is familiar with this five-blind drill you can put diversions and gunning stations in between the blinds (as you did with the Double T) to work on the concepts of blinds past guns and marks. Training is a constant process that you will build upon throughout the working life of your dog, particularly if you elect to run hunt tests, field trials, or Super Retriever Series (SRS) events. But make no mistake and never underestimate that these skills are also handy in many hunting situations when you have multiple hunters in the field or marsh.

Once blind work has become a real part of your dog's training it should be balanced with marking—which to review, is the act of retrieving birds the dog has seen fall—sessions so that your dog does not become stale in one or the other. The more blinds you run with your dog, the more teamwork you will build and the better your dog will become on blinds and all that they entail, including lining and casting. However, it is up to you to keep your dog's marking sharp in the process. Also remember that you can often combine marks and blinds when training, but like anything, don't fall into the trap of doing this all the time. No matter what method you have employed, once your dog is running blinds it is up to you to continue to advance his ability and to keep him sharp. This comes from reading your dog and knowing when to push forward and when to ease up—even when to simplify—in the name of success and progress.

Flushing Dogs

As we know, flushing dogs should (1) seek and find game, (2) flush the game within the range of the hunter, and (3) retrieve the game when ordered to do so. Young spaniels by this stage should be hunting well. Specialized work can encourage flushing with the use of dizzied birds (birds that are dazed by the trainer and then planted in the field so they'll hold for several minutes), or by using remote release launchers that contain pre-loaded birds. (Take care not to release a bird when the dog is too close to the launcher.). In addition, some dogs need more advanced zigzagging work on quartering, sometimes with the help of a rope, a whistle, hand signals, and some planted birds to set up success.

When working on the flush keep in mind that a slow flush is OK for many hunters and hunting situations but is not desirable in the trial dog.

Many spaniels are required to retrieve, and the section on retrieving in chapter 25 can be applied to any spaniel. In addition, spaniels have the ability to learn to do blind retrieves, and the section devoted to the skills necessary for handling in this chapter can be applied to spaniels, too.

The advanced trained spaniel should "Hup" (or sit) to flush. For many, this means to hup when the bird actually flushes, but some hunters want their dogs to hup on command, or when they shoot, as opposed to hupping on each flush. Whatever the case, the spaniel that hups as trained and is steady until commanded to retrieve is a joy to hunt over and work with, no question about it. Some hunters do not want their dogs steady to shot; they want them in motion as the bird is falling, thinking that these dogs will recover more cripples.

Pointing Breeds

Unbeknownst to many folks, the pointing breeds can be taught to handle—take lines out into the field for birds with no known location, stop on whistle, and take hand signals to the bird—just like retrievers and spaniels, although the training is often not as intense and is more subtly worked into the hunting routine.

Beyond that, pointers need experience with birds and with hunting. Many pointing breeds need to learn to work within gun range but even the big running All-Age-type dogs can learn to foot hunt with their owners. It all depends on your consistency and effectiveness in communicating what you want to your dog.

Staunchness on point should be honed in training on pigeons, and a checkcord can be very helpful for working on this. Keep adding distractions with birds and begin work with controlled coveys of pen-raised quail (first bought at twelve to sixteen weeks) in training with the use of a recall pen (see p. 226). Backing should also be honed and can be worked on with the addition of another dog or a dog silhouette. Work your dog on a checkcord until he learns that he must honor another dog's find.

A barrel or a styling beam can be used to teach proper stance on point and can accentuate and enhance tail carriage. (See diagram p. 220.)

One difference often found between trial dogs and hunting dogs is the steadiness to wing and shot. Ideally, top dogs should be steady to wing (remain motionless when the birds fly) and shot (stay still when the gun is fired), and, arguably, marking the fall area of shot birds is better done while the dog is stationary. That being said, many hunters allow slack on steady to shot, feeling that dogs on the move as the birds are coming down will recover more cripples. You be the judge on this one, for your dog has to please just you, unless you begin to trial.

Recognize that once you begin hunting wild birds your dog may move on point as he becomes used to the new environment and the actions of the birds. The dog may break, or take off prematurely, to wing and shot no matter how steady he is in training. Because of all the added excitement of the real thing, you may need to put the dog back on a checkcord to advance these skills in hunting situations, or at the very least, go back to training.

Introduction to Water—All Breeds

As a general rule, most retriever puppies are introduced to water and boats at a young age and properly encouraged to build a positive water attitude. However, most other breeds of hunting dogs see very little of water when they are young, yet most of them will encounter water when hunting as adults. Some of them will have to deal with it on a regular basis, such as foxhounds, coonhounds, big-game hounds, and beagles, but this also includes the spaniels (these dogs can be excellent water dogs) and all the bird dogs, pointing breeds, and continentals.

Proper introduction to water is not rocket science but should be mentioned because it is so often overlooked. If your dog simply won't entertain the thought of getting his feet wet, try turning him loose for recess on a hot day near a pond with several good water dogs. Another method is for you to get wet and encourage the dog to join you. You may need waders or a pair of shorts or a bathing suit. Using "running water"—water not so deep to require swimming, but shallow enough so that your dog can run—is helpful until your dog overcomes any initial water phobia, but swimming water must be conquered for any hunting dog to truly be equipped to handle what comes along in the course of a day afield. Make the water scene exciting by proving you can be amphibious, and again, add other dogs for additional action.

Older Dogs Acquired with No Training

You've often heard it said that it's fine to get a year-old dog with no training because he's unspoiled and hasn't been ruined by improper training. However, these dogs are often way behind the eight ball, especially if they haven't had much if any socialization. If they've been languishing in a kennel or on a chain for the better part of that year, you've got your hands full.

First of all, chances are your new dog will have a learning disability, true as it sounds, because he has not learned how to learn. Second, the dog likely has no interest in birds, or rabbits, or raccoon, or foxes, or whatever game you intend to hunt. Third, he may be people shy, gun shy, and even shy of other dogs. What are you going to do?

You've got to find a way to awaken your dog's instincts to birds or game, and that is usually best done by putting your dog in situations to let him "chase." Now, granted, chasing birds is often the least desirable way to get a bird dog started, but when you have nothing to start with you therefore have nothing to lose. For that matter, many people do employ this method with young dogs. Get his bird instinct in gear so that you have something to work with. This method applies to pointing breeds, flushing breeds, HPRs, and retrievers.

With hounds of all types it may help to use an enclosed training pen, such as a rabbit pen, a fox pen, or a coon-training pen. In this manner you can turn your dog loose, possibly with other dogs, and in this way they can learn to chase the game you want. Granted, other types of game and creatures are probably in the pen and your dog might start chasing them as well as the one you want him to become interested in, but since you have nothing to begin with, let them chase—awaken that desire to hunt.

You are going to have to start at square one when it comes to training, just as if your twelve-month-old dog was a seven-week-old puppy. This is the best way to teach him the rules of life and to lay the foundation for effective communication. The time you spend with your dog may help him overcome his fears about people, places, and things in life. Notice that I said "may" because some dogs are lost causes. You won't know until you give it a try, but your effort may become a supreme investment before it's all over with. You would do well to acknowledge this in advance.

In addition, it's almost a given that you will have to teach quartering with a checkcord to those breeds of dogs that will need this skill when hunting, as you've missed the golden time of puppyhood to teach quartering in a natural, uncomplicated fashion.

Terrible Twos and Other Times of Rebellion

As you train your dog you will find at least three stages in which he shows at least a little rebellion or acts like an idiot and seems to have forgotten just about everything you've taught him. The most notorious of these stages is the "terrible twos" as I call it and not that unlike the same term we apply to our children. This stage in dogs can occur right at or near the twenty-four-month mark, or a little before or after, approaching up to three years of age. Sometimes, when this stage rears its head, you are best served if you put your dog up for a few weeks or even a month and let him ride it out. Keep the dog exercised during this time, but little is gained to continue working a dog that is going to potentially dig a deep hole for himself in training and in hunting.

There are two other stages where your dog will either test you or act like he's never been trained, and those include the sixteen-week age, as we saw back in chapter 22, and around the twelve-month age, although this one will vary depending on when your dog really begins to mentally mature. The dog will begin to test your position as his coach, and he will often think he knows better than you how to conduct himself and live his life. Use your smarts to outwit him with as little pressure as possible until the dog outgrows this stage, but don't let him run over you or you may have serious trouble regaining the leadership you need and must have for a successful lifelong relationship with your dog.

Teaching the "Hunt Dead" Command to Dogs

Many dogs have an aversion to getting into an area and rooting out dead birds even though they will retrieve birds they've seen fall. These dogs won't persevere in a thicket or tough cover to stay in there and recover a bird. One of the best tricks to overcome this is to use live, wing-clipped birds.

Many people will immediately disagree because they don't want their dogs retrieving live birds—they want them pointing them and retrieving the dead ones—but I submit to you that this is the best way to get that bird instinct back in drive. The smart dogs quickly learn the difference in their work. You have commanded them to find a dead bird as opposed to them being out ranging and hunting and coming upon scent. When using a wing-clipped pigeon for teaching your dog to "Find" or "Hunt dead" in a piece of cover for the purpose of finding a bird, you can fire a shot with your .22 training pistol or a shotgun just prior to the "Hunt dead" command. Dogs are much more keen on a bird that is warm and fluttering than on a cold, dead find. Once they get the hang of it the transition is easier made to the dead bird.

Woodcock, Geese, Fur, and Cold Game

While most dogs have no problem with working or retrieving different types of game, some will balk at certain species and require additional work to overcome this. Examples include the woodcock, which obviously must smell different to our dogs, as many of them are quite adamant about avoiding woodcock and also refusing to retrieve them until they become used to them. The same phenomenon happens with geese for many dogs.

Many dogs won't pick up cold game, yet this is often a necessity in training. An example would involve retrieving. After your dog is retrieving tennis balls, socks, bumpers, wing-clipped birds, and freshly shot birds, you'll need to supplement his training with dead birds. Encourage your dog to retrieve these cold, dead birds just like any of the other objects he is required to retrieve. If your dog will also be required to retrieve fur, chances are you will have to introduce the fur, often in a series of steps just like any other training.

Use of Birds

It has become fairly mainstream these days for bird dog trainers and retriever dog trainers to keep at least a small bird pen in the backyard—whether you are an amateur trainer or a professional—and pigeons are an inexpensive alternative to ducks and pheasant and are hardier than quail. Dogs trained primarily on birds keep a keen attitude and maintain a better mental frame of mind during stringent training phases that may contain some "boring" activities, although certainly bumpers should be used when convenient. The use of birds delivers a big reward to retrievers, spaniels, bird dogs, and continentals.

Proper Bird Care

When buying ducks and pheasant for training purposes be certain to keep all paperwork and make sure all birds are properly tagged or marked as pen-raised birds. It is common practice to keep shot birds in a freezer for more longevity of use (you may want to invest in a small freezer in your kennel building or garage to keep birds away from human food items, or wrap them in bags before storing them in the freezer if

Dogs trained on birds whenever possible turn out to be much more focused in the field. (Author Photo)

you must share space), but even birds in a freezer must have the necessary documentation for possession of them to be legal.

Trash-Breaking Pointers, Flushers, Hounds, and Versatile Breeds

Probably one of the most universal problems among dogs that work and run "on their own" after birds or game is that of running trash. These are, after all, "hunting" dogs and the best ones truly love to hunt. Sometimes that means until they find out exactly what they are supposed to be hunting, they may be a bit loose on specialization. However, when the chips are down you don't want your foxhound running rabbits, or your beagle running deer, or your coonhound running fox, or your bird dog running any of those things.

Breaking dogs off trash should be handled with care. Make sure that you know exactly what offense your dog is committing and also be certain he is guilty when you pass judgment. Moreover, when you do deliver a punishment, use one that fits the crime without overwhelming your dog.

Several methods can be used, the first of which is likely the least stressful but does not always work. That is the use of commercially made (or homemade) breaking scents that are applied liberally to the dog's head and neck every day for as long as it takes to turn him off running his chosen trash. Some dogs respond well to this treatment by giving up their vice, while others just shrug the scent off. For the latter case, there are more severe variations of this breaking method.

The second method is physical punishment applied in the manner of a thrashing for the crime when the dog is caught in the act. Caution should be used, however, as most physical punishment goes on long after it has created an effect on the dog. After the first few licks, all the rest are generally "for the trainer, not the dog" and are just to make the trainer feel better for "showing the dog the trainer's displeasure," but the ability of the dog might suffer. This is direct pressure for running trash, and the dog may slack off on his hunting drive for a while after receiving such correction.

Another method is use of the e-collar, and this technique can be broken down into two categories. In one, the dog thinks that the trash (deer, for example) is responsible for the sting from the e-collar, and in the other the dog knows that you, his boss, is very unhappy and is letting him know that. In either case the dog must understand the e-collar, or he could be ruined from pressure that he doesn't understand and for actions he doesn't know to be wrong. That is not to say that the dog *will* be ruined, but it is a possibility. Also, too much correction could hamper his hunting drive for a night, a week, a month—it's difficult to predict. Again, you must be absolutely positive that you are correcting the dog during the act of running the trash, and you should never press that button just because you think the dog might be trashing. There are a number of ways to accomplish this, from working in the daytime (even with coonhounds) on the problem to using a live deer when one is accessible to using a series of steps beginning with scent, then progressing to a confined live deer, and ending with turning your dog loose with some deer dogs on a deer track (using deer as an example, of course). Eventually the dog will turn down temptation of the race and go hunting on his own for the game he is supposed to run, or find.

There is yet another method but I do not condone it because it is too extreme, and the potential for harm or injury is quite high. This rough method consists of putting the dog in a mechanical tumbler with some piece or portion of the off game, and then spinning the tumbler with the intent of making the dog too ill to ever mess with that game again. For the welfare of our dogs this method should be stamped out.

Makin' a List and Checkin' It Twice

One of the most beneficial things you can do is make a list of the types of hunting you will encounter each year and add this to your training journal. In this way you can review the things you've done with your dog and determine if you need to add anything to his training in additional preparation. If you will encounter a ground layout blind on a goose hunt, practice with one ahead of time. If you will be hunting in thick swamps, find a place that comes close to simulating that before you go. Have you done enough work with decoys? Will your dog ride in a boat? Is your dog proficient at jumping fences? Do you hunt near rivers with strong currents?

Constantly review your progress with your dog. Look for things that you might be overemphasizing and others you might be overlooking or shortchanging. Strive for balance. Don't overtrain. Whether your dog is a little puppy or an old veteran, end a day of hunting or training with the dog wanting more. Always do your part to set your dog up for success while pushing the envelope to advance his skills.

CHAPTER
TWENTY-SEVEN

Solving Training Problems

Despite your best-laid plans and intentions, and no matter how conscientiously you go about the training of your dog, there will be times when you encounter problems along the way. The sailing will not always be smooth no matter how gifted and intelligent your dog may be. What are you going to do when you encounters these bumps in the road? Some folks elect to grit their teeth and forge ahead, come hell or high water, but as you have immediately guessed, that is usually the wrong way to proceed and will only create more problems most of the time. But what, then, is the best way to proceed? How does one learn the answers, the formulas for tackling training problems?

Read Your Dog

First of all, remember the golden rule of learning to walk in your dog's paws. Read his mind as best you can—you will constantly improve on this skill as you go along and continue to focus on your dog—and learn to stay one step ahead. If you see something starting to break down, make book. The first instance of a bad action is often "on the house" as many trainers say. However, if your dog does something negative on two occasions, this would signal the beginning of a bad habit. Now it is up to you to figure out why this is occurring and what you can do to counter it or wipe it out entirely. Sometimes the "why" matters not, but you must devise a solution.

You see a problem developing and perhaps have given a correction or two, but the problem persists. Or, the correction has done no good and effected no change in behavior. What are you going to do?

Develop a Plan

The first step is to analyze the problem and develop a plan. You may have to do this on the fly while you are in the middle of a training session. In a situation such as this if you really do not have a clue what should be done, it might be wise to put your dog back up in his kennel until you can consult with someone who has more experience. You may even want to consult a pro.

Often the best solution is to conclude the immediate training session and then go back to the "yard" or a controlled training atmosphere where you can re-create the problem situation and "talk it out" with your dog. Show your dog the desired response, which is generally easier to do back in the yard or where the dog has learned obedience and/or e-collar conditioning as well as basic field skills. Your dog understands that you are communicating with him and showing him the desired response.

For example, let's take a dog that is dropping his bird or bumper on the way in from a retrieve. If you go charging out at the dog in a field working setting, hollering at him to "Hold" or "Fetch" or any number of other things, pretty soon you will create a dog that comes in with trepidation, slowly, if at all. Take the dog back to the yard and work specifically on delivery. Remind the dog what is expected and then, once he is performing reliably in the yard, go back to the field. At this point you will have to play things by ear. If the dog again acts up in the field, you should yet again retreat to the yard for another session, but perhaps this time—since you've recently refreshed his memory on delivery in the yard—you can most effectively break the situation down in the field to get the dog's clearest understanding of what you want. These things are not and cannot be written in a book. You must feel them out and figure out the best solution that will be the easiest for the dog to understand and with the least resistance or pressure. (You might also use the solution on return, coming up shortly.)

Another situation may come up when you are out hunting and your dog refuses to come to you. Let's say he's pretty new at hunting and he's simply having too much fun. You are even using an e-collar and the dog is just blowing you off and won't pay any attention. Well, it's a safe bet that this dog was not properly conditioned to the e-collar in the first place, and is now learning to "run through the stim" and that "pressure of correction has not exceeded the pressure of cause" (Rex Carr, from personal correspondence with author). The distractions that are present in the field far surpass the correction from the e-collar. Your dog might be a bird dog bumping birds instead of holding point or he might be a hound that simply doesn't want to quit hunting or grinding a track and doesn't take you seriously at all.

In either case, the dog should be returned to the yard, put back on a rope, and schooled properly on "Here" in this controlled setting. Once you have done this, gradually add distractions, such as birds or new surroundings. Note that this can be done whether or not a dog is e-collar trained. If he is not an e-collar dog but is still blowing you off, the dog should be returned to the yard, just like the improperly conditioned e-collar dog, because in any event, he is not prepared for the level of distraction present in the field or the woods. Rope work and compliance on "Here" must be reliable in the yard, and then in different areas and with increasing degrees of distraction, before the rope is removed—with or without an e-collar—before you can ever expect your dog to be reliable out in the real world of hunting.

Simplify

Often you can take this same yard principle and apply it in the field on the spur of the moment by zeroing in on one facet of the training situation where the problem has surfaced. Take the hunting or training situation and break it down into components. Choose the most important facet of the skill that has broken down and invent a very explicit drill to work on the problem as it occurs. Why try to carry out an elaborate sequence of events if your dog is munching on the bird? The dog may make that awesome retrieve or slam into that dazzling point, but if he crushes the bird once he gets it, your dog is learning to destroy your next meal while getting higher and higher over his misdeed in the process and therefore all the more prone to destroy the next bird, and he will soon do it again and again. Don't let your dog get away with this even once, as the mouth problem is a severe infraction and should never be allowed to continue without being addressed by you, or you may have to resign yourself to keeping a dog that won't bring your birds back in satisfactory condition for the table, or resign yourself to the prospect of having to replace him with a better dog. And that may not be an option for you.

No matter how your hunting day or training day is going, take your dog and the bird and work on "Hold" right then and there. Make the dog hold the bird and then walk with the bird without even so much as moving one jaw muscle in an attempt to munch on the bird. If the dog does try to mess with the bird, even ever so slightly, go back to the truck and get out a training bumper and do some hold drills using the bumper to replace the bird.

If you are lucky, you may get out of this potentially disastrous situation with these few steps. If not, the solution may require redoing the entire yard process about how to hold a bird, from the beginning, whether or not the dog is force fetched. Indeed, a nonforced dog may require the force procedure to overcome the hard-mouth problem, although this is not always the case. Most definitely you will have to do some work and see this training through to the nth degree. Your dog must not mess with that bird.

Now, let's take another variation of this same scenario. Your dog is coming in with the bird and mouthing it along the way. He's rolling the bird back and forth instead of holding it in a firm, solid, secure yet soft grip. The dog is lollygagging his way back while mouthing the bird.

This situation presents a potential mouth problem, but you might have the opportunity to erase it without pointing your finger directly at the problem and potentially making it worse. Instead of going to the dog and commanding "Hold," remove the dog from the situation—and this can be done by just relocating a few feet or yards—and put the dog on an extended sit, without the bird in his mouth, about ten yards from you. If you are not using an e-collar, attach a rope to the dog's collar. Now, command "Here," and either nick the dog with a low intensity on the collar before he has a chance to comply or give the dog a tug with the rope, and then when the dog heads toward you, say "Good" and reinforce the action by repeating the command. The object here is to focus your dog's concentration on his knowledge of the here command and that he should get back in to you as quickly as he possibly can, since that is what he was trained to do. Now, put a bumper in his mouth and do the same thing, focusing on "Here," although now the dog is also delivering an object. Finally, put the bird in the dog's mouth and repeat these steps.

Back out in the field or when hunting, if you see your dog perhaps even thinking about mouthing that bird, get on your whistle for the come command or issue a stern "Here" to get his mind on the return. More often than not this is exactly what will happen and you will have avoided a potential confrontation with the bird and mouth problem and solidified the here command with a positive experience in the field.

Situations like these are what training is all about. You must constantly be evaluating what is going on with your dog and then figuring out how to best counter and react in ways that can accent success and avoid failure whenever possible. It is often far easier than you might think, but this requires the ultimate in concentration and anticipation on your part. Not an easy task for the novice, but one that comes more smoothly as you gain experience with your dog.

Think. Read your dog. React. Make book. Figure out how to simplify and how to communicate exactly what you want to your dog. The more you are able to do this the better off you both will be and the quicker you can advance to even bigger and better things, and eventually that lofty goal of hunting trips afield with no training issues—nothing but pure hunting enjoyment for you and your dog. Those are the best of times, and they are not out of reach but are attainable through your consistency and thoroughness in training your dog.

CHAPTER
TWENTY-EIGHT

When to Consider Professional Help

Professional training is available for every hunting dog breed, and the time may come when you elect to seek help in training your own dog. Perhaps you bought a puppy, and although you've given it your best shot, you have finally faced the music. No matter how hard you've tried to make quality time to spend with your dog you just can't cut the mustard. Work is consuming the better part of your days and weekends, leaving precious little time for other pursuits. You don't want your puppy's potential to be wasted, so you begin to consider the help of a pro.

Or you've been dealing with all the puppy stuff remarkably well, but now that it's time for more advanced work, you are not quite sure how to proceed. You've decided that you want to force fetch your dog, but hey, you've never done it and you aren't convinced you want to do that part of it yourself anyway. Why not leave the dirty work for someone else?

Then again you might be progressing admirably with all parts of your dog's training and suddenly one day you both seem to hit a brick wall. With every passing day your dog seems to be slipping backward and you cannot figure out what has gone wrong, much less what to do about it. Should you continue to try to bulldoze through the problem, maybe digging a bigger hole, or back up ten and punt then call for help?

All of these situations are good examples of when services from a professional trainer may be in order. If these things apply to you, take heart, for you are not the lone ranger. Many other folks have been in your shoes and agonized over the right thing to do. Of course you'll be without your dog for the duration of the training time that you choose, but in certain situations this decision is the right thing to do and pays big dividends over the lifetime of your dog and your hunting career with your dog.

Training Programs

Professional trainers generally offer a variety of programs to choose from. With all levels of retrievers and bird dog breeds these usually include finished training up through a couple of different levels. For example, a retriever trainer may offer a basic gundog program and an advanced gundog program. The difference between the two is that dogs in the basic program will be trained for general work such as steadiness to shot, delivery to hand, and basic multiple marks on land and water. Advanced gundogs will also possess handling skills where they do blind retrieves by stopping on a whistle and taking hand signals. Some kennels offer introductory programs that include obedience schooling and force-fetch-trained retrieve. Bird dog trainers also offer a variety of programs. Time frames yield different results.

Hound kennels often offer a starter program that includes a minimum of hunting exposure along with basic obedience and training on additional commands such as "Load." Hunting by the month with another dog or solo can be contracted, usually with a higher price when your dog is hunted alone.

Virtually all professional trainers, regardless of breed specialization—unless they are stay-at-home trainers—also offer professional handling for your dog at organized events such as field trials, hunt tests, or night hunts. Day training is often available, and some trainers offer phone or Internet consultation.

Spot Training

Some trainers will consider taking in a dog on a skill basis. In other words, you have a few things that you would like worked on as opposed to an entire skill set or training program. Discuss your needs with various professionals that you have chosen and perhaps this special request can be accommodated.

Facilities: What to Expect

When you choose a professional trainer you may want to meet the individual in person and see the kennel area and/or training grounds. This is a reasonable request, but by all means please show some respect for the pro's time by calling in advance to make an appointment. I have seen plenty of ink devoted to this subject and invariably the advice is "to just drop in . . . then you'll really see how things work."

First of all, if you have any questions about the ethics or conditions of the pro and the kennel you have chosen, you should continue looking elsewhere. For any business relationship to work you must trust and respect your professional. Therefore, dropping in unannounced is neither warranted nor necessary. Indeed, you may end up making a long trip out to the kennel with the intention of dropping in only to discover that the trainer is out with the dogs at a piece of property another hour away in the opposite direction. Plan ahead!

Pro trainers have busy schedules, just like you do, and when someone shows the lack of courtesy by dropping in unannounced, the entire day can be set into a tailspin. Would you like to be treated this way? I suspect not. Most pro trainers have their entire week planned in advance and must adhere to a strict schedule to achieve the goals set for that week.

During an initial meeting, ask all the questions you can think of that might concern you. Inquire about visitation, regular hours, whether you can attend training sessions, and how to go about that. Ask about day-training policies. Be satisfied with the overall condition of the pro's kennel and the trainer's dogs. A brand spanking new facility in the multimillion-dollar range is not necessary, but the kennel should be clean, water buckets should be spic and span, and dog transport equipment should meet standards in cleanliness and upkeep. Training gear should be organized. The dogs should be in excellent physical condition and with a good mental attitude. It's easy to spot well cared for, contented dogs in training. If you get any sort of alarm sound from that little voice of yours, you might consider looking elsewhere for help.

What should be expected with regard to training fees and additional fees? Normally there is a monthly training fee, usually payable at the first of each month. It is pretty customary for most kennels to expect the entire month in payment even if you take your dog home for part of that time, because it is not feasible for the trainer to fill your dog's empty spot for a few days or a week. If you contract a month's training, expect to pay for it. Some trainers have a reservation policy with an advance deposit due. Others will not take a dog for less than a specified time and will expect you to commit to that time frame.

Additional expenses can include birds such as pigeons, ducks, pheasant, quail, or chukars; heartworm prevention; flea/tick prevention; airport charge for pickup or delivery; veterinary trip charge if a visit to the doctor becomes necessary; all veterinary expenses; grooming and baths when needed; and sometimes there are charges for requested special care over and above normal kennel policy.

Some trainers offer winter training trips for northern clients and summer training trips for southern-based clients. Basically a North-based pro goes south for the winter to train throughout the winter months, and the South-based pro goes north in the summer months for the same reason, to escape the southern summer heat and ensure year-round training. Usually when these trips are contracted for training there is the monthly fee with an additional trip fee to help cover road expenses.

The best professional trainer/owner relationships are built on mutual respect. Do your homework as solidly as possible before you visit a potential pro and determine the person's style and type of training and whether the trainer's methods blend with your own. If you are in doubt about the way the pro trains dogs, ask specific questions until you are satisfied. Some trainers will work most of their dogs with e-collars but will consider working yours without if that is important to you. Others won't make such concessions because of the potential time conflict throughout any day's training. The only way to find out is ask. Some trainers are very flexible and train each dog individually, while others expect each dog to conform to a standard program.

The bottom line—choose a trainer with the training methods that suit you and your dog best. Be secure in your decision and give the pro respect. You will be treated likewise, and your dog will be all the better for the professional training and the abilities he gains as a result.

CHAPTER
TWENTY-NINE

Maintaining Performance in Older Dogs

Most working hunting dogs have life spans from ten to four-teen years. Sometimes we get lucky and our dogs live longer than that, but not always. Many times we are shortchanged and our pals are taken from us prematurely. Just as preventive measures help us as we draw closer to our golden years, so too are certain things we can do to help increase the quality of life in our older dogs.

Regarding Training, Hunting, and Maintenance

Chances are you've become hooked on training and hunting with your dog—in fact the hook was set way back in puppyhood and it just sunk in deeper from then on—and now it's become kind of a lifelong thing. That's easily understandable because you've grown to cherish the time you spend with your dog, and training extends that special bond.

However, you've begun to notice little changes in your buddy, things that you may or may not have also noticed in yourself depending on your age, but it helps to make note of those subtle changes as you see them take place. Your dog's well-being could be at stake. Seven years is the generally accepted threshold as the senior period for large breeds of dogs, while nine is the time frame for medium-sized dogs. Believe me, it will creep up on you without warning and suddenly you realize with a start that your beloved hunting companion is growing old on you. Perhaps his muzzle is showing some gray, or maybe there's not quite the same spring in his step. Your dog may begin having trouble seeing or hearing or both. These are all unmistakable signs of aging.

Often older dogs are less apt to need honing and training but will benefit more from physical exercise between hunts or events. I've thrown events in here because many of you will have ventured down the path of competitive dog games along the way. Perhaps you have a hunt test dog or a field trial dog, or a nite-hunt competition hound. A savvy hound that is up in years may not need hunting every night to perform well on the weekend, but he does need his health and solid physical conditioning. The same goes for all of our sporting breeds. Well-chosen training tests in moderation will keep them sharp, but they don't need to be run on every test that comes down the pike or that we can dream up along the way. They've gone far past that point having reached a secure, consistent place in their lives.

Changes in Needs

A number of things can be done that not only increase your dog's life span, but also contribute to his comfort once aging sets in. With the passing of years you will begin to realize the importance of the quality diet you've fed your dog since he was a puppy. You'll see how your dog maintains his condition, physically and mentally, over other dogs you are familiar with that seem less fortunate in all ways, and you see the importance of a year-round exercise plan for your dog and how it has paid off as he grows older.

I've been in that boat more times than I can count, and although it's true that genetics plays a part in how a dog ages, there is no question in my mind that the importance of excellent diet and regular exercise play a close second. Every older dog I've owned has belied his or her years by moving better than other dogs of similar age; by maintaining a shiny, healthy coat; by defying the debilitation of age until past what seems realistic or fair. One of my dogs was in fact gray all over but constantly drew comments about his incredible ease of movement and athleticism in the field at 12 years of age.

One of the most important things you can do for your older dog is continue to provide a quality diet high in protein. I know, I know—the alarm bells sound off like chimes in a steeple whenever someone hints at the possibility of feeding an older dog a high percentage of protein, but the old adage that high protein will burn up a dog's kidneys has been disproved, provided the dog is otherwise healthy. That, of course, is the key.

And it's far more complicated than that. Older dogs actually benefit from higher protein in their diet as opposed to lower percentages for several reasons. The first is that they cannot metabolize protein as effectively, so they need more in order to come out even, much less ahead. Next, higher levels of digestible protein will enable your older dog to recover from injuries and muscle strain more quickly, to ward off stress and the threat of some diseases more efficiently than without this benefit. This is because dogs without the protection from higher protein in the diet have lower protein reserves and less ability to maintain proper immune system function.

How does this work? Some amino acids, which are commonly called the "building blocks" of protein, are made by the dog's body, but others are not and must be supplied in the diet. These are called "essential" amino acids. We've already seen back in chapter 10 how proteins are broken down into amino acids through digestion and then distributed through the blood to cells that rebuild the amino acids into body protein. Protein turnover constantly occurs as these body proteins are broken down and also produced. When adequate protein is lacking in the diet, the body will compensate by slowing down its internal protein turnover. The end result is not all that inviting when you view the menu: reduced ability to ward off trauma, stress, cancer-causing agents, you name it. Sounds like a pretty good reason to provide a diet high in quality digestible protein to me.

Other things? In addition, older dogs tend to feel extremes in temperature more keenly than their younger counterparts. This means you may need to take extra measures during the dead of winter as well as the broiling heat of summer to help keep your buddy comfortable. Try to keep all the things your dog has become accustomed to as constant as possible. This includes his routines and familiar schedules.

Be conscious of the fact that as your dog ages he may have to go outside more often than normal. When traveling, your dog may need more frequent pit stops than you'd like, but it will add to his comfort and well-being. Invest in a quality mat, perhaps of the supportive orthopedic variety, and put one in the dog box of your truck or SUV. If your dog spends any time in a crate in the house, use an orthopedic pad there also, or replace his regular bed with one that offers more support.

When you go out to train or on hunting trips, either invest in a tailgate ramp to assist your dog in getting in and out of your vehicle or physically help setting him on the ground. Do not allow your older dog to jump down and jar those aging, possibly arthritic, bones.

Watch for weight gain. Just like us, our dogs experience a reduced metabolic rate as they grow older and therefore are more prone to pack on extra pounds. If you keep your dog active and in shape this should not be much of a problem.

Training need not be nearly as strenuous as in the dog's younger years. Older and wiser, your dog has likely figured out the best way to do things anyway, and in many ways will be smarter than you in that regard. It is more important to keep your dog physically fit. If you have a few dogs that you are training and you take your older dog along, run him on one training setup to the youngsters' three or four setups. Pick your old pal's workouts wisely.

Finally, be mindful of every hunting excursion. Take more precautions about where you take your older dog and the kind of weather you hunt in, as lengthy adverse conditions could be tough. Plan ahead for little ways to make the dog's time afield more comfortable. Your dog will appreciate it as once again he can count on you to be fair and conscientious about his needs.

PART FIVE

Dog Games

CHAPTER
THIRTY

Breed and Working Certificates

Some of you will remain hunters with your dogs, with no further aspirations. But some of you will feel a nudge to do more with your dogs, as I've hinted periodically. So—you check out the dog games.

An option within some breeds that is less involved than hunt tests or field trials allows you to work your dog toward field recognition. Some breed clubs offer the Working Certificate (WC) and the Working Certificate Excellent (WCX) programs that test your dog's ability to retrieve on land and water and award these efforts with a suffix certification (explained in chapter 4). Flat-coated and golden retrievers have WC and WCX events wherein the breeds can run events interchangeably. The Curly-Coated Retriever Club of America has a similar program. Also, the Labrador Retriever Club of America has a working certificate program and further mandates that no member use the CH (bench champion) prefix on a dog's name until WC requirements are met.

While requirements are easier than hunt tests, this program has merit in allowing dogs to prove field competence. Some show dogs even perform in this program. From someone who's been there and done that, I started out with a dog that would retrieve birds when hunting but needed lots of help, and one day I ended up at a breed test with my dog. Years later, I've been to the top of the field trial game. That worn motto applies to you and me: you've got to start somewhere. The working certificate program is an excellent place to begin.

Requirements include tasks such as executing a straightforward land double (two birds thrown before the dog is sent) and back-to-back water singles (one bird thrown and retrieved and then another bird thrown and retrieved) on birds in the WC level. Dogs demonstrate marking ability and willingness to retrieve two birds on land with the tenacity to swim on command for two singles. The WCX level tests advanced trainability, memory, and perseverance by executing a land triple (three birds thrown before the dog is sent) that includes two dead birds and a live shot flier; water work involves a double mark with an honor (dog must sit still while another dog's birds are shot) for another dog's work.

WC program requirements can sometimes be satisfied by completing one of each land and water series at an AKC-licensed field trial, by placement of first through fourth place in a stake or receipt of the Judge's Award of Merit (completion) at an AKC-sanctioned trial, completion of the Junior Hunter (JH) title, or one leg of the Senior Hunter (SH) or Master Hunter (MH) title.

Much effort is put into these programs to preserve the natural instincts and abilities for many field breeds. Should you decide to explore the dog games you should have arrived at a reasonable starting point for testing your training skills. Once you try your hand, you may want to step further into the organized field event direction, or you may be perfectly content with what you've achieved here. And that is fine, too. It's all about the things we can do with our dogs.

CHAPTER
THIRTY-ONE

Hunt Tests

In years past the only available dog game was the field trial. This wasn't a bad thing—and field trial dogs can exemplify the best of the best—but while field trials were born from hunting dogs, actual conditions became less like a normal day's hunt as bird dogs' and retrievers' abilities improved.

Sporting dog enthusiasts wanted a new game in town without the competitiveness of field trials, one that would test dogs on a working standard more akin to real-world hunting. Hence, the hunt test was born. The mid-1980s saw these fledgling programs begin to develop into their own.

Boykin Boy Hunt Test. (Pamela Kadlec)

Hunt tests have come full circle in the dog game world by filling a void in the wake of the expensive, challenging field trial game. Unfortunately, as the program grew, some supporters felt the need to slam field trial dogs and people. This was unnecessary—there is room for both games. The dogs and people can complement each other far more than they can tear each other apart.

Hunt tests are games whose time had come. It's my belief they would've prospered without manufacturing negative baggage. Many top hunt test bloodlines come from mainly field trial stock, and many of the dogs in both games originate from the same veins. Some enthusiasts play both games with their dogs and still hunt.

Currently, AKC and UKC support hunt test movements in all types of hunting dogs, from pointing breeds to Airedales. Hunt tests were defined so that people can work their dogs in conditions similar to hunting. Instead of using an elimination process to determine ultimate placements, dogs work toward a standard.

In hunt tests for bird dogs, all participants must walk. For the average hunter, this works well. However, dogs must be used to horses, as the judges and marshal will be mounted to better view the dog's performance. Still, in some hunting tests judges and the marshal may walk throughout the event. Dogs must demonstrate a keen desire to hunt, be bold and independent of its brace mate, and show desire to find game and point, skills that are escalated in ability as levels increase, up to the Master title where the dog must show a "completely finished" performance.

Retriever hunt tests were designed so the dog owner ends up with a good, solid hunting dog with a place to perform. The dog is not competing against other entries but against a "standard." Beginning levels test marking ability, while top levels require that the dog demonstrate exceptional marking ability and handling and honoring skills, reflecting a truly finished and experienced hunting retriever. All test levels should emulate true hunting situations with natural hazards, obstacles, decoys, and hunting equipment.

Hunt tests for spaniel breeds judge dogs on their natural and trained ability to hunt, flush, and retrieve their game on land and water, while the best dogs must work under control, must handle well, and must be steady to wing and shot.

Are you interested? Chances are your curiosity is piqued just a bit. Remember, you may be able to get your feet wet in WC/WCX programs before exploring hunt tests. Also, check with your local clubs; find those within driving distance that host tests. You might consider joining a club if you're not already a member. You'll gain new friends and maybe training partners!

Check out hunt test seminars. You'll become familiar with the standards that will be tested, requirements, and helpful tips. Come as a spectator to one or more events before you enter your dog. You'll learn what general things you'll need to polish in your dog's training and you'll see things you'll be required to do as a handler. Then when you attend your first event as an entrant, you'll feel a bit less like you have two left thumbs than if you had entered cold turkey.

In pointing and spaniel hunt tests, clothing should include comfortable footwear and blaze orange attire. Retriever hunt test handlers will run their dogs from the same area and should wear dark or camouflage clothing. Sometimes ear protection is recommended when guns are fired within close range of handlers, judges, and dogs.

Other hunting dog breeds have hunt test programs within their parent breed clubs, such as the Airedale Terrier Club of America, which organized its first hunting/working series in 1994. This program showcases upland bird skills, retrieving, and ability on fur.

NAVHDA belongs in a class of its own, known for its testing format for the continental HPR breeds. Until 1971 these "tests" were known as trials.

NAVHDA chapters sponsor four kinds of tests, including the Natural Ability Test, Utility Preparatory Test, Utility Test, and the Invitational Test, NAVHDA's highest level, open to qualified exceptional animals that have demonstrated a superior level of training and advanced skill. NAVHDA states that tests for versatile hunting dogs must meet certain criteria and be conducted in an environment that reflects actual hunting conditions and situations to showcase the best qualities of a good versatile dog.

If you're interested, find one of these events pertaining to your breed and check it out. There's nothing like the real thing, and you may find a way to spend some of your extra vacation time or your retirement. Time spent with your dog? Priceless.

CHAPTER
THIRTY-TWO

Sanctioned Events

Tree Dog, Pack Dog, or Earth Dog?

The tree dog performs by settling on the side of the base of a tree, announcing the presence of game cornered high above in the branches. The pack dog chases a rabbit or fox in packs or braces. The earth dog tracks game and wriggles through underground tunnels in pursuit of small game above and below ground.

Coonhound "Nite" Hunt Events

"Nite" may seem like a misspelled word, but it is what the coonhound competition world calls its games that take place at night. Hunting with hounds is one of the oldest of the organized dog sports. However, it wasn't until the 1940s that the coonhound world's first registry, American Coon Hunters Association (ACHA), was formed to stage wild coon hunts for determining the best dog. In 1951 the first official nite hunt rules were paired with four-hour casts, compared to the two-hour casts of today.

The sport has exploded so that today many different registries offer nite hunt programs and other events. Often high purses are at stake, as are prestigious World Hunt titles. Registries include UKC, AKC, PKC, ACHA, and the National Kennel Club (NKC). Events are restricted to six recognized coonhound breeds: black and tan, redbone, treeing Walker, English coonhound, bluetick coonhound, and the Plott hound. PKC also provides for crossbreeds and curs, while UKC has a cur/feist treeing contest.

351

Modern nite hunts are run in casts of two hours each with four dogs and four handlers per cast. Dogs are judged on a point system that acknowledges how hounds strike—or open on track—and the order in which they tree game. Some of today's events are benefit hunts that support such worthy causes as St. Jude's Children's Hospital.

Beagle Events

Another North American sport steeped in tradition is organized beagle hunts or trials, held exclusively in the United States and Canada and dating from 1890. Main registries include the American Rabbit Hound Association (ARHA) under the auspices of NKC, and AKC and UKC programs.

ARHA has four divisions of testing, including Big Pack, Gundog Division (including Gundog Pack and Gundog Brace formats with Open, Champion, and Grand Champion classes), the popular Little Pack venue, and Progressive Pack (the latter two also have Open, Champion, and Grand Champion classes). UKC's progressive beagle program includes Large Pack and Small Pack, limited to pack sizes of seven dogs, although the Winner's Pack could include nine dogs.

AKC's beagle program is considered a field trial program and is more than one hundred years old. The oldest format, Brace, judges dogs on their accuracy in trailing a rabbit; Small Pack Option (SPO) divides the dogs into packs of seven to pursue rabbits; and finally, Large Pack trials turn all dogs in the class loose to find and track hares.

Foxhounds

When you hear the term foxhunting, what images are conjured? You may envision a large hound pack accompanied by red-coated riders, and you're on track, no pun intended. Foxhunting is widely known as the sport of mounted riders chasing wild quarry with hounds. The Masters of Foxhounds Association of North America (MFHA) provides an eloquent description of the elements involved in an orchestrated hunt (see Resources).

North American foxhunting enjoys deep roots dating from colonial times. In general terms, "foxhunting" could include the pursuit of the red fox, gray fox, coyote, or bobcat. Today the MFHA is the governing body of organized fox, coyote, and drag hunting in the United States and Canada.

Foxhunts may be held using private packs, owned and supported by an individual, or subscription packs, where members pay a fee to hunt and the hounds are owned by a club or hunt committee. The latter case remains the most common American hunt, with subscription and organization similar to successful golf clubs. One pays a fee to participate and the money is used for hound care and hunt-associated expenses. Since no one knows where a wild fox may go, large areas of land are required for a successful hunt.

According to the MFHA Web site, "The popularity of foxhunting continues to grow. Currently there are 171 organized clubs in North America. There are many reasons for its popularity. There is an old adage that says, some people ride to hunt, others hunt to ride. Certainly the thrill of galloping over the countryside on a fine horse who meets his fences well, is a thrill for anyone. Also, the sight of a pack of hounds in full cry is breathtaking." (See http://www.mfha.com/abfo.htm.)

Another form of fox hunting is run by the National Foxhound Association, where dogs from as few as fifteen to several hundred are turned loose at once and judged on speed and drive, hunting, trailing, and endurance. The Standard Foxhound Stud Book is maintained by *The Hunter's Horn* magazine.

Earth Dog Events

Farmers once used small terrier breeds and dachshunds to pursue rodents to ground. These sporty little dogs had to measure up—or down—in body shape and mental tenacity to go where dogs hadn't gone before, into an animal's home turf. (Hounds go to ground after raccoon and other game.)

Nowadays few dachshunds and terriers are actually hunted on the game they pursued for hundreds of years, but organized earth dog events provide simulated action. Terriers and dachshunds now have legitimate outlets for their energy in training and competition. Tests by design awaken instincts in dogs of this working division, established in 1971, with AKC's program commencing in the 1990s. An introductory level, Introduction to Quarry, advances to Junior, Senior, and finally the Master Earth Dog levels where each dog must exhibit many advanced skills. UKC's earthwork program involves real hunting for wild quarry.

CHAPTER
THIRTY-THREE

Field Trials

The best of the best. Commonly viewed as the aristocratic extension of sporting breeds, field trials are responsible for the perpetuation of priceless qualities including style, boldness, and class in our modern-day breeds. While it's true that the modern game has evolved far beyond its original intent of duplicating a normal day's shoot or simulation of time afield, dogs have continued to rise to the occasion as genetics and trainability have improved one hundredfold.

When no other games existed, field trials shouldered the necessity of accurate record keeping and the responsibility of showcasing the best dogs in each breed. Field trials provided the means to track the accomplishments of well-bred dogs, an important way to determine worthiness of breeding stock for breed improvement. Field trial blood is found within most hunt test breeding stock.

Those opposed to field trials state that dogs consistently in the winner's circle are apt to ruin the breeds we love, accusing them of being well trained and well handled only because of the skills of their trainers. It's a common misconception that these dogs need no natural talent to reach the top of their game. I beg to differ—vehemently. It's pure rubbish to believe that consistent winners can finish, place, and win in today's exceedingly competitive environment without an abundance of natural talent enhanced by continually improving training methods.

It's tough to compete in modern-day field trials. But, if you can't run with the big dogs, stay on the porch. Appreciate these dogs for what they are—very talented athletes that are an asset to their breed. Whether you choose to compete is your choice. Just know that many field trialers began as hunters—me included—and most of us still hunt.

The ultimate question remains: Can All-Age pointing bloodlines function for foot hunting and can All-Age retrievers excel in duck blinds? The answer is *yes*; the key is how they're trained and handled.

Retrievers

Retriever trials began in the 1920s, with the first U.S. trial in 1931. Standards have changed enormously since then. Today's highly trained, stylish, intelligent field trial retrievers are truly impressive to watch.

International retriever working test. (Bill Beckett)

Weekend licensed events include trials for young dogs and advanced All-Age competitors. All-Age stakes include multiple marks—which are marking tests with birds thrown in various configurations—and blind retrieves, often several hundred yards distant. Placements in All-Age stakes award points that count toward the FC and AFC titles and contribute to qualifying for yearly National Championship events.

Bird Dogs

Great Britain held the first pointing dog field trial in 1876; eight years later the first U.S. pointing dog trial was held near Grand Junction, Tennessee. Two recognized bodies govern pointing dog trials in the States, American Field and AKC. American Field's history with pointing dogs dates from 1874 and incorporates horseback stakes and walking events on upland game birds, including quail, pheasant, prairie chickens, grouse, woodcock, chukars, and Hungarian partridge. AKC also offers Open All-Age and Gundog stakes. *American Field*, published weekly, remains the oldest continuous sporting journal in America.

There's nothing more exciting than observing an All-Age dog that knows its stuff. The intense, bold, fast dog that slams on point with class and style brings a thrill beyond words to the most casual observer.

The National Shoot-to-Retrieve Association has also reached admirable levels of participation by handlers and prowess in dog work.

Spaniels

Field trials for spaniels began in 1924 and currently offer several stakes for competitors. Qualities tested include steadiness to flush, shot, and command; marking ability; willingness to take hand signals; and style in delivery. These animated dogs are an absolute joy to watch when they are at the top of their game. If you've never seen well-trained spaniels at work, attend a trial.

Basset Hounds

These low-slung, lovable dogs are classified in the field trial division by AKC. The basset is a trailing hound whose purpose is to find game, to pursue it in an energetic and decisive manner, and to show determination. Basset hound field trials are designed to select hounds with sound quality and ability. They're run by Large Pack, Brace, or Small Pack Procedures and must possess searching and pursuing ability, accuracy in trailing, proper use of voice, endurance, and adaptability. Patience, independence, cooperation, competitive spirit, and intelligence are desirable qualities.

Dachshunds

All field trials should be run in braces on rabbit or hare, and classes include Open All-Age Dogs, Open All-Age Bitches, Field Champions, or Field Champion Dogs and Field Champion Bitches. Dachshunds should demonstrate obedience to commands and willingness to go to ground.

CHAPTER
THIRTY-FOUR

Events Made for Television

Recently some television networks have begun to include hunting dog shows in their programming. Airtime might mean short, two-minute segments on training tips, special episodes, or entire shows on dogs, hunting, and training. Actual hunting experiences spotlight choices for the upland bird hunter and waterfowl specialist, with additional programming giving special attention to hunting dogs such as hounds. Some outdoor shows feature dogs as cohosts, such as Minnesotan Ron Schara with his beloved black Lab female on *Minnesota Bound* and *Backroads with Ron and Raven*. Other pro-

SRS Hot Springs competition. (SRS Staff Photo)

The Super Fly competition is always a fan favorite. (Credit TK)

gramming highlights events tailored for television, such as the popular Super Retriever Series (SRS) and the crowd-pleasing Big Air Dock Dogs, Super Fly, and Extreme Vertical jumping competitions.

Super Retriever Series

SRS began in 1998 when Justin Tackett, Bill Fitts, and Shannon Nardi developed a spin-off retriever game from the traditional field event for ESPN. ESPN's *Great Outdoor Games* was born, and SRS has since evolved on its own merits. In SRS the goal is to complete the cleanest run (lowest score) on successive courses designed by judges. Tests simulate hunting conditions and use hunting props. Since its onset SRS has been run with "rubber" ducks and Avery True Birds (ATBs) (Dokken Dead-Fowl Trainers, described in chapter 18), and top qualifiers advance to a yearly Crown Championship. Crowds at SRS events have exceeded five thousand. This series is aired on Versus prime time (formerly OLN).

Dock Dogs and Super Fly Events

These dogs can jump! Big Air dogs "long jump" as they launch over water for retrievable objects. It's exciting to watch those dogs race down a dock and bravely launch themselves over water—this sport has universal appeal. Competitors include Labs, Chessies, border collies, and greyhounds. There's no restriction on breed, and Dock Dogs recently added a division for lap dogs.

Jumping events began under Shadd and Melanie Field's tutelage for ESPN's *Great Outdoor Games*. Big Air was born and has gone in many directions since then. Today's Dock Dogs and Super Fly events reward the dog with the longest jump. It's a team event. The presence of the handler and the precision of the handler's toss of the retrievable object over the water will affect overall jump performance. Dogs race down the simulated dock (forty feet long by eight feet wide, and twenty-four inches above water level) and then hurtle into the air after Dokken's ducks, Kong dowels, bumpers, tennis balls, Frisbees, and corn cobs, ultimately landing in a tank of water; jumping distances are measured.

Dock Dog Open Waves and Big Air events and *SRS* Super Fly competitions are the growing rage for grassroots retriever games. They provide a stimulating outlet for you and your dog to train and compete for monetary rewards

Water Dog TV

Innovative television producer Shannon Nardi began producing a new hunting show called *WaterDog* that originally aired on ESPN in 2001 and has since moved to Versus. Her goal was to design a series of shows based on a man and his dog and their trials and tribulations while hunting. Starring Justin Tackett and the female Lab Yella, the show has traveled to locations including Saskatchewan, Louisiana, and Maine. Good hunts and bad are depicted on camera with sportsmanship and camaraderie stressed regardless of the hunting success. In its fifth season, *WaterDog* shows it all.

Hunting with Hank and Dash in the Uplands

Upland hunting enthusiast Dez Young graced OLN (now Versus) for nearly a decade and has a loyal audience that first watched him hunt America's wild bird coverts with Hank, his Llewellyn setter. Later, Hank's son, Dash, starred in *Dash in the Uplands* with Dez. These shows are regularly watched by men and women who enjoy hunting vicariously with a fellow wing shooter. *Hunting with Hank* has been published as a book.

PART SIX

The Real Deal—Hunting in Style

CHAPTER
THIRTY-FIVE

Types of Hunting

Upland Hunting and Waterfowl Hunting

Bird hunting for upland game is one of the most popular forms of hunting in the world. Pointing, HPRs (the continentals), and spaniel breeds are commonly used in a variety of different methods to target everything from woodcock, bobwhite quail, Gambel's quail, Mearn's quail, scaled quail, mountain quail, California quail, chukars prairie chickens (native of India), ring-necked pheasant (native of Asia), ruffed grouse, sage grouse, sharp-tail grouse, blue grouse, Hungarian partridge (native to Sweden, Germany, and Russia) and ptarmigan (native to the Arctic, sub-Arctic, Iceland, Greenland, Japan, the Pyrenees, and Alps) to mourning doves and wood pigeons (ringdove). This last one is not a game bird technically speaking, but is often called a "sporting bird," because by all accounts it is one of the most popular birds for shooting in Europe. A colorful fast flyer of moderate size, there is no closed season on this one. Other European game birds include gray partridge, red-leg partridge, red grouse, and black grouse. Woodcock and snipe seem to be found the world over. In South America, the Picazuro and spot-wing are similar to the ring dove. Mexico has the popular white wing dove.

Most forms of upland hunting in the States require good physical conditioning on the part of the hunter and the dog since much walking in difficult terrain is usually necessary for a good day's hunt. In the United States birds are concentrated in various parts of the country; unless you travel you may never see or hunt many of them. Wild bird hunts and preserve hunts have both come into their own regarding most all species found in the States. In addition, some private shooting clubs have European or "tower" shoots with released pheasant that require guns and also dogs similar in fashion to the United Kingdom's pickers-up.

In the United Kingdom "hunting" is with hounds, and "shooting" is with pointing, HPR, spaniel, and retriever breeds. Shooting is further broken down to driven pheasant shoots, rough shooting, and wildfowling. Driven shoots include the guns, the beaters (usually spaniels and most of those English springer spaniel, but also sometimes Labs) that flush pheasants toward the guns, and the "pickers-up," the people who retrieve the downed game. Most pickers-up use Labs and often have several at heel all throughout the day.

Rough shooting (walk hunting), on the other hand, is the equivalent of upland game hunting in the States, with Labs and springer spaniels being the most popular dogs, although the use of cocker spaniels is on the rise. There are not many pointers except on the moors of Yorkshire or Scotland. Any game birds in season are taken on these shoots, or rabbits and wood pigeons year-round. In addition, deer hunters are known as stalkers and they use "stalker's dogs" to track and trail shot deer. Most of these dogs are Labs with a few German shorthaired pointers, continentals, and dachshunds.

Waterfowling varies slightly depending on the terrain of any given country. In the United States there is virtually every type of waterfowl hunting, from sea duck hunting to pothole shooting to hunting on inland lakes and more. Duck hunters might use sneak boxes, float blinds, portable blinds, johnboat blinds, or blinds built in flooded timber, or they may "jump shoot" on little hidden ponds. Nova Scotia duck tolling retrievers employ an entirely different method. These neat little dogs toll game along the shoreline where large numbers of ducks or geese are rafting offshore. As the dogs run and play they lure the ducks to shore where the hunters shoot and the dogs retrieve downed birds.

In the United Kingdom most waterfowl hunting is on the seacoast in estuaries and tidal marshes, and unlike the United States, in the United Kingdom no point of land is over eighty miles from any coast. Inland duck hunting across the pond is limited to inland lakes and ponds, similar to the United States, and geese decoy on land as they do in the States. Hunting blinds are called "hides" in the United Kingdom.

Species of waterfowl in countries such as Iceland, Ireland, and England include the pink-footed goose, greylag goose, white-fronted goose, Canada goose, mallard, teal, wigeon, pintail, shoveler, tufted duck, gadwall, and pochard, scaup, and oldsquaw. Iceland has a season on black seabirds such as the rasorbill, guillemot, Atlantic murre, Brunnich's guillemot, black guillemot, and the puffin. South American ducks include the rosy-billed pochard, white-checked pintail, yellow-billed pintail, brazilian duck, silver teal, red shoveler, and the cinnamon teal, which winters there.

Furred Game

Already mentioned are the rabbits and hares taken during rough shooting in Europe. Rabbit hunting is a popular pursuit in America and is usually aided with the use of beagles or bassets. In addition, it should be noted that rabbit dogs can and often are taught to retrieve so that they can deliver shot small game to hand or to the area of the hunter. Telemetry is widely used with hounds and helps eliminate the possibility of lost dogs.

Fox hunting, which includes gray and red fox, coyote, and bobcat hunting (mentioned below) has deep roots dating from hundreds of years. The most popular form of fox hunting includes the pack of hounds with mounted riders that race throughout the countryside in pursuit of their quarry, all the while observing decorum and tradition. Fox pens are a popular form of hunting, also.

Hunting for the elusive wild boar is popular in different parts of the world from southern areas of the United States to most of Europe, including Italy, Spain, Germany, Hungary, Bulgaria, Poland, Belgium, and France, and also Africa, South America, and Australia. Wild boars are hunted in most parts of the world. A number of tenacious breeds are used for this dangerous sport, including Jagdterriers, Drahthaars, griffons, Irish and Scottish wolfhounds and deerhounds, dogo argentinos, mixed hounds long of leg and ear, and others. In France the use of dogs quite resembles bear hunting in parts of the States where if pressure is not kept on the boar by the hounds the bear will surely escape. Also, when the boar is brought to bay the dogs must use caution or they will be injured, just as with a bear.

North American bear hunting also requires a pack of gritty dogs, which may include Plott hounds, blueticks, treeing Walkers, and mixed breeds. Young dogs will often switch off on an easier track, similar to some of the instances trainers of dogs run into when hunting boar in Europe, and this is undesirable. The dogs should stay with the bear track they start and increase pressure on the bear until treed. A track may be found at a bait pile or at a road crossing. Bear races often go for miles through unforgiving terrain and may run over the course of a day or more.

Cougar, or mountain lion, hunting is also popular in much of the western region (where legal) of North America, and tough hounds are needed to trail and tree these majestic beasts. Hunting conditions are usually taxing and grueling for both dogs and hunters who are often on horseback. Really good dogs can trail tracks several days old and eventually jump the track into a race.

One of the most popular types of hunting in North America is coon hunting with hounds. It is usually done on foot although in some hilly and mountainous regions the use of mules is popular. ATVs are sometimes used, as are boats in massive swamp areas. Raccoon are highly adaptable animals and are found in nearly every state and Canada. Hunting of squirrel, another form of game that trees, is also gaining strength in numbers of both dogs and hunters.

Bobcat hunting takes a special hound that is fleet of foot, very athletic, and also tough footed to take the pounding in snow and ice. Coyote hunting is also growing in leaps and bounds; usually sight hounds (such as greyhounds and Scottish deerhounds) are used to hunt coyotes in the plains states. Curs, feists, terriers, and hounds are used to squirrel hunt throughout North America.

Falconry

A centuries-old field art that can be constantly refined, falconry is best described as the hunting of wild quarry in its native habitat with a trained raptor, and also, for our purposes, with a dog. There are hawks that are flown straight from the fist when quarry is flushed, and there are falcons that are taught to wait, hovering on high, and come down vertically at extremely high speeds to overtake the fast-flying game birds from behind. Dogs are used with both of these types of hawking to find and point quarry, flush on command, or reflush game as needed. Falconers are somewhat divided regarding dog choice over the biddable setter, the hard-charging pointer, and not to be excluded, the versatile continental HPRs. Ultimately it's a matter of personal preference.

Falconry sounds simple and straightforward enough, but of course nothing is that easy. Once a falcon is released, if you cannot flush the quarry at exactly the right time and without fail, the bird will eventually leave the falconer to hunt on its own somewhere else downwind. And since the quarry can see the falcon overhead, it tends to flush at the wrong moment or sit tight and not be found at all.

To counter this obvious drawback, many falconers train pointing dogs as part of the hunting team. Interestingly, some of the best dogs for falconry can actually be those deemed gun shy and therefore considered useless to the gun hunter. In the field, the falcon is not put up (released) until the dog is on solid point. Within a few minutes, if the falcon has been well trained, it may be as high as 1,000 feet overhead waiting for the flush. The dogs should be steady to wing and hold solid through the initial flush, since there are usually more birds in the group and the falcon can remount to try again if the first attempt is a miss. In past centuries, before fences and other barriers complicated life, this type of hunting with falcons and dogs was done from horseback, and in many parts of the world this remains true today.

Telemetry is used on both the falcons and the dogs since the hunt can take either one far out of sight while they are in the act of chasing quarry.

The ancient sport of falconry—hunting with birds of prey—is alive and well and incorporates the use of dogs to work up the game for the bird. Many individuals practice falconry and are quick to point out that if you keep any bird of prey but do not hunt it, you are not a falconer. The visual blend of dogs, horses, and birds working in harmony to produce success in this sport is something to behold and experience.

CHAPTER
THIRTY-SIX

Hunting and Habitat

Continued successful hunting, not just in the short term but for the longevity of the sport, requires land and habitat management as well as strong conservation programs. All species of life need suitable space, food, water, and support to survive. Many state and federal agencies exist solely for the purpose of land management. Add to that the nonprofit conservation agencies that work tirelessly to implement sound practices that will protect habitat for various species as well as to secure new properties and land for these species, and the picture may not be as bleak as some would have us think. In addition, these agencies and organizations develop educational programs that help bring new interest into these hunting sports and also expand awareness for those of us already in the fold.

A number of government properties including state and federal land and game management areas have hunting opportunities, but it is up to us as sound, conservation-minded hunters to protect our rights to use these lands for the future. This means that we must self-police and care for public management areas in the same way we should maintain the private lands we are fortunate enough to use for training our dogs and hunting. "Treat the land as though it is your own" is always the best policy.

Ethics and respect go a long way toward furthering and solidifying any relationship; nowhere is this more true than on our wild lands. This means a variety of things, including stewardship of the places we love. Observe all game laws. Don't poach or break the laws, and encourage others to do the same.

Don't drive on the front lawn. Get out and walk. Use perimeter roads. Better said, don't destroy things for those that come behind you or it could be taken away from each and every one of us. Stay on roads and two-tracks, and unless any portion of property is designated for off-road use, observe the rules and regulations. Park your vehicle and walk in.

Police the lands. Whenever you can, pick up the trash left behind by thoughtless others. Empty bottles and cans can cut or otherwise injure you or your faithful canine hunting companion. If you see it and have a place to put it, pick it up and dispose of it yourself. Looking the other way—in this instance—is not the same as the adage many of us grew up with called turning the other cheek. Take the bull by the horns and continually do your part to preserve and protect the lands that we all use, the same lands that are inhabited by the game species we admire and hunt with respect.

It just takes one, and although this may seem lame at times in the face of wanton disregard by a few bad apples for the things we hold dear, each singular effort we expend can help overcome the negative influence of those few. When you take a moment to clean broken beer bottles or pick up a whiskey flask from a creek bank or the edge of a pond, you may be influencing someone else to do the same.

Certainly, this is not meant as a lecture to anyone, and I sincerely hope that everyone reading this is already a perfect example of this kind of behavior. However, it is so important to the future of our sport, not only for us, but so that our children and their children have the same opportunities to share time in the outdoors with a hunting dog and perhaps a special friend in pursuit of elusive quarry that often remains just that—but wherein memories are forged regardless of the successfulness or lack thereof on any given trip.

Hunting Gear and Gadgets

The difference between men and boys is their toys. Of course this includes girls and women, too, make no mistake! When it comes to the sport of hunting the list of available items to make hunting more enjoyable with your dog is not only a long one, it is growing longer, thanks to innovative technology. An overview of the gear and supplies necessary and optional for a successful hunt is not only helpful but will allow you to be better prepared once you hit the road. Take this list and add to it to accentuate your personal needs.

Hunting Paraphernalia

Most any hunting trip—of any kind—involves venturing into the wild outdoors. Usually, there are no helpful road signs and maps on every corner in the woods and fields you'll be canvassing. Indeed, often there are no roads at all, unless you count game trails. Directional equipment can make any trip a better one by giving you the means to find your way back home.

Compass—In today's market there are scores of sturdy, well-made compasses available in a variety of models that can be carried in a pocket or around your neck.

GPS unit—The Global Positioning System is a high-tech instrument that can be programmed, operates off space satellites, and when used properly will tell you where you are in relation to your starting point and how to get back there. Note: Carry extra batteries—you don't want to be stranded by a dead GPS when you need it most.

Radios and cell phones—Communication is often key to a successful hunting trip. With the advent of cell phones this is often more easily accomplished, but there are many areas where cell phone reception is poor at best or nonexistent. In these areas handheld radios are invaluable. Many models are available with up to several miles of range depending on terrain. Note: Again, carry extra batteries, even if you have a rechargeable unit, just to be on the safe side.

Waterproof matches—A handy packet or two of waterproof matches may never be used, but it sure is nice to have them when you need them. Put this item on your list and get a supply, just in case the need should arise.

Game calls—For hunting purposes you may want to invest in applicable game calls. In certain types of hunting, electronic-type calls are allowed, but know your regulations before you buy.

Space blanket—These emergency blankets come packaged in a little cellophane or in plastic wrap and are about the size of a standard deck of cards. Again, you may never need one, but it takes up very little room and only costs a few dollars. Put one or several in your truck with other hunting supplies.

Flashlight—Invest in a good waterproof flashlight. Models are available from several different companies with extremely bright special bulbs in all sorts of convenient sizes. Some models can be attached to your forehead and thus are conveniently out of the way.

Belt light—Used for night hunting sports, these lights wrap around the waist with a single battery pack attached or a series of batteries weighted through the belt itself. A hard "bump" cap is usually worn with the "headlight" piece for hands-free operation, and an additional "spotlight" can be used when exceptionally bright light is needed. Many makes and models and voltage sizes are available.

Combination tool device—An item such as the trademarked Leatherman always manages to provide that little extra convenience when you need it. A suitable choice should include screwdriver ends, pliers, wire cutters, knives, can opener, and corkscrew.

Handsaw—Usually these gadgets come with two types of cutting blades and are useful for squaring up a camping area as well as just about any trimming need.

Rope—Different size cotton and nylon rope for emergencies is a good idea.

Twist ties or Velcro strips—These can be used to cinch up and repair equipment when in a bind until you can get back to civilization.

First-aid kits—You'll need two versions, one for yourself and your hunting buddies, and another for your dog.

Canteen or hydration container—A portable water supply is a necessity more often than not. Invest in something that is easily carried on your person.

Backpack, fanny pack, or belt pouch—A variety of different-sized storage items will make your choice as simple or as advanced as you'd like for carrying necessities with you in the field or woods.

Boot dryer—This electric contraption comes in several different sizes and uses warm, forced air to dry your boots from the inside out.

Clothing

Footwear—Virtually no other item is as important for your body as a well-made, comfortable pair of shoes or boots. Poorly made or ill-constructed footwear can make you miserable in less time than it takes to tell you about it, destroying your hunt and perhaps your overall comfort for weeks to come. Invest in footwear that suits your needs and the terrain. Look for proper soles, insulation or lack thereof, waterproof or not, and convenient types of lacings. Not all footwear is created equally.

- Hiking shoes—available in leather or canvas in a variety of heights
- Shoe boots—constructed of durable leather, may be waterproof
- Knee boots—rubber, various types of leather or snakeproof material
- Hip boots—from rubber to breathable extensions sewn to knee boots
- Waders—available in rubber and a variety of waterproof breathable fabrics

Socks—Your choice of sock is vital to comfortable footwear as well. Today's hunting supply stores carry a wide variety of well-made cotton, wool, and blend socks in various weights and heights.

Electric socks—These are just as the name implies.

Wader booties—Usually of down or Thinsulate, these are wonderful to have during extremely cold weather when wearing waders.

Underwear and outerwear—During cold weather, suitable undergarments are as important as well-made outerwear garments. Layering is often the best bet for optimal hunting comfort.

Undergarments—Silk, cotton, thermal, and synthetics are all available in different weights and thicknesses.

The following are also suggested:

- Layering shirts, sweatshirts, sweaters
- Appropriate raingear
- Jackets and coats in different weights and insulation
- Camouflage and blaze orange items
- Vest with game pouch
- Jacket with game bag, which can be removed
- Gloves for the season

Additional Items

People and dog snacks can make any long day or night of hunting more enjoyable. Choices include power bars, trail mix, nuts, chocolate, and fruit for you, as well as honey and performance diet kibble for your dog. Other conveniences that are easy to carry would be Chapstick, sunscreen, a pocket-sized pack of facial tissues and one of Wet Wipes, and a travel-sized bottle of hand sanitizer.

CHAPTER
THIRTY-EIGHT

An Art to This Game

Successful hunting with your dog requires a knack, inside knowledge, and a good eye. It helps to know about the places you'll be going, and as a hunter you should of course possess an insight on the birds or game you will pursue—things such as their feed and activity habits—to increase your odds of at least seeing game. Much of this information is best learned through the annals of personal experience and the lore and priceless tips passed along by mentors over the years. Practice observant behavior everywhere you go, whether you are actually hunting or just training your dog. Be familiar with your gun and shoot it often. You can hone your shooting skills at your local skeet, trap, or sporting clays range.

But there is more to it than that. The art to this game comes not just from the knowledge you will build up in the passage of time. Rather, put the spotlight on your dog and watch him develop into a hunting fool that knows where to look for his game. It is a universal thing about a hunting dog—if you allow a dog to develop to his full potential, not only will he be in tune with the quarry but he will learn about scent and the wind and how to make things swing in his favor. The dog will know where he has been successful before and he will check those kinds of places again and again, always building more in his memory banks with each trip to the woods or field. Hunt your dog in a big wind, in the rain, with a front moving in, on a bluebird day or night. He is like a giant sponge, constantly learning more with each time you take him hunting, and those things simply aren't learned sitting in a kennel. (Note: While we are frequently talking in singular form, all of this applies to the solo dog, yes, but also to dogs hunted in packs. Dogs learn in the woods, in the field, in the swamp, and if they could talk we'd be the better for it—but they darn sure don't learn sitting on concrete.)

With all this, however, comes a deep, abiding respect for the wildlife we pursue and the dogs that are a part of us—or the wild country we share with them in the chase. Hunting is far more than a bottom line and is not measured by the amount of harvest, but by reverence for the game we seek and the sporting chance we give it . . . and the thrills we receive in return, albeit often empty-handed.

Know Your Quarry and the Habitat

Study your game. Bear hunting? Know how they move, what they eat, how they react when dogs strike a track and begin pursuit. Some areas have spring seasons and fall seasons, others just have fall seasons. Hunting with hounds is just one of three methods for hunting bear, the other two being setting on a blind over bait and stalking. Bear hounds usually wear tracking collars, and a race can take the better part of a day and cover miles of ground. A big bruin will often pass up many chances to tree while looking for suitable big timber; it may also charge the dogs any number of times, scattering them. They will regroup and resume the chase. Found North, South, East, and West, bear take on formidable country such as southern cypress swamps, northern cedar swamps, and everything in between.

Mountain lion hunting? Cougars are found in the western United States and western Canada. Actual hunting takes place in the winter months, usually from December through March, and is extremely physically demanding, whether in the southern or northwestern states. Hunters use horses and ATVs, and in the high country they use snowmobiles and snowshoes. Become familiar with everything about mountain lions— know their behaviors inside and out. (Reports of cougar sightings have been made in several midwestern, eastern, and southeastern states. The Florida panther resides in southern Florida and is protected.)

Fox hunting? What will the wily creature do, and what should you expect from all the dogs, and from other hunters and horses? Few organized activities are as thrilling as riding to the hounds through wild countryside, where you must be one with your horse over all types of terrain including formidable fences, streams, and riverbanks. The full coursing cries of the hounds will stir your blood and waken your senses, whether you are on horseback or on foot.

Rabbit hunting? Some mornings are diamonds, others are dust. Rabbits and hares are found throughout the world and are hunted predominantly with beagles but also with spaniels and even mixed-breed hunting dogs. Rabbits can zig and zag in and under pretty thick cover and are very excitable to the dogs; indeed, any number of hunting dogs that are supposed to be after other game cannot pass up the chance to run a rabbit. Rabbit hunters are very addicted to their sport, but then, addiction is a part of this hunting with dogs, no matter the formula. Good rabbit dogs know their stuff and are a joy to hunt behind.

Squirrel hunting? Curs, feists, terriers, and hounds are used to put the limb-rat skyward. Squirrels have a habit of not adhering to a strict schedule, and some outings may produce lots of action while on other days barely a squirrel is seen. The best squirrel hunting is in the fall and winter months. Squirrels prefer hardwoods and swampy areas that produce an abundant food source in acorns and nuts. When a squirrel is treed and the hunters approach the tree, the squirrel is very good about staying on the opposite side of the tree trunk from any hunters. Squirrels often build large nests of leaves high up in the branches of trees near the trunk and cannot be seen in their nests.

Raccoon hunting? What is on the menu for Mr. Ringtail at any given time of year? In July it might be blackberries and wild cherries; in October, peanuts; in December, pecans; and whenever handy, frogs and crawfish. Raccoon can be found just about everywhere in North America and have even been relocated to mainland Europe. In some parts of the States, they are classified as furbearers and in others they are a pest; seasons and limits, or lack thereof, are made accordingly. This sport can be pursued by one man and one dog. A pack of hounds is not necessary for success. Although raccoons are nocturnal, early morning hunts often offer quite a bit of action. The racketeering raccoon is able to pull a fast one on many a hound and seemingly vanish into thin air.

Regarding virtually all game—where are the water sources? While some types of game require very little water to survive, they may dine on grasses or smaller creatures that live near water. How does the land lay? Terrain—hollows, swamps, hills, creeks, flat woods—what is the prevailing wind? Are there any major game trails? What are the major and minor feed times—do you follow the moon and tide tables?

Know the birds. Bobwhites—perhaps the most popular and widely known game bird—won't be found in open fields so why train there? When you are using planted birds, put them where the bobwhites will be, such as fencerows, briar patches, stream banks, and along a wood line and those infamous "edges." The edge might be where two different types of cover meet or the edge of various types of growth around a pond or swampy area. How do bobwhites react when pushed by dogs? Bobwhites and Mearn's quail (in the southwestern United States) are very similar in the way they hold. In contrast, most western quail will run. Indeed, the blue-scaled quail is an all-out runner, although a covey will sometimes hold relatively well in cover. The blue-scaled quail is the most speedy, to be sure, but all other western quail are likely to stay on the move, too, and some bird dogs counteract this by learning the art of circling, especially when at least two dogs are being worked, to hem up the birds.

Pheasant can really cover some ground, too, and they are an example of how birds adapt under hunting pressure. I remember hearing stories about how pheasant would hold as well as Mr. Bob (white), but this was decades ago, like maybe in the 1940s. Over time, these birds have become much more wary and elusive. They will sneak, duck, and run, but you can often eventually catch up with them by stopping your dog until you can catch up with him and then sending the dog after the bird again. This takes some doing and some pheasants will be lost, but you'll get some of them, too. Cornfields and sorghum fields are hot spots for birds, as are the surrounding fencerows, especially thick ones and cover-strangled ditch banks, but an often overlooked favorite haunt of the pheasant is a slough. Find a marsh or slough in pheasant country and you are likely to be in the birds. Hopefully you will be properly dressed or you may get wet, but don't pass these places up. Also, once the snow falls, pheasant will burrow and savvy dogs learn this as well. (As do ruffed grouse—they will burrow in the snow or roost in conifers.)

Grouse dogs should work closely and need to pull up at the first hint of scent because most all grouse will otherwise explode, possibly out of range. Ruffed grouse hang out in thick, heavily wooded areas, in poplar stands, and along two-tracks with cover. Since woodcocks also fancy these wooded, dense places, as well as muddy swamps, a good grouse dog will usually double well on woodcock, provided you can interest him in a woodcock. And talk about hard to hit! Both of these birds will challenge your skills on your best day. You'll need your dog to locate the birds and also to find them after the shot. Trust me, they are nearly impossible to find otherwise, and that is if you are lucky enough to connect. Also, many a grouse/woodcock hunter puts a bell on his dog—yes, the cover and woodlands can be that thick.

Doves, including mourning and white wings, are one of the most prolific birds we have, as they lay clutches of two about four times a year, and one of those will also be raising young within the year. Doves like water sources, tree lines, and grain fields, such as sunflowers, peanuts, and corn. Seasons often encompass at least a hefty portion of hot weather, though, so bring water and ice for both you and your dog and stay on top of your dog's condition. Don't overdo it. Doves will fly in rain, but that same rain, if cold and inhospitable, will move them on to greener pastures. The next morning they are usually gone. A word of caution about doves: they fly like kamikaze pilots—really. They will humble many a good shot after any but the first few early-season shoots.

Ducks are hard to predict, at the very least, during most of the season. Different parts of the country produce some of the same species and many different ones. For example, cinnamon teal are largely inhabitants of the Pacific flyway—I had never seen one of these beautifully striking ducks until my first trip to California—while mallard concentrate on the coasts and in the middle of the States, such as Louisiana, Mississippi, and Arkansas. Mallard frequent flooded green timber as well as unlikely peanut fields on land in Oklahoma. Old-squaws, wigeon, teal, and scaup are found from Iceland across Europe. Duck hunters keep crazy hours for often limited opportunities at shooting, and at certain times of the season we also brave difficult and inhospitable weather for this pleasure. Yes, I count myself in this largely temporarily insane bunch of hunters—during duck season, that is.

Goose hunting seems to withstand changes in the lifestyles of the birds themselves. I remember as a child being called out by my father to witness the magic of those first flocks of geese migrating south; there was forbidden magic and mystery in their eerie calling as they flew, often by moonlight. Canada geese prefer cornfields while snow geese choose rice. Shooting is often quite sporting. Geese may be large birds but they aren't patsies to hunt, and can be very challenging for the dogs as well when called upon to retrieve.

Know the Dogs

As your dog learns his craft, you in turn should cultivate the art of learning to watch him closely, not as you do when you train the dog, but as a fellow hunter and teammate. Often he will tell you things about your game before you perceive them yourself.

Retrievers learn to watch the skyline, and they virtually always see incoming ducks before you have a clue anything is headed your way. Same thing for doves—your dog will see them first, once he gains just a little experience in the field. Watch your bird dog for the slightest makings of a scent cone off a bird and snap to—get ready. Zero in on the signs from your flushing dog or your beagle, as well.

Decipher the different voices of your hound. If you listen, you will learn. Compound the learning experience by getting out there in the timber behind your dog. In this manner you will quickly discover what types of terrain your hound is working through as he follows his quarry. Translation: A hound will usually give different tongue when working through a tough, muddy swamp than he does when crossing an open field or when working through hardwoods on a hillside or weaving through a corn or soybean field. You'll be able to tell when your dog hits a marked tree but goes on with his hunt and when he finally locates and trees his game. You'll know when he falls treed on a layup coon (one that hasn't been down on the ground for quite some time, but remains up in a tree). You'll eventually be able to tell when your dog is running off game and when he switches over to his straight game.

Stay in tune with what is happening when you are out hunting. If you are after ducks over a swift river, you may need to send your dog before your bird hits the water because the bird will drift rapidly out of reach and keep going. Are you hunting in ice and snow? Is there danger to your dog?

Know the Weather

Any time we set foot into the wild outdoors we are at the mercy of Mother Nature, and never should we underestimate that fact. Not only will her extremes of weather have the potential to affect our hunts, but they also compromise our safety.

Know the projected weather forecast, and anytime there is the slightest hint of foul conditions approaching, continually monitor updated reports for changes and potential threats to your well-being and the hunt. A portable battery-operated weather radio is a wise yet inexpensive investment that will pick up local forecasts from virtually any location you may be hunting. Bottom line—always respect the elements. Keep the safety of yourself and your dog the main priority of any hunt.

CHAPTER
THIRTY-NINE

Hunting with Dogs

Few experiences in this world rival the unique and special relationship a hunter and his dog share with the wilderness each time they venture into the outdoors for a spot of hunting. Indeed, what makes the sport so seductive, so intangible, and so surreal is that no two encounters with the wild will be the same. Our inner spirits crave the reckless abandon and freedom we feel with a gun in our hands and a dog by our side. Adventure beckons beyond each hollow and around the creek bend or over the next mountain, ne'er predictable and always memorable, right down to the first spectacular sunrise and that last blazing sunset.

Hunting Alone with Your Dog

Not everyone has the luxury of a hunting partner—the *Homo sapiens* variety, that is. Certainly it is true that I don't, and as such I've learned an awful lot the hard way about what to do and what not to do when hunting alone. When hunting gets in your blood, it is high near impossible to turn down the urge to get out there just because a hunting buddy is unavailable. Off you go into the wild blue yonder, or black night, as the case may be. A little forethought and preparation goes a long way to a successful hunt alone.

Any time you set out on a solo expedition, make an effort to let someone know approximately where you will be going and when you should return. This way in the event your vehicle breaks down, or worse, if you have an accident, a time will come when you will be missed. At that point, would-be rescuers have some information to organize a search.

You should have a complete extra change of clothes for yourself no matter the time of year, and perhaps an extra jacket stashed behind the seat of your vehicle. A clean, dry towel, a blanket, waterproof matches, spare snacks for you and your dog, a compass that you know how to operate, and a flashlight—or spare hunting light if you are night hunting, in case your main light malfunctions—all these things often become life-savers in the face of an emergency. Carry a supply of water for you and your dog as well. A working cell phone, as mentioned earlier, is often the biggest lifesaver of all; carry a list of important phone numbers including those of your personal physician and your dog's veterinarian.

Use caution when you are tempted to plow across that beaver pond, or swim that river, or climb that tree. Accidents can and do happen when you are alone—well, you get the picture—and you must be able to look after your beloved dog as well. You can't do that very efficiently if you are hurt or injured, possibly rendered immobile at least until found.

Keep your wits about you at all times. Know where you are and what it will take to return to your vehicle. Be mindful of the passing time and the threat of any approaching bad weather. Awareness of your limitations and that of your dog will be your most important act of self-protection, whether you consciously realize this fact or not.

If you should get lost, don't become distracted. Before you set out blindly in a rashly chosen plan of action, consider your options and what best percentages of rescue might be in your favor. Figure out ways to leave "signs" behind for folks that will be looking for you. And trust your dog, for he often knows better than you how to get back to where you started, and in some cases, how to find the way home.

Hunting with Friends

On the other hand, when you set out with hunting buddies, there is a certain amount of etiquette, usually of the unspoken kind. Perhaps your buddy has a dog. Is the dog well-trained or a brute in the duck blind? Has he been taught the finer aspects of hunting afoot or is he oblivious to wonders such as hidden coverts and other magical woodland places? Will he focus on finding and running a rabbit or does he want to aggravate all the other dogs on the ground? Is he serious about hunting or does he potter and dally about?

Any time you contract a hunting trip with a friend, whether on the neighbor's back forty or several states away, it is your responsibility to bring a trained dog that won't strain the relationship, and your buddy should do the same. Suppose you have a young dog that has been doing well in the yard and you want to see how he handles his first hunting situation, and then suppose the dog falls flat on his face, doing nothing right, everything wrong, and generally making an overbearing nuisance of himself. Perhaps you should consider putting your dog back in the truck for the remainder of the day and until you're able to execute more training with your young protégé. Now, if you are lucky and you have a true friend who wants you to take advantage of the time out with your green youngster, go for it—but let your friend know in advance about the experience, or lack thereof, your dog has at that time with regard to hunting.

When hunting in a place with numerous hunters, such as a dove field, make sure that your dog picks up only your birds and possibly those of nearby hunters without dogs that request the help of your dog. Make a wide berth for any renegade dogs disrupting the entire dove field with disobedience and downright vagrancy.

If you will be using hunting props that you suspect your friend's dog has never seen before, you might offer an introductory lesson or two to help ease any uncomfortable feelings on your friend's part. Explain the use of a boat platform to assist your efforts in getting the dogs in the boat, or a tree ramp for flooded timber. Bring an extra lead in your pocket in case your friend forgets to bring one and ends up really wishing one was handy.

Be sure to complement your friends' dog for a job well done, when applicable. Inquire about the dog's breeding and his overall ability and experience. Perhaps set up a training session to work on problems that your friend's dog or your dog exhibited throughout the course of the day, or night, and you may have a new training partner as well.

There may be times when you have a young dog and the other folks in your hunting party have fully trained dogs. Be sure to carry a checkcord and show consideration if your youngster proves to be a little too overeager. Don't let your dog spoil the hunting for your friends. You'll have years to work it, God willing.

Often with bird dogs or retrievers, on those first times out you may want to plan on letting someone else do all the shooting so that you can concentrate on your young dog's finds, his points, flushes, or retrieves, and work the dog on being steady. Concentrate on your dog instead of worrying about your shooting and take the chance to work on making sure your dog gets it right, out there where it counts.

Extremes and Your Dog

We must consider that any hunting trip, even the shortest ones, usually require a ride to and from the hunting location. During extremes of hot (such as during portions of dove season) and cold weather, additional care must be taken to ensure your dog's safety and comfort unless he is in the same air-conditioned or heated vehicle interior as you. Modern technology has developed certain accessories intended to help us keep our dogs cool in hot weather. Some examples include cooldown crate mats filled with polymer cooling crystals that will work for several days at a time and can be reused over and over. Dog collars made of the same stuff are available. Battery-operated fans can be attached to the doors of crates and dog boxes for additional comfort when your dog is confined. Some people prefer to freeze two-liter or gallon jugs with water to place in the dog box when the vehicle is stationary, but beware of doing so in a moving vehicle where such a frozen, weighted object may become harmful in the case of an accident. Note: The practice of clipping some longhaired breeds in the summertime will make them more susceptible to sunburn. Many experts feel that a long hair coat actually insulates against heat and that shaving during the summer can compromise the dog's comfort. You be the judge for your own dog, or consult your veterinarian.

Conversely, extra care is also needed during extreme cold. Other types of crate pads can be used to provide warmth during cold weather. Bedding types help, as well.

Heatstroke concerns were covered in chapter 12, but keep in mind that dogs can suffer frostbite, too, just as we can. It appears on the extremities such as the ears, the tip of the tail, the feet, and on the scrotum in males. Signs of frostbite include sloughing of epidermal skin surface tissue, white or grayish tissue, reddened tissue, and symptoms of shock. If you see these symptoms, try to get to your veterinarian. You must warm the affected areas as quickly as possible. Do not rub or massage these places. Use warm water but not hot water and apply warm, wet towels to the areas.

If you run or cycle with your dog, be mindful of hot asphalt and pavement with regard to his foot comfort in the summer, and also of ice and snow caking between the toes of his paws in winter. Deicers put on roads can irritate the pads of the feet as well. Always keep a close check on your dog's paws throughout the year.

Constantly monitor the physical condition and well-being of your dog while you are out hunting. Certain times of year the weather can quickly become too warm or too cold or too formidable to continue a hunt, for your sake and that of your dog. Your dog cannot speak for himself, not in so many words, anyway, which is why you must be in sync with what he is telling you in dog talk.

Consider that no matter where you are, if things begin to deteriorate, you still must make it back to your vehicle, or to a cabin or campsite, for assistance or help or to go home. Never push the envelope beyond wise limits or it could spell disaster for you or your dog. Read the signs of the day and act accordingly. This might mean cutting big plans in half, but doing so could save your life or your dog's life. And, God willing, there will be another day.

The Total Package

"Cherish" is the word I use to describe all these feelings that I have overflowing from inside . . . for this world I've been blessed to explore with a faithful hunting companion by my side.

It is one thing to tackle the wilderness and match your wits with Mother Nature and all she throws in your path, unleashing violence in her wrath and revealing brilliance in her splendor, in places never seen from the comfort of a sofa. It is yet again quite another thing to experience these things with the companionship, skills, and togetherness of your special pal, ever anxious as you to round the next bend or cross the next hill, sharing it all. To experience this oneness in Nature's backdrop truly is the total package.

CHAPTER
FORTY

Changing of the Times

I find it very interesting when I read stories from one and two centuries ago and I see passages about concerns for animal habitat and hunting grounds. Of course this subject is constantly talked about in most hunting circles today, and with good reason, but to realize that these same worries plagued our forefathers is notable, at the very least. Then again, their circumstances were different from ours, depending on the time frame, as there were market hunters for ducks and geese and an all-out slaughter of buffalo, deer, and caribou. Because of hunting pressure the passenger pigeon became extinct.

Times have changed and with the advent of applied biology principles, management, conservation, and good hunting practices, most species have not only rebounded, but are thriving and increasing in population. We need to fiercely protect what we have, and to always conscientiously set good examples as hunters with dogs, and we need to encourage young and old alike to join our ranks in training our beloved dogs and in hunting in the outdoors. Keep our sport alive and well—it begins and ends with us.

Nevertheless, our forefathers were correct. Civilization marches ever onward and outward, and we must constantly adjust to the pressure and find new areas to train our dogs and cultivate opportunities for places to hunt. More associations may be formed such as the California Retriever Trainers Association, which has purchased several thousand acres of land for the training of hunting and trial dogs and for holding field dog events, whose membership is fee based. Remember, this group didn't do it alone, but had the help of other state and federal conservation-based organizations, all working together for common goals. We may see more of that in the future across all types of hunting. And working together to accomplish these things? That is certainly a good thing.

Training Areas

We not only face the possibility of continued shrinking areas for training as civilization continues its encroachment on rural life in all parts of the world, but we must be mindful of the grounds we do have for use and how they affect the training our dogs receive. Are we being short-changed, and if so, what should be done to compensate? Has the quality of these grounds changed, and if so, for better or for worse?

The best example that comes to mind regards water for training retrievers. Not too many years ago, sculpted training grounds with fancy ponds complete with spits, points, and islands was a rarity in the United States. Indeed, even the necessity of training on private land was largely unheard of, and most training took place on public lands. Most water on public property consists of lakes, ponds, rivers, and floodwaters, with the emphasis on "natural" water and generally lots of it.

Private land for training is becoming more the norm, and pond building is at an unprecedented boom as the popularity of retrievers, duck and upland hunting, hunt tests, and field trials continues to escalate. As a result we see less and less "big water" and "natural water," and the performance of our dogs reflects this. Fewer dogs are experienced with boat marks or marks that fall in big, open water, and fewer dogs can tackle the "out-to-sea" concept so necessary for ocean, sea duck, and Great Lakes hunting.

While our retrievers are known as "water" dogs, many types of that very stuff, water, can be intimidating to them without proper exposure. It does not all come naturally. Alternate training grounds can be located with some effort, and many things can be done to prepare your dog for this type of work. Without it, some dogs will refuse big water, whether hunting or testing, make no mistake about it. Water work is difficult. It can be taxing for both the dog and the trainer. It is more time consuming and requires special equipment in many cases. But the rewards you reap will be many in the years to come, if you plan to hunt your dogs in the water.

And, let me tell you, it is an experience beyond words to have your dog brave that really big water, as well as the wind and the current that usually goes along with it, and retrieve those hard-earned ocean ducks on your trip of a lifetime, or to forge out into that wind-whipped lake you've ached to hunt on for years to retrieve that incredible one-in-a-million shot you made that only you and your dog witnessed—these are memories that will stay with you forever.

On the same train of thought, no pun intended, the areas used to work any of our hunting breeds of dogs should contain enough variation so that our dogs can work virtually anywhere we take them and do so with the aplomb that their genetics and trainability make possible in the wild.

Hunting Areas

Sometimes the training areas we are able to use during off-season months transforms into our hunting ground as of opening day. Whenever you have the opportunity to train your dog where you can hunt, you can give him the opportunity to learn more about the vegetation, the smells, and the habits of the game, and get a general working knowledge of all things helpful to success, or at least to a good day afoot.

When you are planning a hunting trip to an unfamiliar location, find out what you can about the birds or the game you will be pursuing and what types of terrain are predominant in the area. Then create training situations in places close to home that have one or more of the characteristics where you'll be hunting. Anything you can do in advance to prepare your dog for your trip will be helpful once you arrive with the highest of hopes.

As awareness of wildlife management continues to rise we may face better and better hunting grounds, although their actual size may decrease. Only time will tell. The more we know about the necessary habitat and food sources for our game and implement those findings, the better off many of these species will be for the future.

More pay-hunt areas are cropping up, which may be another sign of the times. Private landowners may be more conscious of their wildlife resources, but it takes dollars to properly maintain and grow those resources. Hunters can help offset huge costs. In some areas, hunting clubs are springing up that are managed not unlike golf clubs and other exclusive membership groups, but this is not necessarily a bad thing. The more facilities and grounds available for all types of hunting, the better our footing and our reputation will be in the general population.

What Lies Ahead

Will we be privileged to enjoy our hunting rights ten years from now? Twenty? What about our children and their children? Trouble has been brewing for many years, primarily in the form of opposition to hunting from animal rights "terrorist" groups and antihunting factions. Yet, many of us are content to drift along on cruise control, oblivious to the threats that different types of hunting receive on a regular basis. We think that it won't happen to us, and this complacency could be our downfall. It's past time to wake up and smell the roses. Stand up and be counted. Vote for candidates who support the rural way of life and the important role that hunting plays in conservation and wildlife management.

Who would have ever thought that England would lose the right to foxhunt? What about Queensland, Australia, banning all duck and quail hunting as New South Wales and western Australia had already done? How many of you know that People for the Ethical Treatment of Animals (PETA) is in our schools in the good old United States of America, distributing coloring sheets to children that depict the evils of hunting, while previously accepted hunting magazines are banned from many school libraries? We've got to counter these efforts in every way we can.

In the United States some interesting developments are afoot. Bear hunting seasons that were revoked, largely because of actions from animal rights and antihunting groups, have been reinstated in a number of areas. Cougar hunting, for instance, was outlawed in Oregon, but is undergoing scrutiny for possible reinstatement because of the subsequent influx of mountain lions into residential areas once hunting—an important part of wildlife management—was banned. In most areas of the United States the majority of the population have realistic views about the traditions of hunting, the role it plays in conservation management, and the dollars brought in from the industry to retail businesses and into government agency coffers from licensing revenues.

We play a part in the opinion of the nonhunting public, and we must realize that now. Every time we make hunting trips and are exposed to people along the way, the things we do and say and the ways we conduct ourselves will influence voters that can support us or denounce our ways. All of these things apply not only to us but to our dogs. The way we treat public and private property will reflect upon us as a whole. The courtesy we give others can come back full circle to our sport. If you know someone abusing our rights and blackening our eyes, stand up and be counted—do something about it!

Support of organizations that work tirelessly on our behalf, such as the National Rifle Association and the U.S. Sportsmen's Alliance, as well as state and national organizations such as Delta Waterfowl, Ducks Unlimited, Pheasants Forever, Ruffed Grouse Society, Quail Unlimited, California Waterfowl Association, and others not necessarily dog-related such as the National Wild Turkey Federation, will help to perpetuate the hunting life we love.

We must get involved, from the grassroots level all the way up to national politics and beyond. One of the most influential things within our grasp is to bring new people into our sport, and an important key to this success is by bringing more men and women into our hunting, shooting, and dog training activities. But we shouldn't stop there. The children and young people of the world, voters and hunters of tomorrow, should be encouraged and taught sound hunting and conservation principles today. They are our future.

CHAPTER
FORTY-ONE

Magical Memories

Hopefully, somewhere along this journey you've taken with your dog you elected to keep traveling down more training roads and adventures along the way. Your relationship with your dog has the potential to constantly evolve into something better than it was yesterday, last week, or last year. Indeed, by now you can pretty much tell what your dog is thinking and you can predict his actions. Chances are your dog can say the same about you.

The Team

Over the course of time, commitment, and sharing special adventures, the two of you have fused as a team. One is not complete without the other. You both have a mutual respect that radiates from deep within. Not only is this sort of connection a deep relationship that transcends the superficialities of this world, but its presence is readily apparent to your hunting partners and your peers—they can see the bond you share, and more than a few of them will be at least a little envious, truth be told.

There is something else you've come to realize. Although you've been told for years that dogs don't think, you suddenly know one day that in fact, they do, and you have countless examples to draw from as proof of this fact, given to you by not only your own dog, but others you've been privileged to know over the years. In school you may have learned that centuries ago, Descartes and assorted philosophers of the times published papers as fact stating dogs could not communicate as we can, that they could not think, and that ultimately they had no souls—and people believed what they read. Fairly recently in history, Darwin and others have proposed vastly different theories based on the premise that dogs do have the ability to think and make decisions on their own. Does this mean dogs are people? Of course not. Does it mean the subject might be multidimensional? Quite possibly, but we already know that our dogs can think. We don't need proof from experiments and studies—we've seen tangible proof ourselves, over and over again.

One Human, One Dog?

The time will come, if it hasn't already, when you want to get another dog, and there may be any number of reasons for this monumental decision. Perhaps your dog is nearing middle age and you want to bring along a youngster to spell the dog as he gets older. Perhaps you've been watchful of a special upcoming breeding and it's time to put up or shut up with a deposit. Perhaps you feel that you need at least two dogs to hunt with. You might just want additional companionship to complement what you've experienced with the pal you've already got. The list goes on and on.

Should you make the plunge and become a multidog household? Wrestle with your situation honestly, and if you feel that you are considering this life-changing commitment for all the right reasons, and if you have the room and the time to invest in another dog, then bite the bullet! Go for it. Of course remember that your next dog, and the one after that, may never measure up to the one you now have and at the very least will likely be quite different in personality and trainability. No two dogs are alike, and if you keep that in mind and wipe the slate clean when you approach another training schedule for your new addition, you will do just fine. Apply all the sound principles you have learned about training as well as the things you've learned about dogs and hunting along the way. With each dog you train you will sharpen your own talents as a dog trainer and you will continue to increase your insight and abilities to that end.

Hunting Journal Excerpts

19 October, 19—, Grand Rapids, Minnesota—Gray day, blustery wind, temperature in the low 40s, we hunted on paper-company land and those birds were blustery, too, always out and away before we could get a shot. By the end of the hunt I had two grouse and one timberdoodle and felt exceptionally lucky to have them, wouldn't have the woodcock at all if not for the English Setter, Lacey, who proved the others wrong on my shot by returning with my bird . . . a tenacious dog with a superb nose . . . I brushed out her tangles when we got back in.

22 October, 19—, Tower, Michigan—Cold, still night. Bitter cold for October. A million stars in the sky, and the northern lights came out and put on a brilliant show. Dogs got on a track that wouldn't end. . . . Everyone on the hunt had their own versions of what the dogs were running, but when they finally came treed our hunting party was so spread out over miles that it was up to me to go to the tree. Tucker gave me a radio and told me the river should be knee deep where I would cross. Wrong! It was up to my chest, nearly my neck, bracing cold and rushing current . . . with the aid of a stout limb for a walking stick I made it across and climbed up the river bluff to the tree. My dog, Haywire, and two other dogs all going crazy and me too, shouting into the radio, until I realized that there was no coon in this tree. . . . I gradually realized that the silhouette taking shape near the truck was . . . no, it couldn't be . . . I kept blinking and squinting and then stepped back and looked for any telltale signs on the tree trunk . . . it seemed impossible—it was a black bear.

18 December, 19—, Egg Harbor, New Jersey—A nor'easter is coming in and we were lucky to get the boat out to the island before the bay became too treacherous to navigate. We've battened down the hatches on the cabin, but the howling wind threatens to burst inside and scatter us over the sedge. Morning will come early. *19 December, 19—,* Egg Harbor, New Jersey—Cold, raw, salty wind. We made it out to the layout blinds over an hour before daybreak, and one minute the morning suddenly appeared . . . there was no sunrise. And what a morning it was! Black ducks! How they test the hunting skills! One magnificent red-leg to my credit and what a shot it was. . . . My dog, Ten, made a spectacular retrieve battling the tide as the black was swept away. . . . This is a beautiful bird, no orange legs here, but instead of the truest red hue.

8 January, 20—, Los Banos, California—High winds, temperatures in the low 20s. Meeting at the duck shack to draw blinds. My hunting partner, Anthony, and I pulled blind #8—on the 8th day, so maybe good luck!—and we were situated in our submerged barrel blinds well before daylight. Talk about birds! Mostly pintail, many of them stayed high, and cinnamon teal, wigeon, lots of spoonies about. . . . We both limited out and had some of the best shooting; backwards overhead and passing shots; Reba, at 12 years old, proved she didn't know how old she was as she retrieved every duck we shot and two cripples from another blind . . . and was ready for more.

I urge you to keep a hunting journal to record the details of your trips into the wild outdoors. One will become another and another, and yes, it will take some time to write the entries, but one day you'll be so glad you did! You'll learn to condense each experience into meaningful words that will—at least to you—re-create each memory in living color as you relive them through the pages of your journal. But more than that, you can eventually see patterns in the times of year, the seasons, and the weather, and helpful hunting tips such as what the game is feeding on. (Something I try to do whenever possible, or at least when I remember, is record information about the type of food any animal or bird is eating at the time of the journal entry.) I always include notes about the dogs, too, which ones were along, and any comments.

Those Special Places

Your dog will take you places. Seems a bit backward, I know, since you are the one driving the truck, but if you don't already know what I mean by those few words, you will soon. Those words have a double meaning because the places will not just be destinations, but also where you go in your mind because of the bond you've forged with your dog and the intangible dimension this has brought into your life.

When I think about the adventures shared with my dogs it really never ceases to amaze me . . . the incredible wilderness and wild country seen over several decades of hunting and competition. We've been to the mountains of Idaho, Nevada, Utah, Wyoming, Colorado, and Montana, as well as the canyons of California and rugged places in Arizona and New Mexico; to rice fields and quail country in Texas; rice and flooded timber in Arkansas and Mississippi; the bayous of Louisiana; vast sweeping cornfields in Kansas; the potholes of North Dakota; the timber country of Minnesota and Michigan; the raw waterfowling country of the Northeast and the Great Lakes; swamps in Alabama, Georgia, South Carolina, and Florida; hardwood country in Kentucky, Ohio, Indiana, Illinois, and Missouri; the majestic pine country—quail country—of southwest Georgia and North Carolina; the plains of Canada; and all kinds of special places in between, every place cherished for the unique aspects brought to my life. God willing I'll be able to share more experiences like these over years yet to come and will vow to always hold each place and each adventure dear to my heart.

I cannot take enough deep breaths of these contrasting places—the dank mud and black water of moss-draped cypress swamps, the invigorating pungent spice of spruce in grouse country, the aromatic smell of sage in the high country—each place holds its own scent, even to my limited olfactory capacity. Imagine what our dogs inhale and process as they sort out the things in their world! I'm convinced they know these places by their smells, just like we do, and probably so very much more.

And in this fast-paced world we live in, it seems that our dogs play a special part in helping us slow down and smell the roses, or rather the fresh-dug peanuts, and the falling leaves of autumn—the seasons and the vitality the world has to offer—if only we'll look.

My parting thought: You've done your best by your dog and trained him to the utmost of your ability, now it's time to follow through—with exposure and experiences in the real world of hunting. Enjoy the journey!

Resources

Medical Sources
———————————————

American Veterinary Medical Association (AVMA)
Web site: http://www.avma.org

Canine Eye Registry Foundation (CERF)
Lynn Hall
625 Harrison Street
Purdue University
West Lafayette, IN 47907-2026
Phone: 765-494-8179
Fax: 765-494-9981
Web site: http://www.vmdb.org
E-mail: CERF@vmdb.org

Optigen, LLC
Cornell Business and Technology Park
767 Warren Road, Suite 300
Ithaca, NY 14850
Phone: 607-257-0301
Fax: 607-257-0353
Web site: http://www.optigen.com
E-mail: genetest@optigen.com

Orthopedic Foundation for Animals (OFA)
2300 E. Nifong Boulevard
Columbia, MO 65201-3806
Phone: 573-442-0418
Fax: 573-875-5073
Web site: http://www.offa.org

University of Pennsylvania Hip Improvement Program (PennHIP)
http://www.pennhip.org

First Aid

Creative Pet Products
P.O. Box 39
Spring Valley, WI 54767
Phone: 877-269-6911
Web site: http://www.petfirstaidkits.com

Ruff Wear
2843 NW Lolo Drive
Bend, OR 97701
Phone: 888-783-3932
Fax: 541-388-1831
Web site: http://www.ruffwear.com

Pet Insurance

http://www.petinsurance.com
http://www.pet-insurance-info.com
http://www.24petwatch.com
http://www.petplan.co.uk
http://www.healthy-pets.co.uk

Registries and Associations

American Kennel Club (AKC)
Operations Center
8051 Arco Corporate Drive, Suite 100
Raleigh, NC 27617
Phone: 919-233-9767
Web site: http://www.akc.org

Australian National Kennel Council
Web site: http://www.ankc.org.au/
(Navigate to State and Territory Info)

Canadian Kennel Club (CKC)
200 Ronson Drive, Suite 400
Etobicoke, Ontario
M9W 5Z9 Canada
Phone: 855-364-7252
Fax: 416-675-6506
Web site: http://www.ckc.ca
E-mail: information@ckc.ca

Hunting Retriever Club (HRC)
100 East Kilgore Road
Kalamazoo, MI 49002
Phone: 269-343-9020
Web site: http://www.ukcdogs.com

Kennel Club—United Kingdom
1-5 Clarges Street
London
W1J 8AB Great Britain
Phone: 012-9631-8540
Fax: 020-7518-1058
Web site: http://www.the-kennel-club.org.uk

Masters of Foxhounds Association of North America
P.O. Box 363
Millwood, VA 22646
Phone: 540-955-5680
Fax: 540-955-5682
Web site: http://www.mfha.com

National Kennel Club (NKC)
134 Rutledge Pike
P.O. Box 331
Blaine, TN 37709
Phone: 865-932-9680
Fax: 865-932-2572
Web site: http://www.nationalkennelclub.com
E-mail: nkcregistry@bellsouth.net

National Shoot-to-Retrieve Field Trial
   Association (NSTRA)
226 North Mill Street
Plainfield, IN 46168
Phone: 317-839-4059
Fax: 317-839-4197
E-mail: nstrfta@ameritech.net
Web site: http://www.nstra.org

North American Hunting Retriever
   Association (NAHRA)
P.O. Box 5159
Fredericksburg, VA 22403
Phone: 540-899-7620
Fax: 540-899-7691
Web site: http://www.nahra.org

North American Versatile Hunting Dog
   Association (NAVHDA)
International Office
P.O. Box 520
Arlington Heights, IL 60006
Phone: 847-253-6488
Fax: 847-255-5987
Web site: http://www.navhda.org
E-mail: navoffice@navhda.org

Professional Kennel Club (PKC)
P.O. Box 4759
Evansville, IN 47716
Phone: 812-868-1900
Fax: 812-868-1909
Web site: http://www.prohound.com

United Kennel Club
100 E. Kilgore Road
Kalamazoo MI 49002
Phone: 269-343-9020
Fax: 269-343-7037
Web site: http://www.ukcdogs.com

Victorian Canine Association Inc. dba DOGS Victoria
Locked Bag K9
Cranbourne 3977
Victoria, Australia
Phone: 030-9788-2500
Fax: 030-9788-2599
Web site: http://www.dogsvictoria.org.au/
E-mail: office@dogsvictoria.org.au

For more registries, including Japan, Chile, Holland, Sweden, Ireland, Scotland, Norway, New Zealand, the Netherlands, Uruguay, Czech Republic, France, Estonia, Portugal, Denmark, Finland, and Italy, go to http://dogs.about.com/od/kennelclubsandregistries.

National Organizations and Museums

American Field Stud Dog Book
http://www.americanfield.com/Pages/FDSBinfo.html

American Rabbit Hound Association
255 Indian Ridge Road
P.O. Box 331
Blaine, TN 37709
Phone: 865-932-9680
Web site: http://www.birddogfoundation.com

Bird Dog Foundation, Inc.
505 West Highway 57
P.O. Box 774
Grand Junction, TN 38039
Phone: 731-764-2058
Web site: http://www.birddogfoundation.com

National Shooting Sports Foundation (NSSF)
11 Mile Hill Road
Flintlock Ridge Office Center
Newtown, CT 06470
Phone: 203-426-1320
Fax: 203-426-1087
Web site: http://www.nssf.org

Breed Clubs

Airedale Terrier Club of America
April Clyde, secretary
403 Walnut Court
Dagsboro, DE 19939
Web site: http://www.airedale.org
E-mail: longvue@mchsi.com

American Black and Tan Coonhound Club, Inc.
Web site: http://www.abtcc.com

American Bloodhound Club
Susan Paine
8810 E. G Street
Tacoma, WA 98445-1926
Web site: http://www.americanbloodhoundclub.org

American Blue Gascon Hound Association
3415 Virgil Goode Hwy.
Rocky Mount, Va, 24151
Phone: 540-489-3755
Web site: http://www.abgha.org

American Brittany Club, Inc.
Carterville, IL 62918
Web site: http://clubs.akc.org/brit

American Chesapeake Club, Inc.
Kimberly Forhart
23016 64th Avenue SW
Vashan, WA 98070
Web site: http://www.amchessieclub.org

American Foxhound Club, Inc.
1648 FM 2144
Weimar, TX 78962
Web site: http://www.americanfoxhoundclub.org

American Pointer Club, Inc.
Debra Freidus, DVM
388 Burlington Road
Harwinton, CT 06791
Web site: http://www.americanpointerclub.org

American Spaniel Club, Inc.
Web site: http://www.asc-cockerspaniel.org
E-mail: Asc.secretrary@gmail.com

American Water Spaniel Club
4005 Ben Lomond Drive
Palo Alto, CA 94306-4503
Web site: http://www.americanwaterspanielclub.org

American Wirehaired Pointing Griffon Association
1924 Sweetwater Road
Gypsum, CO 81637-9413
Web site: http://www.awpga.com

Basset Hound Club of America (BHCA)
1743 Route 206
Skillman, NJ 08558-1914
Phone: 908-359-1372
Web site: http://www.basset-bhca.org

Boykin Spaniel Society
P.O. Box 2047
Camden, SC 29020
Phone: 803-425-1032
Web site: http://www.boykinspaniel.org

Clumber Spaniel Club of America, Inc.
Web site: http://www.clumbers.org
E-mail: secretary@clumbers.org

Curly-Coated Retriever Club of America
Web site: http://www.ccrca.org
E-mail: crlycoated@aol.com

Dachshund Club of America
Andrea O'Connell, secretary
1793 Berme Road
Kerhonkson, NY 12446
Phone: 845-626-4137
Web site: http://www.dachshundclubofamerica.org
E-mail: amtekel@hvaccess.com

Dogo Argentino Club of America
840 CR 431
Pleasanton, TX 78064
Web site: http://www.dogousa.org

English Cocker Spaniel Club
   of America, Inc.
Shannon Loritz
903 Lake Street
Fremont, WI 54940
Web site: http://www.ecsca.info

English Foxhound Club of America
Emily Latimer, secretary
230 Equestrain Trail
Welford, SC 29385
E-mail: englishfoxhound@att.net

English Setter Association of America, Inc.
17842 Club Vista Drive
Surprise, AZ 85374
Web site: http://www.esaa.com

English Springer Spaniel Field
   Trial Association, Inc.
Mary Parszewski
E 9538 Kanaman Road
New London, WI 54961
Web site: http://www.essfta.org

Field Spaniel Society of America
Maxine Reed
3515 Kerley Cors Road
Tivoli, NY 12583
Web site: http://fieldspaniels.org

Flat-Coated Retriever Society
    of America, Inc.
13208 Mandarin Road
Jacksonville, FL 32223-1746
Web site: http://www.fcrsainc.org

German Shorthaired Pointer Club of America
Susan Clemons
5400 Spotted Dog Trail
Chino Valley, AZ 86323
Web site: http://www.gspca.org

German Wirehaired Pointer
    Club of America, Inc.
Sarah Cowell-Herz
32446 Barber Road
Agua Dulce, CA 91390-4871
Web site: http://www.gwpca.com

Golden Retriever Club of America
Barbara Branstad
P.O. Box 20430
Oklahoma City, OK 73156
Phone: 800-632-5155
Web site: http://www.grca.org

Gordon Setter Club of America Inc.
Sharon Hultquist
13332 Redding Drive
Fort Wayne, IN 46814
Web site: http://www.gsca.org
E-mail: Springsong1@comcast.net

Greyhound Club of America
Dani Edgerton
7115 W. Calla Road
Canfield, OH 44406-9454
Web site: http://www.greyhoundclubofamericainc.org

Harrier Club of America
Ellen Parr
P.O. Box 503
Woodburn, OR 97071-2145
Web site: http://www.harrierclubofamerica.com
E-mail: ellen@wynfieldhounds.com

International French Brittany Club of America
P.O. Box 104
Pettibone, ND 58475-0104
Web site: www.frenchbrittany4u.org

Irish Setter Club of America, Inc.
William Deily, Jr.
99 Plantation Road
Carriere, MS 39426
Web site: http://www.irishsetterclub.org
E-mail: irishdox@juno.com

Irish Water Spaniel Club of America
Deborah Bilardi
1930 Marion Avenue
Novato, CA 94945-1755
Web site: http://www.iwsca.org

Jack Russell Terrier Club of America
P.O. Box 4527
Lutherville, MD 21094-4527
Web site: http://www.terrier.com

Labrador Retriever Club, Inc.
Christopher Wincek
14686 Grand Army of the Republic Highway
Chardon, OH 44024
Web site: http://www.thelabradorclub.com

Large Munsterlander Club of North America
Rita Merkel
Box 302
Lake Cowichan, British Columbia
Canada VoR 2Go
Web site: http://www.lmcna.org

National Beagle Club, Inc.
Emily Southgate
P.O. Box 642
Middleburg, VA 20118-0642
Web site: http://Clubs.akc.org/NBC

Nova Scotia Duck Tolling Retriever Club
Katie Dugger
3477 NW Countryman Circle
Albany, OR 97321-9622
Web site: http://www.nsdtrc-usa.org
E-mail: secretary@nsdtrc-usa.org
Canadian Web site: http://www.toller.ca

Pudelpointer Club of North America
Lisa McNamee
Phone: 949-863-1500, extension 208
Web site: http://www.pcna.org
E-mail: hdhuntclub@aol.com

Red and White Setter Club of America, Inc.
Web site: http://www.irishredwhitesetterassociation.com

Retrievers Online
1457 Heights Road, RR#3
Lindsay, Ontario, K9V 4R3
Canada
Phone: 705-793-3556
Fax: 705-793-3554
Web site: http://www.retrieversonline.com

Rhodesian Ridgeback Club of the United States, Inc.
Ross Jones
2008 Dorothy Street NE

Albuquerque, NM 87112-3224
Web site: http://www.rrcus.org
E-mail: rossbod@abq-nm.com

Scottish Deerhound Club of America, Inc.
Jana Brilee
2226 Roberts Place
Walla Walla, WA 99362-9851
Web site: http://www.deerhound.org
E-mail: jaraluv@charter.net

Small Munsterlander Club of North America
Irene Thun
444 South Colonial Parkway
Saukville, WI 53080
Web site: http://www.smallmunsterlander.org
E-mail: dthun@wi.rr.com

Spinone Club of America
P.O. Box 307
Warsaw, VA 22572
Web site: http://www.spinoneclubofamerica.com

Standard Poodle—The Poodle Club of America
Mrs. Helen Tomb-Taylor
2434 Ripplewood
Conroe, TX 77384
Web site: http://www.poodleclubofamerica.com
E-mail: pcasecretary@aol.com

Sussex Spaniel Club of America
Danita Slatton
5629 E. County Road 700 S
Greencastle, IN 46135
Web site: http://www.sussexspaniels.org

Vizsla Club of America, Inc.
Kim Himmelfarb
16 Deer Run Road
Canton, CT 06019
Web site: http://vcaweb.org

Weimaraner Club of America
Ellen Dodge
P.O. Box 489
Wakefield, RI 02880
Web site: http://weimaranerclubofamerica.org

Welsh Springer Spaniel Club of America, Inc.
Carla Vooris
783 Ellington Farm Road
Manson, NC 27553-9200
Web site: http://www.wssca.com

Publications and Periodicals

American Cooner
C&H Publishing
P.O. Box 777
Sesser, IL 62884
Phone: 800-851-7507
Web site: http://www.americancooner.com

American Field: The Sportsman's Journal
American Field Publishing Company
542 S. Dearborn Street, Suite 1350
Chicago, IL 60605
Phone: 312-663-9797
Fax: 312-663-5557
Web site: http://www.americanfield.com

Bird Dog & Retriever News
563 17th Avenue, NW
New Brighton, MN 55112
Phone: 651-636-8045
E-mail: publisher@bird-dog-news.com

Black's Wing & Clay
(Listing of dog and hunting-related businesses and supplies)
14505 21st Avenue N, Suite 202
Plymouth, MN 55447
Phone: 800-766-0039

Coonhound Bloodlines
100 East Kilgore Road
Kalamazoo, MI 49002
Phone: 269-343-9020
Web site: http://www.ukcdogs.com

Ducks Unlimited
One Waterfowl Way
Memphis, TN 38120
Phone: 800-45DUCKS
Fax: 901-758-3850

Full Cry
P.O. Box 777
Sesser, IL 62884-0777
Phone: 800-851-7507
Web site: http://www.treehound.com/html/fullcry.html
E-mail: fullcry@mychoice.net

Gray's Sporting Journal
P.O. Box 1207
Augusta, GA 30903
Phone: 706-722-6060

Gun Dog
6420 Wilshire Boulevard
Los Angeles, CA 90048-5502
Phone: 323-782-2316
Web site: http://www.gundogmag.com

Hunter's Horn
C & H Publishing
114 East Franklin Avenue
P.O. Box 777

Sesser, IL 62884
Phone: 618-625-2711

Just Labs
2779 Aero Park Drive
Traverse City, MI 49786
Phone: 800-773-7798
Fax: 231-946-9588

North American Hunter
12301 Whitewater Drive
Minnetonka, MN 55343
Phone: 800-688-7611

Pheasants Forever
1783 Buerkle Circle
St. Paul, MN 55110
Phone: 877-773-2070
Web site: http://www.pheasantsforever.org

The Pointing Dog Journal
2779 Aero Park Drive
Traverse City, MI 49786
Phone: 800-773-7798
Fax: 231-946-9588

Quail Unlimited
31 Quail Run
P.O. Box 610
Edgefield, SC 29824-0610
Phone: 803-637-5731
Web site: http://www.qu.org

Rabbit Hunter
C&H Publishing
114 E. Franklin
P.O. Box 777
Sesser, IL 62884
Phone: 800-851-7507
Web site: http://www.americancooner.com

Retriever Field Trial News
4379 S. Howell Avenue, Suite 17
Milwaukee, WI 53207-5053
Phone: 414-481-2760
Fax: 414-481-2743
E-mail: retrievernews@mindspring.com

The Retriever Journal
2779 Aero Park Drive
Traverse City, MI 49786
Phone: 800-773-7798
Fax: 231-946-9588

Retrievers Online
1457 Heights Road, R.R. #3
Lindsay, ON K9V 4R3
Canada
Phone: 705-793-3556
Fax: 705-793-3554

RGS Magazine
Ruffed Grouse Society
451 McCormick Road
Coraopolis, PA 15108
Phone: 412-262-4044
Fax: 412-262-9207
Web site: http://www.ruffedgrousesociety.org

Shooting Sportsman
P.O. Box 1357
Camden, ME 04843
Phone: 800-766-1670
Web site: http://www.shootingsportsman.com

Sporting Classics
P.O. Box 23707
9330-A Two Notch Road
Columbia, SC 29224
Phone: 800-849-1004
Web site: http://www.sportingclassics.net

Upland Almanac
P.O. Box 70
Fairfax, VT 05454
Phone: 802-849-9000
Web site: http://www.uplandalmanac.com

Wildfowl
6420 Wilshire Boulevard
Los Angeles, CA 90048-5502
Phone: 323-782-2316
Web site: http://www.wildfowlmag.com

Wing & Shot
6420 Wilshire Boulevard
Los Angeles, CA 90048-5502
Phone: 323-782-2316

Sportsmen and Lobby Groups

Delta Waterfowl Foundation
P.O. Box 3128
Bismark, ND 58502
Phone: 888-WTR-FOWL

Dove Sportsman's Society
Quail Unlimited (QU)
P.O. Box 610
31 Quail Run
Edgefield, SC 29824
Phone: 803-637-5731

Ducks Unlimited (DU)
One Waterfowl Way
Memphis, TN 38120
Phone: 800-45DUCKS
Web site: http://www.ducks.org

National Rifle Association (NRA)
11250 Waples Mill Road
Fairfax, VA 22030-9400
Phone: 703-267-1000
Fax: 703-267-3994

NRA Free Hunters
http://www.freehunters.org

National Wild Turkey Federation (NWTF)
P.O. Box 530
Edgefield, SC 29824
Phone: 803-637-3106
Web site: http://www.nwtf.com

Pheasants Forever
1783 Buerkle Circle
St. Paul, MN 55110
Phone: 877-773-2070
Web site: http://www.pheasantsforever.org

Ruffed Grouse Society
451 McCormick Road
Coraopolis, PA 15108
Phone: 412-262-4044
Fax: 412-262-9207
Web site: http://www.ruffedgrousesociety.org

United States Sportsman's Alliance (USSA)
801 Kingsmill Parkway
Columbus, OH 43229
Phone: 614-888-4868
Fax: 614-888-0326
Web site: http://www.ussportsmen.org

Web Information Forums

Foxhounds—http://www.masterfox.net
Gun Dog Refuge Forum—http://refugeforums.com/refuge
Retriever Training Forums—http://www.retrievertraining.net/forums
Shooting Sportsman—http://www.shootingsportsman.com
Squirrel Dog Central—http://www.sqdog.com/forums
Upland Journal—http://www.uplandjournal.com
Versatile Dogs—http://forum.versatiledogs.com
Working Retriever Central—http://www.working-retriever.com

Whelping Boxes: http://www.xocom.com/fr/whelping.htm

Hunting and Dog Training Supplies

Doctors Foster and Smith—800-381-7179
www.drsfostersmith.com

Dogs Afield—800-863-3647
www.dogsafield.com

Gun Dog Supply—800-624-6378
www.gundogsupply.com

Lion Country Supply—800-662-5202
www.lcsupply.com

Nite Lite Company—800-332-6968
www.basspro.com
www.cabelas.com
www.gandermountain.com
www.huntsmart.com

Wick Outdoor Works—800-325-2112

References

Acker, Randy. *A Field Guide to Dog First Aid: Emergency Care for the Outdoor Dog.* Belgrade, MT: Wilderness Adventures Press, 1994.

Begbie, Eric. *Gundog Training Made Easy.* Self-published. United Kingdom. 2005.

Bennett, Bill. *Beagle Basics: The Care, Training, and Hunting of the Beagle.* Wilsonville, OR: Doral Publishing, 1995.

Brown, William F. *Retriever Gun Dogs: History, Breed Standards and Training; Upland Game and Waterfowl Specialists.* New York: Barnes, 1945.

Carlson, Delbert G., and James M. Griffin. *Dog Owner's Home Veterinary Handbook.* New York: Howell Book House, 1980.

Dahl, John, and Amy Dahl. *The 10-Minute Retriever: How to Make an Obedient and Enthusiastic Gun Dog in 10 Minutes a Day.* Minocqua, WI: Willow Creek Press, 2001.

Derr, Mark. *Dog's Best Friend: Annals of the Dog-Human Relationship.* New York: Henry Holt, 1997.

Dornin, Tom, and Velta Dornin. *Breeding a Strain of Better Beagles.* New Wilmington, PA: Son-Rise Publications, 1991.

Erlandson, Keith. *The Working Springer Spaniel.* Shrewsbury, Shropshire, UK: Swan Hill, 1995.

Fergus, Charles. *A Rough-Shooting Dog: Reflections from Thick and Uncivil Sorts of Places.* New York: Lyons & Burford, 1991.

———. *A Rough Shooting Dog: The First Season of a Hunting Spaniel.* New York: Main Street Doubleday, 1995.

Fisher, Dave. *I'd Rather be Rabbit Hunting.* Smithfield, PA: LinDavid Productions, 1997.

Goodwin, Butch. *Retrievers . . . From the Inside Out.* New Plymouth, ID: Northern Flight Retrievers, 2003, 2005.

Graham, Evan. *SmartWork for Retrievers.* Liberty, MO: Rush Creek Press.

Hardaway, Benjamin H., III. *Never Outfoxed: The Hunting Life of Benjamin H. Hardaway III.* Columbus, GA: Benjamin H. Hardaway III, 1997.

Holst, Phyllis A. *Canine Reproduction: A Breeder's Guide.* Loveland, CO: Alpine Publications, 1985.

Hudson, David. *Working Pointers and Setters*. Mechanicsburg, PA: Stackpole Books, 2004.

Humphreys, John, comp. *The Complete Gundog*. Newton Abbot, NY: David & Charles, 1990.

Irving, Joe. *Gundogs: Their Learning Chain*. Dumfries, Scotland: Loreburn Publications, 1983.

——. *Training Spaniels*. Shrewsbury, Shropshire, UK: Swan Hill, 1993.

Isabell, Jackie. *Genetics: An Introduction for Dog Breeders*. Loveland, CO: Alpine Blue Ribbon Books, 2002.

Kadlec, Pamela Owen. *Retriever Training for Spaniels: Working with Soft-Tempered, Hard-Headed, Intelligent Dogs*. Edgefield, SC: Just Ducky, 2002.

Knutson, Paul, and Julie Knutson. *The Pointing Labrador: Getting the Most from You and Your Dog*. New Castle, CO: Clinetop Press, 2001.

Lamb, Vickie. *Dynamics of Hound Training*, 2 vols. Register, GA: Wynd-Chyme Press, 2002 and 2004.

——. *Carr-Dinal Principles of Retriever Training*. Register, GA: Wynd-Chyme Press, 2006.

Masters of Foxhounds Association of North America. *Foxhound Kennel Notebook*, Millwood, VA: Millwood House, Ltd., 1997.

McCurdy, Robert. *Life of the Greatest Guide*. Phoenix, AZ: Blue River Graphics, 1981. 3rd Ed, Loveland, CO: Jess Rodriguez, 2002.

Merck and Co. *The Merck Veterinary Manual*. Whitehouse Station, NJ: Merck and Co., 2005.

Miller, Pat. *The Power of Positive Dog Training*. Indianapolis, IN: Hungry Minds, 2001.

Monks of New Skete. *How to Be Your Dog's Best Friend: A Training Manual for Dog Owners*. Boston: Little, Brown, 1978.

Onstott, Philip. *The New Art of Breeding Better Dogs*. New York: Howell Book House, 1962. (First published by Kyle Onstott 1946 by Denlinger's.)

Osborn, David A. *Squirrel Dog Basics: A Guide to Hunting Squirrels with Dogs*. Watkinsville, GA: Treetop Publications, 1999.

Quinn, Tom. *The Working Retrievers: The Training, Care, and Handling of Retrievers for Hunting and Field Trails*. New York: Lyons Press, 1998.

Robinson, Jerome B. *The Ultimate Guide to Bird Dog Training: A Realistic Approach to Training Close-Working Gun Dogs for Tight Cover Conditions*. New York: Lyons Press, 2000.

Rutherford, Clarice, and Cherylon Loveland. *Retriever Puppy Training: The Right Start for Hunting*. Loveland, CO: Alpine Publications, 1988.

Smith, Steve, ed. *Encyclopedia of North American Sporting Dogs: Written by Sportsmen for Sportsmen*. Minocqua, WI: Willow Creek Press, 2002.

Spencer, James B. *Training Retrievers for the Marshes and Meadows*. Fairfax, VA: Denlinger Publishers, 1990.

Syrotuck, William G. *Scent and the Scenting Dog*. Rome, NY: Arner Publications, 1972.

Tarrant, Bill. *Best Way to Train your Gun Dog: The Delmar Smith Method*. New York: McKay, 1977.

Walters, D. L., and Ann Walters. *Training Retrievers to Handle*. La Cygne, KS: Walters, 1979.

Wehle, Robert C. *Wing & Shot: Gun Dog Training*. Scottsville, NY: Country Press, 1964.

Wick, John. *Walk with Wick: The Tree Dog Encyclopedia*. Montgomery City, MO: Westwick, 2006.

Winge, Øjvind. *Inheritance in Dogs with Special Reference to Hunting Breeds*. Translated by Catherine Roberts. Ithaca, NY: Comstock Publishing, 1950.

Videocassettes, DVDs

Lardy, Mike. *Total E-Collar Conditioning*, VHS. Metamora, MI: Younglove Broadcast Services, 2001.

Mertens, Jackie. *Sound Beginnings: Retriever Training with Jackie Mertens*, VHS. Metamora, MI: Younglove Broadcast Series, 2002.

Smith, Rick, and Ronnie Smith. *The Silent Command System of Dog Training*, DVD. San Antonio, TX: Huntsmith Productions, 2003.

———. *Puppy Development*, DVD. San Antonio, TX: Huntsmith Productions, 2005.

Glossary

All-Age—The top of the field trial ladder in bird dog and retriever pursuits.

Backing—See **honoring**, bird dog example.

Bayed—When the game is located but is not in a tree, such as when a bear or hog is surrounded on the ground.

Big running—As in bird dogs, refers to those dogs that range far, deep, and wide, covering much ground quickly and usually well out of gun range; the hunter or the judges and handler must then approach him when he is on point.

Blind retrieve—When the dog has not seen a bird or other game (such as rabbit) fall and then takes direction from his handler to retrieve and deliver the bird.

Break—With hunting dogs, a few meanings: to take off before being sent for game; or to "break" off trash; or to "break" a dog's spirit or will.

Casting—Giving arm signals and directions to the dog while assisting him to the area of a bird.

Earth work—Otherwise termed "going to ground," where various breeds of terriers, dachshunds, and many gamey breeds of dogs will pursue said game into its den, which may consist of underground tunnels. Some of these dogs are very tenacious and won't leave their quarry; the dogs may need to be dug out.

Face barking—When a dog actually tries to get in another dog's face, invading the other dog's space and barking all the while; this can escalate to aggression. Face barking often occurs at the tree when hounds locate game; as their prey drive reaches a frenzied pitch some dogs want to aggravate other dogs next to them and will turn and bark in their face instead of concentrating up the tree. Face barking can also occur in kennels through the fencing when one dog tries to aggravate another.

Fancier—Enthusiast, such as "bench" fancier (conformation breed shows).

Flushing—When birds are located, some breeds rush in and "flush," or put the birds to air, for the potential harvest by shot.

Flyer or flier—A live bird used in training that is thrown and shot for the dog.

Force-fetch or trained retrieve techniques—One of two generally accepted methods are used to create discomfort so that the dog learns to open his mouth to take an object; this eventually translates into the retrieve action.

> **Ear pinch**—the tip of the ear flap is pressed or pinched to create discomfort.

> **Toe hitch**—a piece of rope is attached around one toe on a foot that will be tightened to create pressure with the same result as the ear pinch.

Fox pen—A man-made enclosed area, stocked with foxes or specified game; these areas are used for training and in many cases also for various competitive events where dogs are turned loose in large numbers and scored on their performance.

Game—Upland birds, waterfowl, small animal or large animal wild quarry.

Gamey—This refers to the hunting dog's level of interest in his quarry or in various types of game.

Handling—Taking direction: Retrievers and bird dogs take casts (directional hand/arm signals) to birds they have not seen fall; hounds learn to come in on command.

Hard mouth—Pertains to any variation where the dog damages game, while holding it in his mouth, during retrieve and delivery other than a perfect delivery where game is "fit for the table." Tooth punctures and damaged or mangled flesh often renders game unusable.

Honoring—The practice when two or more dogs are being hunted or trialed and one is actually working; the other dog(s) remain motionless until released. Examples: retriever being sent for a marked (one he has seen fall) retrieve while other retrievers sit still; bird dog points quarry while other dogs pull up immediately and remain behind (backing).

Hunt dead—Technically different from blind retrieve; the dog is commanded to hunt in a specified area for dead game that he hasn't seen fall.

Hup—This means to "sit" and is a popular command among spaniel trainers and others.

Line—Two meanings; one defines a location for a working area in training or in retriever trials or hunt tests, re: take your dog to the line, send him from the line, move around in the boundaries of the line. The line is often further defined with the use of a mat or marked boundaries.

The other refers to the blind retrieve (see **lining**) and to the direction toward any retrieve, marked or blind, such as "line" to the bird.

Lining; Take a line—This is the terminology when the dog is sent out on a blind retrieve; he must initially be given a direction, or line, to run out into the field or swim out into the water.

Marking—The hunting dog's ability to watch game in the air and as it falls and then to subsequently remember the location of the fallen area and to go to it briskly and recover the game.

No-go—When the dog is sent to retrieve game and refuses to do so.

Off game—Any live game other than that your dog is allowed to pursue. Examples: A coon dog or rabbit hound should not run deer. A bird dog should not chase rabbits or deer.

Opening on track—When a hound periodically gives voice along as he runs a scent trail.

Pointing—Different from flushing; when birds are located the dog locks into position and inidicates their whereabouts; the hunter walks in and flushes them for shot.

Pop—When a gundog turns around and looks to the handler for guidance without receiving any command to do so from his handler.

Quartering—The act of the hunting dog working back and forth in front of the hunter or handler, ideally within gun range, in pursuit of wild birds, or planted birds when training.

Runner—Wounded game that moves from its original fallen location.

Scent cone—The area of scent radiating from an object or from live game. Environmental conditions and terrain will affect the actual size and distance pertaining to the scent as it drifts from the object or game.

Silent on track—When a hound remains silent, or gives no voice, during the running of the track.

Staunch—Same as steady.

Steady—Remaining motionless in the face of great distraction such as when birds are being shot (steady to shot).

Strike a track—When a hound or hunting dog gives voice to signify that he has scented a game trail.

Titer level—Refers to a level in the dog pertaining to vaccination protection or disease resistance or disease buildup.

Trash-breaking—Any number of different procedures that result in the dog being convinced to leave off game alone.

Treed—When a hound changes voice as he locates the correct tree, the game has gone up and then stays treed until the hunter or handler arrives.

Whoa—To stop instantly and stand motionless.

Wing and shot—A term used to describe what happens during bird hunting where the bird flushes or otherwise takes to the air and then is brought down by a firearm. Also, "steady to wing and shot" means that the dog being hunted remains motionless as the bird takes wing and as the bird is subsequently harvested and falls to the ground or water.

Wipe the eye—When one hunting dog is sent in to retrieve and cannot locate the game and then a second dog is commanded to the same area and recovers the game that the first dog couldn't find; also applies to locating game by pointing or flushing that previous dogs missed when working the same area.

Index

Munsterlander
  colors, 17
  prong collar, 217
  size, 17
Muscular myopathy, 95

N
Names, 85–91
Naproxen, 166
Nardi, Shannon, 360, 361
National Foxhound Association, 353
National organizations
  support, 393
National Rifle Association, 393
National Shoot-to-Retrieve Associ-
    ation, 357
National Wild Turkey Federation,
    393
Natural water, 390
NAVHDA. *See* North American Ver-
    satile Hunting Dog Association
    (NAVHDA)
Neutering, 167
New South Wales
  fox hunting, 392
Night hunts
  professional training, 336
Nite hunt program
  coonhound breeds, 351
  registries, 351
"No," 258, 260, 261, 281, 307
Nonhunting public
  opinion, 393
North American Versatile Hunting
    Dog Association (NAVHDA), 9,
    16, 17
Nose
  human *vs.* dog, 239–241
  moisture, 242–243
Nova Scotia duck tolling retriever,
    44

Nursing routines
  puppies, 172
Nursing stages
  puppies, 173
Nurturing environment, 253

O
Obedience training, 276
  puppies, 252, 264–265
Observation
  dog learning, 188
OFA. *See* Orthopedic Foundation
    for Animals (OFA)
"Off," 258
Off-the-ground kennel, 109
Older dogs
  acquired with no training,
    321–322
  comfort, 340
  maintaining performance,
    339–342
  needs changes, 340–342
Olfactory ability
  medications, 243
  training expanding, 247
Olfactory membranes
  human *vs.* dog, 239–240
One-dog feeders, 141
One human, one dog, 396
On-the-ground kennel, 110
Open All-Age and Gundog stakes,
    357
Operant conditioning, 186
Opossum hunting
  blackmouth cur, 62
Organization
  training, 232–233
Organizations. *See also* specific type
  support, 393
Orthopedic Foundation for Animals
    (OFA), 89

U
Umbilical cords, 77
Undergarments
 hunting, 376
Underwear
 hunting, 376
United Kennel Club (UKC), 16
Unknown blinds, 316
Upland hunting, 299–300, 365–367
U.S. pointing dog trial, 357
U.S. Sportsmen's Alliance, 393
Utilization, 4–5

V
Vaccinations
 importance, 144–145
 protocol, 116
 puppies, 83, 116
 records, 83
Valley fever, 151
Velcro strips, 375
Versatile pointing breeds, 16–27
Vests, 222
 with game pouch, 376
Veterinarian care, 149–166
 hunting dogs, 149
Veterinary clinic
 training partners, 236
Veterinary examination, 77
Vizslas
 sled harnesses, 147
Volhard puppy aptitude test,
  69–77
 elevation dominance, 71
 following, 70
 puppies' ability to deal with
  stress, 69
 restraint, 70
 retrieving, 71
 score interpretation, 75

score meaning, 72–75
scoring the results, 71–73
sight sensitivity, 71
social attraction, 70
social dominance, 71
sound sensitivity, 71
touch sensitivity, 71
Vomeronasal organ, 240

W
Wader booties
 hunting, 376
Waders
 hunting, 375
Walk hunting, 366
Water
 playing in, 45
 training retrievers, 390
Water bowls
 stainless steel versions, 140
Water Dog, 361
Water dogs, 390
Water dog TV, 361
Waterfowl hunting, 365–367
Water introduction, 320–321
Water jugs, 226
Waterproof matches, 374
Waterside terrier, 62
Water sources, 379
Water springer spaniel, 34–35
 size, 34
Water T, 313
W drill, 317
Weasel
 German jagdterrier, 64
Weather
 extremes, 386
 know, 382–383
Weight gain
 older dogs, 342